*For Victoria Schulberg
    in memory of a
three day mountain-climbing
trip with her illustrious
father — who pulled me
out of crevices into which
I sank and away from
avalanches —
    with affection to you
both
            F Scott Fitzerald
        Beverly Hills
        1940*

Tender Is the Night (Collection of Budd Schulberg).

FITZGERALD/HEMINGWAY ANNUAL 1977

FITZGERALD/HEMINGWAY ANNUAL 1977

Edited by

MARGARET M. DUGGAN

RICHARD LAYMAN

Consulting Editor: MATTHEW J. BRUCCOLI

A BRUCCOLI CLARK BOOK

GALE RESEARCH COMPANY ● BOOK TOWER
DETROIT, MICHIGAN 48226

Editors: MARGARET M. DUGGAN
RICHARD LAYMAN

Consulting Editor: Matthew J. Bruccoli
Managing Editor: C. E. Frazer Clark, Jr.

Address all editorial correspondence to the editors at The Department of English, University of South Carolina, Columbia, S. C. 29208.

Address all orders and subscription inquiries to Gale Research Company, Book Tower, Detroit, Michigan 48226.

Library of Congress Catalog Card Number 75-83781
ISBN 0-8103-0909-2

This Volume Is Dedicated To
Alexander Clark, Curator Of Manuscripts,
Princeton University Library:
Marking His Retirement
After Twenty-Five Years Of
Generous Assistance To
Fitzgerald Scholars.

CONTENTS

F. SCOTT FITZGERALD

ERNEST HEMINGWAY

REVIEWS

BIBLIOGRAPHICAL MATERIAL

FITZGERALD/HEMINGWAY ANNUAL 1977

F. SCOTT FITZGERALD

"THE FEATHER FAN"

The F. Scott Fitzgerald Papers at Princeton include the two-page outline and three-page treatment for what appears to have been a projected movie, "The Feather Fan." Both are typed.

The outline, which came first, was originally the story of John Blake who finds a magic "Indian crane skin." Fitzgerald started to revise this outline into the story of Genevra Barr, but stopped after the second item. (Fitzgerald's revisions are bracketted in the transcription). Then he wrote the summary for the story of Genevra and the feather fan that grants her wishes while consuming her health. The reference to *Dark Victory*—a 1939 movie starring Bette Davis—places "The Feather Fan" in the last two years of Fitzgerald's life.

The material for "The Feather Fan" is unpromising because the fantasy plot and the serious theme about the girls of 1919-1920 with their "infinite belief" do not accommodate each other.

"The Feather Fan" is published here with the generous permission of Scottie Fitzgerald Smith and may not be reprinted without the formal permission of Harold Ober Associates.

M. J. B.

[The Feather Fan]

PRINCIPAL CHARACTERS

John Blake
Joe Legendre
Genevra Barr
Lois Bell

RETROSPECT

[Genevra]   [down from Vassar] [her]
1. ~~Blake's~~ coming ~~to New York~~—~~his~~ father ruined by the war,
                    [her]   [conduct]
   leaving him $900. ~~His~~ pattern of ~~study.~~ First meeting with the
   fourteen year old Lois. [poor Blake]
   [Lois]   [Legendre]   [Legendre's]
2. ~~Legendre~~ takes him to see ~~Genevra~~ on Long Island. ~~Genevra's~~
   legend of purity.
3. His passion for Genevra. His different methods of trying to win
   her—the kindness of Lois and her mother.
4. He gets a job of rewriting the memoirs of some stuffed shirt—
   one sees that little Lois is in love with him.
5. The episode of the theatre and how Lois saves him.
6. He goes into Lois' bedroom and spies on her.
7. He gets $1500. from the sale of an island in the St. Lawrence.
8. He tells all to Genevra who coldly throws him over.
9. He and Legendre gamble on the market and make $20,000 and
   he plunges into the world of pleasure, finally losing it all.
10. He goes to a gambling house and then a curiosity shop. He
                                    [feather fan]
    meets the Orientalist and finds the ~~Indian crane skin.~~
11. Blake's first wish—for luxury. Coming out of the shop he meets
    the crowd looking for him. They go to the stockbroker's party—
    the women, Joan and Barbara.
12. Blake wishes to be rich and immediately finds at breakfast that
    he has inherited five million dollars from a grandfather. This is
    the second use of the skin and he notices a slight shrinkage in it.

WE HAVE A TIME LAPSE OF SEVERAL MONTHS

13. His servant reports on his decline to the old professor and John Blake aids the professor by accident—then realizing in terror that the token will have shrunk again.

14. The theatre. Genevra's beauty is outclassed by Lois'. He and Lois fall desperately in love. Desiring her love has made his token shrink so that he has but two months left of perfect happiness. He throws the skin down a well. The gardener finds it undamaged.

15. He consults a zoologist and learns the legend of the skin. He consults a physicist. A machine breaks trying to break the skin. He goes to a foundry. A press breaks trying to break the skin. Finally a chemist fails to get a reaction from the skin.

16. He finds Lois asleep in a sad scene. His health breaks and the doctors argue over him. He is ordered away.

17. He goes to a health resort and guests turn from him. They try to get rid of him. He is inveigled into a duel and uses up one of his last wishes.

18. He meets the people in the mountain.

19. He throws the skin into a fire without success. Lois comes to him as he is dying.

20. He wants her and with his wish he dies.

21. The beautiful epilogue about Lois and Genevra.

THE FEATHER FAN
Time is 1919 [- 1920]
[Fathers failure + suicide - She's 19]

Genevra Barr is coming down from Vassar to New York. Her father has been ruined by the war leaving her $900. She decides that she is going to be a great figure in the dress business and she lays out a course of study for herself—studying advertising, methods of the great wholesale clothes merchants and attends a school of design—everything to prepare herself for being a career woman.

She meets a poor man named Blake, who is very kind to her. He is a hopelessly impractical inventor, dream character of some sort of whom one does not at this moment expect success. She runs into a wealthy girl through her business, perhaps a girl who is doing social work or studying design as a hobby and this girl is also alone and homeless but is better fitted than Genevra, more in the know about New York and how to get around. They are both Western girls. Lois has more money while Genevra is just barely getting along on her $900.

Lois takes her out to Long Island to a man's house. The man is a polo player, romantic type, a confirmed bachelor. His legend is that while he has made love to many women he has never for a single moment allowed himself to become sentimental. She conceives a passion for him and goes through several routines to try and win him. Meanwhile the poor young inventor and his mother with whom she lives are very kind to her and one perceives that the young inventor is in love with her. But he sees that she has her eyes fixed on some high destiny and has nothing to offer.

She goes to the theatre with Legendre and one of her subterfuges which is that she has a good deal of money is almost exposed but John Blake's (the inventor's) discernment gets her out of this mess. About this time in the story she has noticed on sale a very splendid feather fan from Persia which appears in a store window, perhaps Tiffany's and is instantly withdrawn from sale. This is a plant which will develop later.

She goes out to Long Island by herself and follows Legendre around for one whole day in a sort of state of hypnosis watching him play polo, watching him all through the day with fascination. She is enabled to do this by a visit to Lois perhaps. Now she has a spot of luck. She inherits a little money from the sale of an island in the St. Lawrence River which her grandfather owned. Out of this she buys some new clothes and declares her love to Legendre and is repelled as he coldly throws her over. Now on Lois' advice she plunges with the money into the wholesale dress market and makes a killing—something like the famous polo coat killing of 1915. She buys some model from Paris which springs into immediate popularity and clears $20,000., but it seems all to have come too late. She moves up into a luxurious apartment house and spending this money carefully the world of fashion is now open to her but men have ceased to interest her and she thinks only about Legendre who has so thoroughly snubbed her except for that moment—he passes out of her life. Her money goes in luxury and now when she has nothing suddenly she finds a feather fan. It's owner will not sell it but instead will give it to her for a kiss. He tells her its peculiar property. Her first wish is for fun and almost as she is leaving the shop where she has acquired the feather fan, she meets Lois looking for her. They go to a big party and there Genevra finds that she has come into a fortune. She finds this out at 6 o'clock in the morning. She has inherited five million dollars. This is the second use of the feather fan and she notices that it has diminished in size and feathers seem to be missing. She feels a certain awe and premonition.

There is a time lapse of several months.

The dean of Vassar College in New York comes to see her in regard to an endowment, but finds her in a state of terror. She has changed. Her maid tells the dean about the curious change that has come over her. She aids the dean by accident and then realizes that the feather fan has shrunk again. She goes to the opera that night. Two people are present. One is Legendre and the other John Blake, neither of whom she has seen for some time. John Blake in the course of these months has made a fortune and suddenly become one of the most important figures in the business world of New York through his invention. He is also tremendously attractive and she realizes what charm he has and begins to fall in love with him.

Legendre on the other hand, begins to look to her faded and conceited and not worth while. She falls desperately in love with Blake but desiring his love makes the feather fan shrink further still. She feels a diminution of energy in herself. Blake returns her love but a doctor tells her that from her present physical condition she has only two months to live. She throws the feather fan from the top of a tall building but a man finds it in the street and brings it back undamaged.

She consults a zoologist and learns the legend of the fan and a physicist. Every effort is made to try to stretch it and restore it to its original size. Feathers are added but to no effect—perhaps a man is seriously hurt or a machine damaged trying to fix the feather fan. All this is happening during her honeymoon with John Blake, perhaps abroad. Her health is now extremely bad and doctors argue over the situation and finally order her away.

She goes to a health resort and the guests turn away from her. They try to get rid of her. She is inveigled into a contest of will with another woman, perhaps a set of tennis or a game of chance to see which one will live and she wins but it uses up one of her last wishes. She has not desired the contest. The feather fan has become a curse. She wanders up into the mountains near the health resort and talks with some simple people envying them. On her return to New York she throws the feather fan into a fire but it doesn't burn. She is dying now. John Blake comes to her. She wants him with her and this is her last wish as she dies. For a little while we follow the two men that she has cared about. Legendre becoming more and more worldly and more unhappy while Blake who must always have been an utterly charming and unworldly character goes ahead in his own line always carrying with him her image.

This is really a character study of a very fine girl who has the ideal of success and who tries it in the long view without getting anywhere and then from the short view. She is a symbol herself of the girl of 1919-1920. The world is her apple but she butts up against it with the result, in the case of her fruitless passion for Legendre and misses the real love which was always hers for the asking.

Now suddenly that thing that we all want comes to her. The feather fan which is a symbol of the ancient wishing ring—of a token which will give us everything which humanity longs for. It is the answer to the desire of modern woman. It is the world offered her. But alas we have to take what we get because this token brings with it death and mortality. She gets wealth, yes, but what is wealth without health. But more than that she gets released from her thraldom to Legendre, her hopeless love for him, but finding that he is not even faintly worthy of it and she has even that final goal of a perfect love but the perfect love which is the summit in the crown of all that could be wished is defeated because of the means with which she obtained it. If she had taken it when it came to her naturally all would have been well but it is part of that power given by the fan that all things touched by it will be tainted. It is even sadder having the love and knowing that it cannot last—that is is only given for a day.

Then comes her fruitless and dramatic fight against death almost like that of the girl in "Dark Victory" though of course different and her death which symbolizes something that seems to me to have happened to women of that very generation of the twenties who thought that the world owed them happiness and pleasure if only they had the courage enough. The sanitariums are full of them and many are dead. I could name many names and after those wild five years from 1919-24 women changed a little in America and settled back to something more stable. The real lost generation of girls were those who were young right after the war because they were the ones with infinite belief.

MARGARET M. DUGGAN
=====

A NEW FITZGERALD BOOK REVIEW: The Boy Grew Older

In Fitzgerald's scrapbook III (*Tales of the Jazz Age, The Vegetable, All the Sad Young Men*) is his review, entitled "The Defeat of Art," of Heywood Broun's novel *The Boy Grew Older* which was published during the week of 21 October 1922. Fitzgerald's review may be regarded, in part, as an answer to Broun's earlier assessments of *This Side of Paradise*. Broun had twice devoted his column to commenting unfavorably on Fitzgerald's novel in *The New York Tribune* (11 and 16 April 1920), attacking the author's immaturity as well as the "authenticity" of the novel's atmosphere and characters. In his essay "Early Success" Fitzgerald recalls that: "In a daze I gave out an interview— I told what a great writer I was. . . . Heywood Broun, who was on my trail, simply quoted it [*New York Tribune*, 7 May 1920] with the comment that I seemed to be a very self-satisfied young man, and for some days I was notably poor company."

By citing Broun's enthusiasm for *The Moon-Calf* (New York: Knopf, 1920), Fitzgerald also used the occasion of this book review to indict Broun's critical acumen as well as the literary merit of Floyd Dell's novel which Fitzgerald felt had been "promoted" by certain critics and its publisher into an unwarranted success. Fitzgerald, uncharacteristically, seemed actually to resent the popularity of Dell's novel, perhaps, because *The Moon-Calf* was most often compared with *This Side of Paradise*. On 30 July 1921 Fitzgerald sent Maxwell Perkins an ad for *The Moon-Calf* hailing it as "The most

9

brilliantly successful first novel of many years" with the comment
that "You've [Scribners] let everyone forget that my book once had
this title. Knopf's statement goes quite unchallenged."

The following is a transcription of the Fitzgerald review with a
reproduction of the clipping from the scrapbook. A search of those
newspapers (*New York Evening Post, New York Tribune, New
York Herald,* and *St. Paul Daily News*) in which Fitzgerald reviews
appeared in 1922 has failed to yield its location.

University of South Carolina

Fitzgerald scrapbook III, Princeton University Library.

F. SCOTT FITZGERALD

"THE DEFEAT OF ART"

THE BOY GREW OLDER, by Heywood Brown.   G.P. Putnam's
Sons. New York. $2.00.

By no less an authority than that of our leading humorist, Heywood Broun has been pronounced the best all-around newspaper
man in America. And he is. He can report a football game, a play, a
literary dinner, a prizefight, scandal, murder, his own domestic
interests, his moods, the konduct of the klan and the greatness of
Charlie Chaplin with the same skill and the same unfailing
personality.

"Now," says Heywood Broun, "every scribbler in Christendom is
writing an immortal novel while I continue my ephemeral output. I
shall crystallize some of this so-called personality of mine into a
novel and preserve it against the short memory of man."

The result is called "The Boy Grew Older."

Before I talk of this novel I want to list Heywood Broun's most
obvious insufficiencies. His literary taste, when it is not playing
safe, is pretty likely to be ill-considered, faintly philistine, and often
downright absurd. He seems to have no background whatsoever
except a fairly close reading of fashionable contemporary novels by
British and American novelists. He seems unacquainted with anything that was written before 1900, possibly excepting the English
units required for entering Harvard.

This lack is, in an American novelist, a positive advantage insofar
as it puts no limit on the width of his appeal. There is nothing in
"The Boy Grew Older" to puzzle a movie director or a scenario
writer. It is a book free from either the mark or the pretense of
erudition.

Once upon a time, in the early days of the American literary
revival, Mr. Broun mistook the fact that "Moon Calf," by Floyd

11

Dell, was a seriously attempted novel for the fact it was a successful piece of work. "Drop everything and read 'Moon Calf,'" said Mr. Broun to the public. "Drop everything and read Henry James," said the Dial to Mr. Dell. But the public trusts Heywood Broun and because of his shove "Moon Calf" dragged in the wake of "Main Street" to a sale of 30,000 copies or more.

So when I began to read "The Boy Grew Older" I feared that, in the "Moon Calf" tradition, it would be thick with dots and bestrewn with quotations from Tennyson, Eddie Guest and the early poetic efforts of Mr. Broun. On the contrary it is a competently written, highly interesting and somewhat sketchy story which concerns the soul of a newspaper man named Peter Neale. And the book is about Peter chiefly—about a simple and rather fine man who has somewhat the same devotion to his profession that Mark Twain has to his piloting or Joseph Conrad to the sea. What does it matter if Peter Neale's gorgeously ethical newspaper world is imaginary? By such books and such men as the author of "The Boy Grew Older" such an idealized concept is made a reality. After Kipling, every private in the British army tried to be like "Soldiers Three."

With a boyish hatred of emotional sloppiness Mr. Broun has utterly failed to visualize for us the affair with Maria. When she leaves Peter I was sorry. But not sorry that she was gone—not with the feeling that something young and beautiful had ceased to be—I was only sorry Peter was wounded.

Peter gets drunk. In the best "cafe fight" I have ever read about, Peter is slugged with a bottle. He meets another woman. Mr. Broun hesitates for a moment whether to be correctly the Harvard man and public "good egg" or whether to make Peter's second affair human and vital and earthy and alive. Somewhere on a dark staircase the question disappears and never emerges from its obscurity.

The boy grows older. The reality he possessed as a portrait of Heywood III fades out when he grows older than his model. At Harvard he plays in 1915 in a football game that took place in 1921. He comes to New York and works for a while under an excellent pen portrait of a famous liberal editor. He has a voice, so his mother takes him away and leaves Peter to his work and to his rather fine concept of honor and to his memories—which, if the incidents had been just a little more emotionally visualized when they occurred—would have made the book more moving at the close.

But Heywood Broun can write. If he will forget himself and let go, his personality will color almost every line he chooses to set down. He is a real talent that even the daily grind of newspaper work cannot dull. His second book is decidedly worth waiting for.

—F. SCOTT FITZGERALD.

FREDERIC E. RUSCH

ADDENDA TO BRUCCOLI: FOUR FITZGERALD DUST JACKETS

For his *F. Scott Fitzgerald: A Descriptive Bibliography,* Matthew J. Bruccoli (Pittsburgh: University of Pittsburgh Press, 1972) was unable to locate the dust jackets for the English editions of *This Side of Paradise, Flappers and Philosophers,* and *The Great Gatsby,* and found incomplete dust jackets for the English editions of *The Beautiful and Damned* and *Tales of the Jazz Age.* Recently I came across complete jackets for all of these editions except *Gatsby* in the University Library at Cambridge, England. The descriptions of the jackets given below follow the format used by Bruccoli.

A 5.2.a   THIS SIDE OF PARADISE

First English edition, first printing
Dust jacket: Front has the W. E. Hill drawing that appeared on the first American edition: '[white outlined in black] THIS SIDE OF | PARADISE | By F. Scott Fitzgerald | [orange] *COLLINS' 'FIRST NOVEL' LIBRARY'.* Spine: [black] This Side | of | Paradise | F. SCOTT | FITZGERALD | [orange] 'FIRST NOVEL' | LIBRARY | [white price against black circle] | [black Collins seal] | [black] COLLINS'. Back: 'Collins' New Novels | SPRING, 1921 | [reversed Oxford rule] | [9 titles beginning with *Mainwaring* and ending with *Adam and Caroline*] | [leaf] | Collins' First Novel Library | SPRING TITLES | [4 titles beginning with *Kimono* and ending with *TSOP*]'. Front flap lists 3 novels by Francis Brett Young, 4 novels by J. D. Beresford and 4 novels by Beresford in preparation; back flap has blurb for the sixth impression of *Potterism* by Rose Macaulay.

Location: University Library, Cambridge 1921 ⑦ 1449 (deposit-stamp 21 July 1921).

A 6.2.a   FLAPPERS AND PHILOSOPHERS

First English edition, first printing
Dust jacket: Front has the W. E. Hill drawing that appeared on the first American edition: '[white outlined in black] FLAPPERS AND | PHILOSOPHERS | By F. Scott Fitzgerald | [orange] *Author of* "THIS SIDE OF PARADISE"'. Spine: '[orange] FLAPPERS | AND | PHILOS- | OPHERS | [greenish black] F. SCOTT | FITZGERALD | [white price against orange circle] | [greenish black Collins seal] | [greenish black] COLLINS'. Back: '[greenish black] Collins' New Novels | SPRING, 1922 | [Oxford rule] | [13 titles beginning with *The Return* and ending with *Mainspring*]. Front flap has F&P blurb; back flap has TSOP blurb.
Location: University Library, Cambridge 1922 ⑦ 1066 (deposit-stamp 4 April 1922).

A 8.2.a   THE BEAUTIFUL AND DAMNED

First English edition, first printing
Dust jacket: Front, spine and front flap as described in Bruccoli. Back: 'Collins' New Novels | AUTUMN 1922 | [Oxford rule] | [14 titles beginning with *Pilgrim's Rest* and ending with *The Deaves Affair*]'. Back flap lists 6 novels by Francis Brett Young, 8 novels by J. D. Beresford and 2 works by Walter de la Mare.
Location: University Library, Cambridge 1922 ⑦ 3448 (deposit-stamp 9 November 1922).

A 9.2.b   TALES OF THE JAZZ AGE

First English edition, first printing
Dust jacket: Front as described in Bruccoli. Spine as described except for 'AUTHOR OF | "THE BEAUTIFUL AND | DAMNED" etc.'. Back: 'Collins' New Fiction | SPRING, 1923 | [Oxford rule] | [14 titles beginning with *Love's Pilgrim* and ending with *Henry Brocken*]'. Front flap has blurb for *TJA;* back flap has blurb for the second impression of *B&D.*
Location: University Library, Cambridge 1923 ⑦ 835 (deposit-stamp 6 April 1923).

Indiana State University—Terre Haute

Cambridge University Library.

Cambridge University Library.

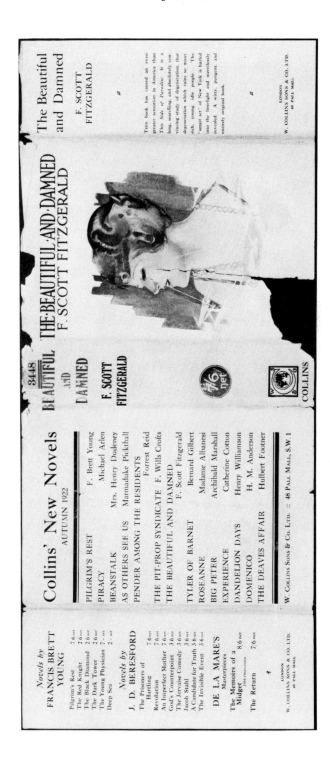

Cambridge University Library.

Cambridge University Library.

W. R. ANDERSON

RIVALRY AND PARTNERSHIP: THE SHORT FICTION OF ZELDA SAYRE FITZGERALD

The recent publication of *Bits of Paradise 21 Uncollected Stories By F. Scott and Zelda Fitzgerald*[1] was, in part, a witness to the growth of interest in the fiction of Zelda Sayre Fitzgerald. *Bits of Paradise* reprints ten pieces which she wrote, alone or in conjunction with her husband. All of them had been published in periodicals during her lifetime, but they were, at last, being accorded the more permanent stature of book publication, in company with eleven of Scott Fitzgerald's previously-uncollected stories. If one eliminates the very brief sketch "The Continental Angle"—arguably a nonfiction essay in gustatory nostalgia, on the order of Mrs. Fitzgerald's lengthier pieces " 'Show Mr. and Mrs. F. to Number —' " and "Auction—Model 1934"—a survey of the stories in *Bits of Paradise* provides a consistent index to the awakening and growth of Zelda Fitzgerald's interest in fiction as a creative art form. This paper makes such a survey.

The objective of the survey is twofold: first, to trace Zelda Fitzgerald's progress as she moved from her first tentative efforts in fiction through a series of increasingly more ambitious undertakings toward her novel *Save Me the Waltz;* second, to explore the interrelationship between her writing and the literary career of her husband. Zelda Fitzgerald also wrote a small body of nonfiction—reviews, essays, articles for women's magazines. These pieces are considered only peripherally in their relationship to the published fiction, as are the references to unpublished and presumably lost

19

stories, references which occasionally surface in the Fitzgeralds' correspondence.[2]

Zelda Fitzgerald has typically been understood as blessed with a flare for brilliant but unsustained creative expression, as a woman possessed with an unstable talent and little esthetic or educational background with which to discipline that talent. Nancy Milford's biography *Zelda* has, of course, largely corrected this glib assessment.[3] Examination of the development of Mrs. Fitzgerald's short stories substantiates Milford's findings that, despite the emotional chaos in which her marriage and her life foundered, Zelda Fitzgerald's groping efforts to find self-definition in artistic achievement resulted in fundamentally consistent growth toward control and purpose in her writing.

That progress was, to be sure, extremely complicated by the intricacies of her relationship, personally and artistically, with her husband. As Milford has shown, theirs was a union marked by extremes—exuberant happiness turning to mutually-destructive rivalry, conflict, and jealousy. Yet, as she also demonstrates with discernment, the Fitzgeralds were, even in their most agonized alienation, dependent on each other, emotionally and otherwise.

One facet of that interdependence surfaced in their writing. Certainly Scott Fitzgerald *needed, used* Zelda Fitzgerald. He seized upon her freshness, her ready acceptance of life, both to reinforce his own romantic worldview, and to provide—from her letters, diaries, and from his observations of her actions—subject matter for his fiction. In her writing, Zelda Fitzgerald was similarly dependent on him. She turned to his work for guidance, discipline, examples, and patterns. She relied on him for suggestions and corrections. Most importantly, as he used their life together as an inexhaustible repository of experiential subject matter, so she increasingly came to draw upon the joys, conflicts, and disappointments of their marriage. Most writers, of course, call on their own experiences as bases for creation. The Fitzgeralds, however, shared a sensibility which depended much more heavily than usual on that artistic wellspring. Zelda Fitzgerald, like her husband, saw life in those intensely romantic, intensely subjective terms which naturally emphasized personal experience, and emotional response to the experience, almost exclusively as the fundamental subject matters of fiction.

With such a sensibility, writing is, in part, a method of self-definition. Two writers striving to find meaning, value, and achievement from a common experience are almost assuredly headed for conflict; such was certainly the case with the Fitzgeralds. Writing fiction became, for Zelda Fitzgerald, part of her intensive struggle for spiritual independence. Like her dancing and painting, her writing took on, in her eyes and in those of her husband, an ominous tinge of rivalry. Thus, as she came closer to writing *good,* serious fiction, the interrelationship, as it is demonstrated in this survey, became more and more complex. Fitzgerald continued throughout his life to assist and encourage his wife's literary efforts; yet, as she became increasingly proficient, he demonstrated increased resentment and annoyance that she was attempting to establish herself in his field, using his expertise, and (most disturbingly) drawing on "his" material—their experiences.[5]

At the beginning, however, Fitzgerald seems to have enjoyed Zelda Fitzgerald's forays into writing. In the early years of their marriage, as they became figures of public interest, she was given the opportunity to contribute brief articles to several periodicals—interviews, a review of *The Beautiful and Damned,* "authoritative" articles on the flapper. These pieces, of course, played on their mutual popularity, and their supposed "Jazz Age" lifestyle together. The process by which these fledgling efforts led to a desire to write fiction is unclear; however, by 1923 Zelda Fitzgerald was engaged in composition of her first short story, which would ultimately find publication as "Our Own Movie Queen," under her husband's name.[4]

The Fitzgeralds were living in Great Neck at that time. Scott Fitzgerald was occupied with the production of his play *The Vegetable,* and with planning his third novel. Nevertheless, he found time to assist Zelda Fitzgerald with the story, which was completed in November. The degree to which Fitzgerald was involved is uncertain. The notations he made in his *Ledger,* his personal account book of his life and literary career, exemplify that uncertainty. He includes it in his "Record of Published Fiction," but notes that it is "Two thirds written by Zelda. Only my climax and revision."—yet credits its entire earnings to himself.[5] In the section entitled "Money Earned by Writing since Leaving Army," however, he notes it as "(half Zelda)," yet credits the entire $900.00 income (after a ten per cent agent's fee) to his own earnings.[6] In the section devoted to "Zelda's Earnings" he also claims half-authorship and divides the income equally, crediting his wife with having earned $450.00 from the story.[7]

At the same time, Zelda Fitzgerald was telling an interviewer about her efforts to write fiction:

> "I like to write. Do you know, I thought my husband should write a perfectly good ending to one of the tales, and he wouldn't! He called them 'lop-sided,' too! Said that they began at the end."[8]

She told an interviewer that she had written three stories, although only "Our Own Movie Queen" survives from that time.[9] The interview also sounded two portentous notes. First, it expressed Mrs. Fitzgerald's interest in finding a creative outlet of her own. She was beginning, albeit with self-conscious amateurism, ventures into a field she would subsequently come to term her "work." The second implication of importance is that Fitzgerald apparently was willing to offer her passing guidance and correction, but did not take her "work" seriously enough to become deeply involved in it.

Taken in conjunction with the *Ledger* entries, then, the interview indicates that Fitzgerald's contributions to "Our Own Movie Queen" were probably not major. What interested him about it was its potential marketability: he first attempted to sell it to the Hearst publishing corporation, as partial fulfillment of a contract with Hearst's *Cosmopolitan* for options on all his stories during 1923,[10] which would explain his sole by-line. The story was finally placed with the *Chicago Sunday Tribune,* where it appeared in 7 June 1925.[11] Undoubtedly, the fact that the *Tribune* thought it was buying a Scott Fitzgerald piece accounted for the high price of a thousand dollars.

A typescript of "Our Own Movie Queen" exists in the F. Scott Fitzgerald papers at the Princeton University Library.[12] It evidences extensive editorial revision in Fitzgerald's hand, almost completely in the form of deletions of words, phrases or passages. The effect is an overall tightening of the story; however, there is no evidence, at this stage, of any substantial addition of passages or of ideas by Fitzgerald. Unless his contributions came at earlier stages, "Our Own Movie Queen" would seem to have been principally Zelda Fitzgerald's creation. Certainly the finished story is not one which would add particular luster to his reputation. It is a brittle, "slick," satiric piece. Its tone and mood are, perhaps, akin to those of Scott Fitzgerald's less-serious magazine stories of the period— "Jemina"—as well as to the glib facetiousness of Zelda Fitzgerald's nonfiction pieces such as the review of *The Beautiful and Damned* which she wrote for the *New York Tribune* of 2 April 1922—the review which contains this sample of Mrs. Fitzgerald's humor:

> It seems to me that on one page I recognized a portion of an old diary of mine which mysteriously disappeared shortly after my marriage, and also scraps of letters which, though considerably edited, sound to me vaguely familiar. In fact, Mr. Fitzgerald—I believe that is how he spells his name—seems to believe that plagiarism begins at home.[13]

As part of its tone of sophisticated wit, "Our Own Movie Queen" adopts a consistently superior attitude, verging on condescension, toward its humorously-named heroine, Gracie Axelrod. She is a poor girl, who wreaks a plebian's revenge on the snobbish Blue Ribbon family. Yet, the reader is invited to see her, within limits, as a woman capable of taking care of herself in the world, by manipulation of her physical attractiveness, and through a certain self-protective predatoriness. To this extent, she is Zelda Fitzgerald's version of the tough, selfish, but attractive young women who populate so much of her husband's fiction. Gracie is not aristocratic or wealthy—few of Mrs. Fitzgerald's heroines are—but she shares qualities of self-absorption, self-sufficiency, and attractiveness with women such as Judy Jones of "Winter Dreams."

Like much of Fitzgerald's fiction, "Our Own Movie Queen" also turns to personal experience for some of its setting—a midwestern locale, patterned, apparently, on the twin cities of Minneapolis/St. Paul. The Fitzgeralds had lived in St. Paul in 1921-1922; Zelda Fitzgerald could draw on her outsider's impressions of her husband's city, as he had drawn on his impressions of her home town for stories such as "The Jelly Bean" and parts of "The Ice Palace."

Whatever the degree of his participation in its composition, "Our Own Movie Queen" certainly shows the mark of Scott Fitzgerald's influence. Despite its rudimentary characterization, trick ending, and overall slickness, he was not ashamed to claim it as his own creation, at least for the sake of selling it. As a beginning venture into writing it must have given Zelda Fitzgerald a sense of accomplishment: it had been accepted professionally, by her literary mentor, and by a paying publisher.

Zelda Fitzgerald was, however, by no means ready to embark on a literary career. For the next five and a half years she contented herself with a continuation of the role of the amateur dabbler, writing occasional magazine pieces, such as "Does a Moment of Revolt Come Sometime to Every Married Man?" and "What Became of Our Flappers and Sheiks?," both of which were published in *McCall's* magazine (March 1924 and October 1925, respectively), or "The Changing Beauty of Park Avenue," which appeared in *Harper's Bazaar* in January 1928.[14] The typescript of the latter, like the typescript of "Our Own Movie Queen," in the Zelda Sayre Fitzgerald papers at Princeton, bears corrections and editing in Scott Fitzgerald's hand, evidence that he continued to take an interest in his wife's writing, as a proud parent would encourage the inventiveness of a precocious child. A measure of the kind of writing she was producing may be derived from the fact that, by 1928, her market was the youth-cult-oriented *College Humor*, a magazine for which Fitzgerald had little respect, considering it only a market for hastily-written or second-rate material.[15] Apparently, however, he had no objection to selling *College Humor* two of Zelda Fitzgerald's humorous sketches, which were published as though written by both Fitzgeralds. "Looking Back Eight Years" appeared in June 1928, and "Who Can Fall in Love After Thirty?" the following October.[16] The *Ledger*, which attributes them entirely to Mrs. Fitzgerald, discloses that the first one was apparently sold directly to the magazine, for $300.00, while the second one brought $200.00, less ten per cent commission—indicating that Fitzgerald's agent, Harold Ober, handled its negotiations.[17]

By Scott Fitzgerald's standards, such prices scarcely warranted his signature—he earned $25,732.96 that year, by his own count[18]—but *College Humor* was apparently sufficiently pleased to commission a series of six articles, of approximately five thousand words each, treating different types of girls. The series is first described in an office memorandum of 14 February 1929, by Fitzgerald's literary agent, Harold Ober.

> Scott Fitzgerald said that Zelda would do six articles for College Humor, that he would go over them and fix them up and that the articles would be signed with both their names. . . . He said we had better leave the price until they did the first article.
>
> They are to be articles about different types of girls. I should think they ought to pay $500 for them, if they are four or five thousand words in length.[19]

The inference from the memorandum is that Fitzgerald had made the preliminary arrangements himself with H. N. Swanson, editor of *College Humor*. What is not clear is whether Swanson realized he would be paying for pieces basically written by Mrs. Fitzgerald; he may not have cared, so long as both names were signed. On the following day, Swanson and Ober met. Swanson suggested a list of types of girls to be evoked—city debutante, young married, modern, Southern, country club, western, and New York society woman.[20] He also requested that the pieces be "story articles," rather than "philosophical discussions," and suggested techniques to be utilized. Ober wrote Fitzgerald of the agreement with Swanson:

> He thought each girl could be given a name and she could be described as a certain kind of girl because at such and such a party, she did so and so. In other words, she could be described by instances in her life, things that she did, rather than things that were said about her, etc.[21]

Swanson obviously wanted short stories, not satiric humor. If he expected Fitzgerald himself to be deeply involved in their composition, however, he was truly bargain-hunting, for Fitzgerald's stories at that time, which were going exclusively to *The Saturday Evening Post,* sold for $3500.00 each.[22]

If, on the other hand, Zelda Fitzgerald could write them, with some guidance and polishing from her husband, they would provide some easy revenue. More important, assuredly, they would provide diversion for her. By early 1929, the growing friction and tension in the Fitzgeralds' marriage had become serious. Fitzgerald was drinking heavily and worrying about his inability to make progress with his fourth novel, the final version of which would be *Tender Is the Night.* Zelda Fitzgerald, frustrated and disappointed in her inability to derive fulfillment from her role as decorative wife of a famous author, was increasingly struggling to find serious creative achievement in her own right. Her effort to become a ballet dancer occupied much of that struggle, but, as Nancy Milford has pointed out, the articles she had written during 1927 and 1928 were also manifestations of her groping search for meaning in her life.[23] Her need for artistic achievement would, in the next few years, become, obsessively, the central concern of her life, what she would later come to term in communications with her husband and her psychiatrists, her *work.*[24] There is considerable significance in that terminology: "work" connotes professional achievement, not amateur expression.

Zelda Fitzgerald's increasingly intense interest in her work, then, coincided with Swanson's requirements, to lead her back to the effort to write fiction. She had finished the first of the "girl" sketches by the beginning of March, while the Fitzgeralds were still living at "Ellerslie," near Wilmington, Delaware.[25] Entitled "The Original Follies Girl," it was brief (around 2000 words) and sketchy in plot and characterization. Nevertheless, Ober sold it to Swanson for $400.00, and was confident he could get $500.00 apiece for the rest of the series.[26]

Almost immediately, the Fitzgeralds sailed to France. For the next year, while they divided their time between Paris and the Riviera, Zelda Fitzgerald evidently threw herself into her writing with increasing intensity—the obsessive intensity with which she pursued ballet studies. By mid-April, she had finished "Poor Working Girl" and had sent it to Ober; "The Southern Girl" followed in June; "The Girl the Prince Liked" in August; "The Girl with Talent" in October; and "A Millionaire's Girl" in March 1930.[27] As a group, they are a record of Zelda Fitzgerald's struggle toward seriousness of expression, of her growth toward competence in literary technique, and of her husband's continuing but increasingly sparing and wary guidance.

Fitzgerald's correspondence and the typescripts of the "Girl" series included in the F. Scott Fitzgerald papers at Princeton—there

are typescripts for all the stories except "The Southern Girl" with
holograph corrections by both Scott and Zelda Fitzgerald—indicate
that, while Fitzgerald continued to play some part in the conception
and planning of the stories, Zelda Fitzgerald took an increasingly
craftsmanlike interest in composition and revision of what was
steadily becoming *her* work.

The extent to which Fitzgerald was involved in originating the
"Girl" pieces is difficult to assess. He was certainly involved, from
time to time, in at least some stages of writing of some, if not all, of
the stories. Harold Ober, in fact, became alarmed that Fitzgerald
might be engaging himself too deeply in the composition of what
were, to him as to Fitzgerald, minor "sketches." On 8 October 1929,
he wrote Fitzgerald:

> I agree with you that it is a mistake for you to use up material on
> these articles that you could use in stories. Of course as this one . . .
> ["The Girl with Talent"] stands, it is more a sketch than a story,
> although it is a beautifully done sketch. . . . if you have any more ideas
> that will make stories, don't put them into this form.[28]

Fitzgerald probably agreed with and for the most part accepted
Ober's advice; he was, at that time, struggling with the material
which would eventually become *Tender Is the Night,* as well as
attempting to write short stories, and he surely could not have had
much time to devote to his wife's work. Nevertheless, he must have
remained involved on at least a sporadic basis right through the last
of the series to be written, "A Millionaire's Girl." Several years after
its composition, he would write to Zelda Fitzgerald acknowledging
that, as with other of their joint efforts, his contributions to that
story had consisted principally in suggesting a theme and revising
the completed manuscript.[29]

While that letter suggests that Fitzgerald was continuing to assist
and guide his wife's writing, the evidence of the typescripts at
Princeton indicates that she was becoming increasingly
self-sufficient, playing a more important part in the revisions of her
work. Fitzgerald may have been suggesting editorial changes, but if
so, they came in early stages of composition. The extensive editorial
revision on the five typescripts at Princeton is almost entirely in
Zelda Fitzgerald's hand, a marked contrast with the revision in her
husband's holograph on the typescripts of earlier work such as
"Our Own Movie Queen" and "The Changing Beauty of Park
Avenue." The titles and by-lines of all five pieces are written in
Fitzgerald's hand, in some cases changing titles which Zelda
Fitzgerald had supplied. For instance, "The Girl the Prince Liked"
originally was entitled, in Zelda Fitzgerald's holograph, "The Story

Book Girl." There are occasional revisions in the typescripts in Fitzgerald's hand—word changes, an added phrase, and in one instance, several words lined through in the black ink in which corrections identifiable as his are elsewhere made. However, these revisions are sparingly made. In fact, two of the typescripts, "The Original Follies Girl" and "Poor Working Girl," apparently bear no revisions at all by him, other than the added titles.

On the other hand, all five typescripts were thoroughly revised in Zelda Fitzgerald's holograph. In most instances, her corrections are minor—reorganizing and tightening wordy phrases; sharpening images; substituting more effective adjectives or verbs. Three of the stories, however, bear evidence of her enhanced interest in the details of craftsmanship, of careful revision. The final paragraph of "The Original Follies Girl," for instance, was added in revising the typescript, adding to the story's tone of elegaic wistfulness:

> Gay was too good a companion and too pretty to go dying like that for a romanticism that she was always half afraid would slip away from her.[30]

She similarly revised "The Girl the Prince Liked," giving it a completely new ending, and apparently discarding the earlier conclusion. Again, the mood of sustained, isolated loss—a mood which may have been suggested by the "dying fall" endings of a number of her husband's stories—is strengthened. The accompanying photograph shows the revised ending.

However, the last of the series, "A Millionaire's Girl," received the most extensive rewriting. Nine of its twenty-seven pages of triple-spaced typescript were heavily revised; four of these include paragraph-length additions aimed at exploring in greater depth the emotional reactions of characters, or heightening descriptive imagery to influence mood. One example may serve to illustrate the kind of craftsmanship Mrs. Fitzgerald was learning to apply. The principal characters are Caroline—a talented and beautiful social climber—and Barry—a wealthy and aristocratic man with whom she has fallen in love. His family, of course, has objected, and has attempted to bribe her to break off their engagement. There is an argument in Ciro's Club, after which Caroline and Barry part ways. The typescript did not explore the nature of the disagreement, leaving the impression that Caroline petulantly attacked Barry for having the sort of family who would insult her. The sense of the typescript version may be derived if one reads the story as printed in *Bits of Paradise*, skipping the middle paragraph on page 257. That paragraph, as may be seen in the accompanying photograph, was added, in Zelda Fitzgerald's hand, to the typescript. It reads:

> Everyone was delighted with so public and melodramatic a *crise* in a romance that had inspired so much envy. Before they left even the waiters in the place had gleaned the story of Caroline's foolish acceptance of a nice big check and an automible from Barry's father. She claimed to Barry that she had not understood it was to have been the reward for letting him go and he claimed in no uncertain terms that she was fundamentally, hopelessly and irreclaimably dishonest. It seems too bad that they couldn't have done their claiming at home because then they might have patched up the mess. But too many people had witnessed the scene for either of them to give in an inch[31]

The addition makes specific the causes of the dissolution of the romance, while it adds depth to the characterization of both principals. Caroline becomes more naively opportunistic, while Barry is made to display more clearly the pompous rigidity of his breeding. Both are exposed as proud, mettlesome personalities.

To be sure, these revisions may have, in whole or in part, been suggested by Fitzgerald as he read the typescripts; however, the fact that there are some minor additions in his holograph to several of the typescripts makes the likelihood strong that the additions in Zelda Fitzgerald's hand reflect her own thinking. This evidence of substantially increased attention to the details of literary craftsmanship, as she began more and more to consider herself a writer in her own right, is matched by the steadily improving skills she was developing, from story to story, as she moved through the series. "The Original Follies Girl" and "Poor Working Girl," the first two pieces she wrote, were scarcely more than sketches. The first one, which was published in the July 1929 *College Humor*,[32] followed, sympathetically, the fortunes of a beautiful performer, Gay, who surrounded her life with objects and fine clothing, to create a sense of position and accomplishment through possessions and the flair for displaying them with panache. Little characterization slipped in, although there were occasional glimpses of Gay's feelings and thoughts.

The second, "Poor Working Girl," was much more flippant, going back to some of the tone of "Our Own Movie Queen." There was no effort to create reader sympathy for Eloise Everette Elkins, a vacuous, poorly-educated girl from a small-town middle class background. The reader merely follows her as she fails miserably as a governess, abandons her vague plans for a stage career, and settles down to a dreary career as the pretty girl in the electric company's offices. A note of pathos was added at the end, as we are informed that Eloise is the end-product of "worn-out stock." Apparently not even Swanson was very happy with this story, since he postponed publication until January 1931, at the end of the series.[33]

11.

·her away as if she'd been something inedible served

from the kitchen. Everybody was delighted~~with joy~~ *public and* ~~declamatio~~

a cross in a romance that had inspired so much envy.

~~R.~~ ~~Two~~ days later Barry shut the bumpings and thump-

that usually follow a complete disillusionment

ings of ~~an~~ *the* embryo delirium-tremens into a golden-oak

suite of one of the biggest Transatlantic liners en

route for Paris. Two weeks later as I was bumping along

the walnut panellings of a transcontinental express on

my way to California I slipped along the rounded corner

and bang into Caroline. I don't know how I had expected

surprised

to find her but I was terribly ~~impressed~~ with her air

of elegant martyrdom. She was royalty in exile. From

the slope of her shoulders to the eloquent inactivity

of her hands her whole person cried out "This is the

way I am and I'm going to stick by it." Now I knew that

Caroline had not a bit of that "fading-violets closing-

that makes people run

from things

episode" note of the minor lyric poet in her erstwhile

personality, and I wondered what determination had sent

"A Millionaire's Girl" (Princeton University Library).

when she's finished with dashing about
disturbing the susceptible, making susceptible
the disturbing, perhaps you will find her one
day enveloped in Ventian shawls hugging
the most elaborate heating system that money
can buy and ending her fairy tales with "I
, of course it's true because
— it happened to me". But she will have
to be a very old grandmother indeed because
she doesn't like talking about herself, and has so
little of the romantic about her that she
took, so the story goes, the bracelet (that she
will always keep as proof that romance has
not passed out of the world) into a jewelers
to have it valued. I wonder if the
reflections of the gray palace being
at the depth of the stones added any to the weight
in the jewelers scale, or if that added importance was
only for Helena, to help her remember her
fairy story when life leaves her time
for telling it.

"The Girl the Prince Liked" (Princeton University Library).

Harriet, the "Southern Girl" of the third sketch, which appeared in the February 1930 *College Humor*,[34] received more sympathy and attention from her creator. While her story retains some of the air of the mood piece, designed to create sympathy for the disciplined, self-sufficient belle, making the best of the straitened circumstances into which her family has fallen, a basic plot was added. In tracing the complications of separate romances between Harriet and a pair of young men from Ohio, Zelda Fitzgerald reconsidered the theme of incompatibility between Southerner and Northerner her husband had studied in "The Ice Palace." A saccharin resolution mars the story, but it was a decided advance over the first two.

"The Girl the Prince Liked" and "The Girl with Talent" were more ambitious efforts. Each was over 3000 words in length, and followed its heroine through a more sustained and complicated plot, as the two women—"girl" was no longer an applicable term— fought to find excitement and happiness outside the confines of conventional, if affluent, marriages. Both move restlessly to Europe, abandoning husband and children in search of adventure and fulfillment, respectively, as the mistress of the Prince of Wales, and as a cabaret performer. "The Girl the Prince Liked," which appeared in the February 1930 *College Humor*,[35] is perhaps the stronger story, in that it closes on a note of ironic self-recognition as Helena is left with her memories, both of her conquest, and of what she sacrificed for it—a self-possessed but toughened international femme fatale. Lou, in "The Girl with Talent," is permitted a more conventional happy ending, as she suddenly, but ironically, finds another husband and has another child, settling down in China to the same kind of bourgois contentment she fled in New York. The "happy" ending was more appropriate for *College Humor,* in the April 1930 issue in which the story appeared,[36] than had been the starker closing of the earlier story; only the endings varied, however. The stories shared otherwise a quality of increased narrative achievement which was the result of Zelda Fitzgerald's increased attention to a number of facets of fictional technique.

The most striking and effective of these technical devices was the development of a narrative perspective which permitted her to create both a sense of involved immediacy with her characters, and a level of detached judgment. At first, as it began to emerge in the "Girl" series, it was little more than an unidentified narrative voice, a first-person author-observer, undefined by sex or character, who described the appearances and actions of Gay, the "Follies Girl," and Eloise, the "Working Girl," as if it were present as an element of their environment, observing, offering ironic closing assessments, but rarely privy to their thoughts, other than in an occasional limited-omniscient glimpse. In "Southern Girl," however, the

voice became at times plural—a narrative "we," more closely
identified with the specific social fabric of the small Southern
community, analogous to the perspective later used, for instance, by
William Faulkner in "Smoke" and *The Town.* Yet the narrator
could become an individual separating from the community to drift
away, as did the protagonist:

> I left Jeffersonville about then, but I can imagine how the winter
> came and the groups about the parlor at Harriet's grew bigger and
> perhaps younger.[37]

The process of individualization of the narrator permitted
flexibility of scene; "I" left Jeffersonville, in part, so that when
Harriet visited New York there would be an observer. A sense of
distance was also achieved, but at the same time, the observer-
narrator also began to participate more immediately, more actively,
in the destiny of the protagonist. In "The Girl the Prince Liked"
and "The Girl with Talent," the narrator became a party—
sometimes conspiratorially, frequently disapprovingly—to the
increasingly self-destructive life-styles of the protagonists, even
attempting to become involved at one point in a subtle marital
conflict between Lou and her first husband.

Zelda Fitzgerald may not have consciously patterened her
narrator after the observer-participants her husband had employed
so effectively in *The Great Gatsby* or "The Rich Boy." Nevertheless,
by the time she had come to composition of "A Millionaire's Girl,"
she had honed a tool which, like Nick Carraway, simultaneously
permitted access to events, judgmental detachment, and, to the
extent that the narrator is sensitive to the ominous self-destructive
nature of a quality of life shared with the protagonist, a sense of
involvement in their struggles.

That element of involvement is even stronger in Zelda Fitzgerald's
stories. Carraway came to know himself and his society through
Gatsby's tragedy, but it was not essentially *his* tragedy; there is, by
the end of the "Girl" series, almost a sense of fusion between
narrator and protagonist, as though the narrative identity were a
self-questioning element of the protagonist's psyche. That identity
is confusingly complicated in "A Millionaire's Girl" by the fact that
the narrator is identified at one point as one of the Fitzgeralds, as
Caroline and Barry become engaged during a visit to a suburban
home jokingly referred to as "Fitzgerald's Roadhouse."[38] Later, the
narrator is found on the same transcontinental train as Caroline,
and becomes her confidant and adviser in Hollywood, sharing to a
degree her romantic confidence in success, but privately doubting

that her marriage to Barry will survive the tempests of conflicting values and ambitions.

As her narrator became more and more important as a focus of evaluation and interpretation, Zelda Fitzgerald was also learning the value of descriptive setting in suggesting mood. The opening passages of "The Southern Girl" and "A Millionaire's Girl" for instance, do far more than simply describe Jeffersonville or New York: they prepare the reader for the kind of personality on which the story will focus, and at the same time economically establish, by accretion of detail, an air of dreamy verisimilitude.

Both the narrator-protagonist fusion and the use of concrete, if romanticised, detail were elements of an increasing proficiency in manipulation of personal experience. It was the growth of a communicated sense of deeply-felt personal struggle which, as much as any quality, lifted the last of the "Girl" series beyond the realm of amateur mood-sketch. In her protagonists, Zelda Fitzgerald was more and more acutely objectifying her own inner struggles for a sense of identity and achievement; simultaneously, through her narrative commentator, she was weighing the consequences of talent subordinated to marriage, or the equally foreboding consequences of a life in which love and romance are subordinated to the search for individual freedom. To be sure, the increased technical sophistication and seriousness of theme could not find full expression in too-brief stories hampered by glib endings— "happy" reversals or sophisticated cynicism. Nevertheless, by the end of the series, Zelda Fitzgerald was writing stories which both her husband and his literary agent recognized as being too good to waste on *College Humor*.

Even as the series progressed, Harold Ober had been able to persuade Swanson to raise the price of the stories, first to $500.00, then to $800.00.[39] However, as Mrs. Fitzgerald came to an increasingly proficient level, calling more and more deeply on a common store of experience which her husband considered "his" material, Fitzgerald wrote to Ober that he felt the price for "The Girl with Talent" should be raised to at least $1000.00.[40] His concern was primarily financial (he suggested, for instance, that, if Swanson would not meet the increase, his name be dropped from the articles); but he was perhaps also increasingly aware of the degree to which Mrs. Fitzgerald's writing was drawing on his professional resources. He was not jealous, but he felt the improved quality demanded more appreciation, and was willing to attempt genteel extortion to obtain it.

This background partially explains the fact that "A Millionaire's Girl" was sold, not to *College Humor*, but to *The Saturday Evening Post*, for a substantially enhanced price ($4000.00), as the product of

Scott Fitzgerald's pen alone.[41] Upon receipt of the typescript, with
its title corrected in Fitzgerald's hand, Ober apparently thought it
was his story alone, and judged it worthy of the *Post*. Ober
subsequently offered profuse apologies to Zelda Fitzgerald, but both
he and Fitzgerald presumably realized that to acknowledge publicly
that the story had been substantially hers would be to risk trouble
with both *College Humor* and *The Saturday Evening Post*. In his
Ledger, however, Fitzgerald took care to ascribe its authorship
entirely to Mrs. Fitzgerald. If she was not permitted the pleasure of
acknowledged success, she could at least take comfort in self-
satisfaction that her story had been accepted as worthy of her
husband, and that it had earned more than all her previous writing
together.[42]

Unfortunately, by the time the story appeared in the 17 May 1930
Saturday Evening Post,[43] Zelda Fitzgerald had undergone her first
major psychological collapse. As she began to recuperate, first at
Valmont, then at Prangins, Switzerland, she apparently
concentrated on writing as a kind of self-protective therapy.[44]
Unable to dance, she increasingly turned to writing as her "work."
Fitzgerald also evidently seized upon her writing as a therapeutic
exercise, taking great pains, through both the Ober office and
Maxwell Perkins, his editor at Scribners, to find publication outlets
for her stories and sketches. As early as 8 June 1930, she had
completed a story, which he was anxious to send off to New York.[45]
By mid-July, he had sent three stories or sketches, probably
including one, to Ober, to be shown, among other possible buyers,
to Perkins for *Scribner's Magazine*.[46] These stories, which were
never sold, have not been found among the Fitzgerald papers. Their
titles—"A Workman," "The Drouth and the Flood," and "The
House"[47]—take on almost symbolic qualities emphasizing
productive labor, structure, and disaster, when one realizes the
conditions under which they were written.

Although Maxwell Perkins, speaking for the editor of *Scribner's
Magazine,* expressed admiration for the imagistic power of the
stories, he wrote Fitzgerald on 5 August 1930 rejecting them.[48] These
are presumably the same sketches which, in November, Fitzgerald
was urging Ober to submit to *Century Magazine* or *The New
Republic,* under the blanket title "Stories from a Swiss Clinique".[49]
On 6 January 1931, Ober wrote Fitzgerald that Edmund Wilson, at
The New Republic, had agreed to keep the sketches for possible use,
although he had not been encouraging, since that magazine rarely
published fiction.[50] Wilson may have simply been acting from
friendship for the Fitzgeralds, of course; but at least Ober's letter
confirms that Zelda Fitzgerald's fiction continued to have potential

for consideration. No further record of these stories, however, has surfaced.

As she became somewhat better adjusted to life at the Forel clinic at Prangins, Zelda Fitzgerald was able to write a story which found better fortune. Fitzgerald sent "Miss Bessie" to Ober sometime in the fall of 1930. By mid-November, Ober had submitted it to *Scribner's Magazine,* which accepted, for the price of $150.00, provided that Mrs. Fitzgerald would revise what Maxwell Perkins termed, in a letter of 12 November to Fitzgerald, her more "remote" and "too numerous" similes and metaphors.[51] Unpublished correspondence of early 1931 between Perkins and Fitzgerald, which may be seen in the Charles Scribner's Sons Archive at Princeton University Library, contains frequent passing reference to the revision, in proof, of "Miss Bessie." Whether from a genuine belief in the merit of the story, or a desire to find some encouraging stimulus for his wife—or a combination of both reasons, Fitzgerald devoted considerable attention to the story, which ultimately appeared under the revised title "Miss Ella" in the December 1931 issue of *Scribner's Magazine.*[52]

A heavily-corrected set of galley proofs of the story exists in the Zelda Sayre Fitzgerald papers at Princeton. The revisions, in a hand which appears to be Zelda Fitzgerald's, are directed primarily at complying with Perkins' requests that some of the more abstract metaphorical passages be made more coherent. In addition to substitutions of words for greater clarity of diction, wordy or vague passages are pared down or rewritten. There is, however, no major reorientation of plot or characterization. Although Scott Fitzgerald may have participated in the revision process, it appears more likely, from the correspondence concerning the story and from the fact that revisions were made in proof stages, that the basic composition is wholly Zelda Fitzgerald's. While her husband may have lent his incisive instinct for diction and phrasing in the revision stage, "Miss Ella" was, more than any of her earlier work, essentially her creation.

The story evidences a creative continuity with the "Girl" series. Point of view is again focussed through a peripheral observer-participant, a young person who seems to be a relative, or intimate, of the family of the protagonist, the spinster of the title. The age and sex of the narrator are never specified, although the nature of the observations offered—details of dress materials, the description of Miss Ella's triangular love story from an essentially feminine perspective—suggests a young girl, receptive to and appreciative of the complexities of Miss Ella's unhappiness.

When he first read the story, Maxwell Perkins was much taken

with treatment of both protagonist and narrator. He wrote
Fitzgerald:

> . . . it did give a very complete strong sense of a character in this
> Southern old maid. It was moving in that way, but it had another
> quality that was still more moving.—In some way it made the reader
> share the feelings of the young girl through whose eyes Miss Bessie
> was seen, so that she was not only real, and in some degree was not
> real, but was as the young girl saw her.[53]

Miss Ella's character is strong because she has continued to
function, despite some mysterious personal tragedy which has made
her a spinster. But it is the sense of *identity,* of sympathy, between
the narrator and Miss Ella which makes the story work. As the
mystery—an effective element of suspense is created as we wait for
the explanation of Miss Ella's spinsterhood—is unfolded by the
narrative voice, the reader is swept into the events. Narrator and
reader seem not merely present but also involved as a rejected suitor
commits suicide on the day of Miss Ella's wedding to his rival,
sealing her self-denying rejection of marriage and happiness. In
effect, the narrator, who had not been born when the events
occurred, and who never reveals how she knows of them, *becomes*
Miss Ella, leading the reader into a mind and soul rigidly bound in
guilty self-denial. The effect is to suffuse the story with a
Faulknerian air of psychological tension; repressed, self-punishing
fury; effectively, if unrealistically, symbolized by the suicide
weapon, deliberately left as a *memento mori* in the summer house.
    Zelda Fitzgerald was continuing to explore the complexities of
the feminine psyche struggling unsuccessfully for mature
fulfillment. "Miss Ella," however, achieved deeper resonance and
integrity through its more consistent sounding of the note of ruin
and waste which had occasionally surfaced in the "Girl" stories. It
was grounded in her own unhappiness, and it attempted to marshal
that unhappiness seriously, without cynicism or artificiality. Miss
Ella had courage and dignity, and a certain romantic glamor, but
they were founded on repressed sensuality and agonized guilt.
Without being at all autobiographical, the story drew its strength
from the sense of lost opportunities and unattained ecstasy which
had come to characterize the lives of both Fitzgeralds.
    The effort to make art of her internal conflicts may have aided
Zelda Fitzgerald in her recuperation. At any rate, by September 1931,
she had been permitted to leave Prangins, to return to the United
States to settle in Montgomery, Alabama, the home town which had
provided the ambience of "Miss Ella." While her husband went to
Hollywood on a screenwriting job, she threw herself feverishly into

her own work. She was also, according to Nancy Milford, beginning systematically to reread her husband's short fiction, both as a means of re-establishing rapport with him and with former happiness, and as a disciplined effort to study and benefit from his fictional techniques.[54]

Milford credits Zelda Fitzgerald with writing, during the next six months, seven short stories, in addition to the first draft of her novel, *Save Me the Waltz*.[55] Of these, apparently only "A Couple of Nuts," her last published short story, has survived. The story may have actually been written at Prangins; if not, it must have been one of the first of this new group of stories, since it was in Maxwell Perkins' hands by mid-October, only a month after Zelda Fitzgerald's release from Prangins. On 21 October, Perkins wrote to Fitzgerald:

> I think there is no doubt that Zelda has a great deal of talent, and of a very colorful, almost poetic kind. In the case of the particular story, "The Two Nuts" I think perhaps the color and all that, rather overwhelmed the story.[56]

Perkins went on to praise the story's metaphorical freshness, although he felt that that quality interfered with its continuity. Nevertheless, he returned it for revision, with the possibility that *Scribner's Magazine* might accept it. Whether Fitzgerald, who was about to depart for Hollywood, was himself involved in the revision is unclear; no manuscript or other pre-publication version is known to exist. In the absence of other evidence, it is quite likely that Zelda Fitzgerald completed her own revisions of this story. The revised story was acceptable to *Scribner's Magazine,* which published "A Couple of Nuts" in its August 1932 issue.[57]

The story is usually assessed as her most accomplished short fiction. Matthew J. Bruccoli terms it ". . . Zelda Fitzgerald's best effort—. . . closer to a real story than any of the others."[58] Nancy Milford finds that in it, ". . . Zelda was in control of her talent."[59] There are no major new departures in technique in the story: point of view is channelled, once again, through an unnamed narrator-participant, who moves in the same decadent world of European cafe society as the protagonists, a young couple named Larry and Lola. To be sure, the narrator's plane of existence differs: she (or possibly even "he") is an established habitue of the salons, clubs, and villas of the Paris-Cannes axis, while the protagonists are adventuresome night-club entertainers, attempting to parlay their talent, youth, and physical charm into success and acceptance.

The narrator follows them through a metamorphosis from a kind of cynical innocence which accepted life—including marriage—as a grand romantic adventure to dissipation and dissolution: they cease to have *adventures* and become mere adventurers.

That process is precipitated by a new character in Zelda Fitzgerald's cast of standards, a charming, wealthy, but thoroughly amoral socialite, Jeff Daugherty, who toys with the transparent ambitions of the couple as idly as he carries out a passing liasion with Lola. Daugherty is a master of social ease and coordination, but about him clings a perceptible aura of what Milford has termed "ruin,"[60] a major thematic component of the story. He is an almost allegorical personification of illusory superficial glamor masking meaningless and psychically destructive unproductiveness. Even flight to the United States cannot preserve the romantic and artistic integrity of Lola and Larry's marriage. A former wife of Daugherty, as decadently predatory as her ex-husband, completes the destruction. Her seduction of Larry leads to scandal, threatened divorce, and his death, appropriately the result of storm at sea.

The narrator (thus vicariously, the reader) has refrained from actively intervening out of lassitude and, perhaps, class loyalty. Consequently, the narrator becomes implicated in the decay and moral irresponsibility represented in the characterization, plot, and setting. Zelda Fitzgerald called on all her practice to suffuse the story with a sustained tone, ominous and sinister, of loss and destruction. Her physical descriptions reinforce the moral qualities of the story. For instance, as Larry bends all his efforts toward retaining a pretence of nonchalant ignorance of a summer affair between Lola and Daugherty, the couple (along with the narrator, of course) remain too long on the Riviera:

> Jeff left with his fatuous coterie. We three shivered alone in the prickly sunshine of the beach. The ocean turned muddy and our bathing clothes didn't dry from one brisk swim to another; we grew irritable with the unspent tang of the sea.[61]

The beach's sudden loss of charm, coincident with the departure of Daugherty, reinforces the illusory nature of his social magic, and prefigures the death of romance and happiness.

"A Couple of Nuts" also displayed Mrs. Fitzgerald's mastery of irony as a device for control. The narrator, with self-deprecating wit, analyzes her unwillingness to act to save the youngsters. More ironically, Lola ends the story by describing Daugherty and his ex-wife as "a couple of nuts," the same phrase Daugherty had used to dismiss Larry and Lola from his consideration. Lola's phrase betrays her almost-total lack of appreciation of the enormity of the evil which had crushed her fragile dreams.

Without writing veiled autobiography, Zelda Fitzgerald had learned to turn her own experience, including internal torment and struggle, to account in creating moving and affecting fiction. She still needed the guidance and correction of others, but she was surely pleased with the maturity and depth of "Miss Ella" and "A Couple of Nuts." She had begun to consider herself a fledging professional. One indication of her increased self-confidence is that she began to send manuscripts directly to Ober, without waiting to submit them for her husband's suggestions and revisions.[62] A more substantial indication was the novel she had begun to write in early 1932. Her progress, from "Our Own Movie Queen" through the "Girl" series had enhanced her narrative and technical capacities to a point at which she evidently felt herself worthy and capable of artistic independence from her husband.

That desire for independence had undoubtedly been spurred by an increasingly ambivalent attitude on Scott Fitzgerald's part. He had always been patient with his wife's attempts to write, particularly as he felt they amused her, or offered therapeutic occupation. But he had from time to time exhibited a sense of possessive superiority, particularly when she attempted more "serious" writing, with its inevitable infringement on a reservoir of deeply-felt personal experience he insisted was "his" material. In 1930, he had written to one of his wife's doctors that, if he had to choose between her health and his profession, the choice would be in favor of his ambitions to be part of English literature.[63] As he struggled more and more desperately to compose a novel based in themes of loss and the decay of dreams, and set in the France of Parisian night clubs and Riviera villas, he may well have begun to consider his wife's work amateurish pilferings from his own writing. He certainly would have that reaction to her novel, when he finally saw its manuscript, leading up to a tense confrontation, in 1933, in which he described her as a third-rate writer whose efforts were robbing him of his material.[64] Thus, the knowledge, in 1932, that he harbored such resentments assuredly played a part in Zelda Fitzgerald's increased efforts toward independence. In explaining to Fitzgerald why she had submitted the manuscript of *Save Me the Waltz* to Scribners without first showing it to him, she wrote:

> Also, feeling it to be a dubious production due to my own instability I did not want a scathing criticism such as you have mercilessly—if for my own good given my last stories, poor things.[65]

The aura of rationalized self-justification is there, of course. Nevertheless, there is also the ring of unpleasant truth in emotion-laden words like "scathing" and "mercilessly." By 1932, the quality of Zelda Fitzgerald's writing had truly improved to a point at which she must have seemed to her husband a kind of ungrateful rival. It is surely not necessary to see her as his artistic equal to recognize that, through the example, opportunities, guidance Fitzgerald had given her, she had been able to nurture her creative flair into literary talent of sufficient merit to threaten his uniqueness in a way that would have serious repercussions as she turned to the novel for which her stories had been preludes.

The body of Zelda Fitzgerald's fiction is too small, and for the most part insufficiently distinguished, to judge whether, with better fortune, she might have truly achieved her goal of professional mastery. Nevertheless, stories such as "Miss Ella," and "A Couple of Nuts" demonstrate that her sporadic apprenticeship to her husband had had very valuable results. By the time she had published her last short story, she was well on her way to a literary self-sufficiency rooted in tempestuous partnership with Scott Fitzgerald. Whether she would ever have achieved a truly independent professional stature is a moot question. That she had the ability to write moving and true fiction is amply witnessed in her last short stories.

Huntingdon College

---

[1]Selected by Scottie Fitzgerald Smith and Matthew J. Bruccoli (London: Bodley Head, 1974); American edition published in October 1974 by Scribners. Observations on Zelda Fitzgerald's short stories are based on the Bodley Head text.

[2]There is apparently only one completed short story extant which has not been published. It exists in typescript in the Zelda Fitzgerald papers at Princeton University Library, under the title "Other Names for Roses." Internal evidence places its composition in the early 1940's, a decade after the last of the published stories was written.

[3]Milford, *Zelda A Biography* (New York: Harper & Row, 1970). This paragraph and the following three are much indebted to Nancy Milford's assessment of the Fitzgeralds' relationship.

[4]Publication details are derived from: *Zelda*, p. 102; and Matthew J. Bruccoli, *F. Scott Fitzgerald A Descriptive Bibliography* (Pittsburgh: University of Pittsburgh Press, 1972), Section I, "Zelda Fitzgerald's Publications," p. 306. (Hereafter *F. Scott Fitzgerald A Descriptive Bibliography* is cited as *Bibliography*.)

[5]*F. Scott Fitzgerald's Ledger A Facsimile* (Washington, D. C.: Bruccoli Clark/NCR Microcard Editions, 1972), pp. 6-7.

[6]*Ibid.*, p. 55.

[7]*Ibid.*, p. 143.

[8]*Zelda*, p. 100. The interview, entitled "What a 'Flapper Novelist' Thinks of His Wife," first appeared in the Baltimore *Evening Sun* (7 October 1923), Section 5, p. 2. A shortened version, containing the material here cited, may be seen in *F. Scott Fitzgerald in His Own Time A Miscellany*, ed. Matthew J. Bruccoli and Jackson R. Bryer (Kent, Ohio: Kent State University Press, 1971), pp. 258-262. (Hereafter this work is cited as *Miscellany*.)

[9]*Ledger*, p. 54, and *Bibliography*, p. 306, refer to a piece entitled "The Super-Flapper," which was sold to an unidentified publication but apparently never printed. It may have been another of Zelda Fitzgerald's early stories.

[10]*As Ever, Scott Fitz—Letters Between F. Scott Fitzgerald and His Literary Agent, Harold Ober, 1919-1940*, ed. Matthew J. Bruccoli & Jennifer Atkinson (Philadelphia: Lippincott, 1972), p. 51n.

[11]*Bibliography*, p. 306.

[12]I am deeply grateful to Mr. Alexander Clark, Curator of Manuscripts at the Princeton University Library, and to his staff, for their assistance in my review of Fitzgerald manuscript materials.

[13]"*The Beautiful and Damned:* Friend Husband's Latest," reprinted in *Miscellany*, pp. 332-334. The quotation is found on p. 333.

[14]See *Bibliography*, pp. 306-307.

[15]See, for example, correspondence between Fitzgerald and his agent, in early 1925, in which Fitzgerald rejected *College Humor's* offer to serialize *The Great Gatsby*. He offered instead to write the editors a nice letter, and to write an article for the magazine. *As Ever, Scott Fitz—*. pp. 73-75.

[16]*Bibliography*, p. 232.

[17]*Ledger*, p. 143.

[18]*Ibid.*, p. 64.

[19]*As Ever, Scott Fitz—*, p. 127.

[20]*Ibid.*, p. 128.

[21]*Ibid.*

[22]*Ledger*, p. 65.

[23]*Zelda*, pp. 132-133.

[24]See, for example, *Zelda*, p. 165, in which Milford cites a letter of mid-June 1930, to Fitzgerald, and p. 257, in which she quotes from an unidentified clinical source: "All I ask to do is to work."

[25]*As Ever, Scott Fitz—*, pp. 130-131.

[26]*Ibid.*

[27]*Ibid.*, pp. 132-133, 135, 142-144, 146-147, 165-168.

[28]*Ibid.*, p. 150.

[29]*Zelda*, p. 150. Milford cites a letter of 13 June 1934, FSF to ZSF.

[30]*Bits of Paradise*, p. 217.

[31]*Ibid.*, p. 257.

[32]*Bibliography*, p. 307.

[33]*Ibid.*, p. 308.

[34]*Ibid.*, p. 307.

[35]*Ibid.*

[36]*Ibid.*

[37]*Bits of Paradise*, p. 227.

[38]*Ibid.*, p. 255.

[39]See *As Ever, Scott Fitz—*, pp. 133, 148, 154.

[40]*Ibid.*, pp. 146-147.

[41]The nature of that negotiation is outlined in correspondence between Fitzgerald and Ober *As Ever, Scott Fitz—*, pp. 165-166, and in the *Ledger*, pp. 66, 143.

[42]As might have been expected, Swanson of *College Humor* was not entirely deceived. He wired Fitzgerald and Ober in May 1930, expressing his displeasure that "A Millionaire's Girl" had gone to *The Saturday Evening Post*. Ober, in a letter of 26 May, counseled Fitzgerald simply to ignore Swanson's anger, but not to submit any more of the "Girl" series to

College Humor. See *As Ever, Scott Fitz—,* p. 171.

[43]*Bibliography,* p. 308.

[44]See *Zelda,* Chapters Ten and Eleven (pp. 147-191) for the most extensive treatment of Mrs. Fitzgerald's first breakdown and recuperation.

[45]*Ibid.,* pp. 162-163.

[46]See *Dear Scott/Dear Max The Fitzgerald-Perkins Correspondence,* ed. John Kuehl and Jackson R. Bryer (New York: Scribners, 1971), pp. 166-167.

[47]*Ibid.,* p. 166n.

[48]*Ibid.,* p. 168.

[49]*As Ever, Scott Fitz—,* p. 172.

[50]*Ibid.,* pp. 173-175.

[51]*Ibid.,* p. 173, and *Dear Scott/Dear Max,* pp. 169-170.

[52]*Bibliography,* p. 308. Fitzgerald's efforts even extended to sounding Perkins out on the feasibility of publishing a book collection of his wife's stories and sketches (See *Dear Scott/Dear Max,* pp. 168-169.). He revived the idea in 1934, at another period when Mrs. Fitzgerald was very much in need of therapeutic self-assurance (*Zelda,* p. 298).

[53]*Dear Scott/Dear Max,* p. 170.

[54]*Zelda,* p. 196.

[55]*Ibid.,* pp. 194 and 399 (endnotes). Milford lists the following titles: "All About the Down's Case," "Cotton Belt," "Sweet Chariot," "Getting Away from It All," "The Story Thus Far," "A Myth in a Moral," and "A Couple of Nuts." Matthew J. Bruccoli, in *As Ever, Scott Fitz—,* p. 179n, suggests that the last two are duplicate titles for the same story, and notes that "Crime Passionelle," another Zelda Fitzgerald story mentioned in a letter from Fitzgerald to Harold Ober, is an alternative title for "All About the Downs Case." Bruccoli's listing of titles varies from Milford's by dropping the apostrophe from "Down's," and by listing the alternative title for "A Couple of Nuts" as "There's a Myth in a Moral."

[56]*Dear Scott/Dear Max,* p. 172.

[57]*Bibliography,* p. 308.

[58]"Preface," *Bits of Paradise,* p. 12.

[59]*Zelda,* p. 194.

[60]*Ibid.,* p. 195.

[61]*Bits of Paradise,* p. 332.

[62]*Zelda,* pp. 199-200.

[63]*Ibid.,* pp. 171-172.

[64]*Ibid.,* p. 273.

[65]*Ibid.,* p. 220.

EDWIN T. ARNOLD

THE MOTION PICTURE AS METAPHOR IN THE WORKS OF F. SCOTT FITZGERALD

In 1936, in the first of his "Crack-Up" essays, F. Scott Fitzgerald stated that the "test of a first-rate intelligence is the ability to hold two opposed ideas in the mind at the same time, and still retain the ability to function."[1] He went on to define this ability in relation to his own life:

> One should, for example, be able to see that things are hopeless and yet be determined to make them otherwise. This philosophy fitted on to my early adult life, when I saw the improbable, the implausible, often the "impossible," come true. Life was something you dominated if you were any good. Life yielded easily to intelligence and effort, or to what proportion could be mustered of both (69).

In the second essay of the same series, he discussed the failure to deal with life on these terms. Then,

> . . . the tendency is to refuse to face things as long as possible by retiring into an infantile dream—but one is continually startled out of this by various contacts with the world. One meets these occasions as quickly and carelessly as possible and retires once more back into the dream, hoping that things will adjust themselves by some great material or spiritual bonanza.[2]

These articles were written toward the end of Fitzgerald's career, and they expressed a hard-won wisdom gained through harsh

43

experience; but Fitzgerald had incorporated the same themes into his works from the beginning, just as they were to be at the center of his final great work, *The Last Tycoon*. And throughout his works, one of his most successful approaches to these themes was achieved through the metaphor of the cinema. Here was a world in which the real and the unreal, the illusion and the mechanics of the illusion not only existed side by side, but actually intertwined in their own complex way. Here he also found two ideal symbols, personifications of two possible attitudes toward life, in the actor, who enters the illusion and is controlled by it, and in the director, who "dominates" the cheap and the mundane around him. For Fitzgerald, the director, not the actor, is the artist,[3] and in the theater or the cinema the director is able to create, at least momentarily, a perfect world in which all things can be ordered, planned and carried out to a "happy ending."

Yet, with that sense of irony which he was never able to deny, Fitzgerald saw that the very possibility of perfection suggested in these creations ultimately only emphasized the imperfection and inevitability of life as it is. Thus, paradoxically, the illusion, for Fitzgerald, often became the means by which a character is made to face reality. It is each character's reaction to this confrontation with reality that determines not his success or failure—for all of the important characters eventually fail—but the tragic intensity of his struggle and hence the glory of his fall.

The concept of the actor is one which Fitzgerald examined in his earliest writings. Such stories as "The Offshore Pirate," "Myra Meets His Family," and "Rags Martin-Jones and the Pr-nce of W-les" use the rather artificial convention of a group of actors being employed for the purpose of deception. The most important of these is "The Offshore Pirate," in which Curtis Carlyle manages to win Ardita Farnam through an imaginative ploy which combines, for a time, the worlds of illusion and reality.

The actor, or the poseur, receives his fullest early examination in *This Side of Paradise* in the character of Amory Blaine. Even as a child Amory is very much a poseur, planning his entrances and romanticizing his actions. He centers his life on what he calls his "favorite waking dreams"[4] in which he firmly establishes himself as hero. He is a richly imaginative child who attempts to impose his created world on the existing world. Nor is this a tendency that he outgrows. At Princeton, for example, he is recognized as a "clever actor" (35) and has no problem winning a role in the Triangle Club play.

Amory carries his thespian abilities into his romances, but is finally upstaged by Rosalind Connage. Rosalind is as adept as

Amory at dramatizing her passions and sorrows, although she is not as likely to become lost in her roles; she is more of a professional. As if to emphasize this characteristic of acting, of posing, on the part of both Amory and Rosalind, Fitzgerald renders the dialogues of their dramatic meeting and farewell in playlet form. Through this indirect comment on their acting tendencies, Fitzgerald carefully undercuts the reader's sympathy toward the lovers.

Following his interlude with Rosalind, Amory's tendency to falsify emotions becomes, in his resultant cynicism (which itself is a kind of act), more pronounced. With Eleanor Savage, for example, he "could, as always, run through the emotions [of love] in a half hour, but even while they revelled in their imaginations, he knew that neither of them could care as he had cared once before . . ." (248). With Eleanor he tries "to play Rupert Brooke" (248), but after their horrifying experience on the cliff, when the harsh reality of death— and of madness—intrudes, Amory finds that "their poses were strewn about the pale dawn like broken glass" (258).

For Amory, then, posing is a romantic exercise, an acting out of his "waking dreams," but it is also a part of his quest, for in posing he is searching for himself, for an identity. Therefore, the pose, while essentially false, is paradoxically a means of his finding the truth. This idea is best expressed and defined by Monsignor Darcy. When Amory tells him, "I was beginning to think I was growing eccentric till I came up here. It was a pose, I guess," Monsignor Darcy gives him this advice, "Don't worry about that; for you not posing may be the biggest pose of all. Pose. . . . But do the next thing" (115). This need to "do the next thing" is the essence of the Fitzgerald hero; Amory, Gatsby, Stahr, all pose, but they also go beyond the pose. To act is not enough; through the act one must become.

This Side of Paradise was published in 1920, before the motion picture had entrenched itself as the primary form of entertainment, and the cinema plays little part in the novel. Amory likes the movies, but primarily because they give him the opportunity to interact with the other members of the audience. Amory's true fascination lies in New York and the theater. New York is his dream city; the theater is the illusion incarnate: "When they walked down the aisle of the theatre, greeted by the nervous twanging and discord of untuned violins and the sensuous, heavy fragrance of paint and powder, he moved in a sphere of epicurean delight. Everything enchanted him" (32).

For Amory, the theater is inseparably linked with, and in many ways personified by, the "wonderful girl," a "stunning young brunette who made him sit with brimming eyes in the ecstasy of watching her dance" (33). Just as the theater, with its "heavy fragrance of paint and powder," betrays an appeal to the sensual as well as the romantic, so the wonderful dancing girl both attracts and disturbs Amory in a physical way that cuts through his idealistic reveries. As he walks with his friend Paskert, who swears that he would "marry that girl to-night" (33) if given the opportunity, Amory momentarily stops to question the dream. "I wonder about actresses," he asks Paskert, "are they all pretty bad?" (34). In spite of himself, Amory is unable to give himself up completely to the dream. He is unsettled by the cheapness which he suspects lies beneath it, in this case, a cheapness associated with sex.

The illusion surrounding the wonderful girl and the theater is further exposed to Amory in his experience with the chorus girl, Axia Marlowe. Axia tempts Amory in an overtly physical manner as she lays "her yellow head" (122) on his shoulder. Just as he is about to give in to her temptation, Amory sees an apparition, a man whose face "was cast in . . . yellow wax . . . a sort of virile pallor" (123), a color which links the evil Amory senses in the man with that he fears in Axia. After fleeing them both, Amory finds that he is no longer able to romanticize this world of the theater. The next day, as he and Sloane walk through the streets of New York, "Broadway broke upon them, and with the babel of noise and the painted faces a sudden sickness rushed over Amory" (127). Having realized this cheapness, this evil, Amory is faced with two choices. He can either retreat into his illusions, into his acts and poses, or he can, having recognized this reality, try to transcend it, make it into something better. This second choice is the philosophy expressed by Ardita Farnam in "The Offshore Pirate:"

> And courage to me meant ploughing through that dull gray mist that comes down on life—not only overriding people and circumstances but overriding the bleakness of living. A sort of insistence on the value of life and the worth of transient things. . . . My courage is faith—faith in the eternal resilience of me—that joy'll come back, and hope and spontaneity.[5]

Amory, like Ardita, chooses to rely on himself, and it is on this note that the book ends: " 'I know myself,' he cried, 'but that is all' " (305).

Whether Amory successfully accepts the challenge of life is left unclear, but in his next novel, *The Beautiful and Damned*, Fitzgerald examined those people who clearly lack the courage and faith in themselves to face life, who, instead, attempt to retreat from it. Anthony Patch, like Amory, is a man repelled by the smell, the noise, the tawdriness of the city and all it represents of reality, but unlike Amory, he is not willing to become involved with it, to try to change it. Rather, Anthony tries to deny its existence by sequestering himself in his own "inner sanctum," his bathroom. This bathroom aptly symbolizes Anthony's attempted escape into a world of romantic illusion. It is a fabulous place, and on its walls are hung "photographs of four celebrated thespian beauties of the day,"[6] non-threatening representations of his romantic dreams. In their presence Anthony is secure; there is no need to act, for in this state he can admire them, and they can admire him, with no demands made on either side. Yet this is an obviously sterile existence; Anthony's ideal is essentially lifeless.

The duality of Anthony's thoughts reveals itself in an argument with Gloria after their marriage. She wants to become an actress, one of those very beauties whom Anthony so admires. Yet when faced with her desire, to put her dreams into action, Anthony is repelled and frightened, and falls back into his pose of snobbish superiority. "But it's so silly!" he tells her. "You don't want to go into the movies—moon around a studio all day with a lot of cheap chorus people" (214). Despite this condemnation, Anthony does his own "mooning" around, and his own girlfriends are both linked, at least peripherally, with the theater and cinema. One—Geraldine— is an usher, a simple girl, but more honest, and more decent than the superior-seeming Anthony. The second, Dorothy Raycroft, first meets Anthony at the Bijou Moving Picture Theatre, and he seduces her with promises essentially as false as the film on the screen. In the dark theater, which becomes his place of assignation, Anthony fantasizes as much as either of these girls. In the light of reality, the actress-goddesses of Anthony's imagination are revealed as rather sad, pathetic and common. His dream is too weak and too corrupt to be rewarded with any greater prize. His decline is directly related not to any action on his part, but to his very lack of action—both his dream and his soul are victims of atrophy.

Anthony's friend, Richard Caramel, is also unable to maintain his dream. After a highly promising start as a writer, Caramel betrays his talent by becoming a hack, writing for money. He, like Anthony, is at first contemptuous of the motion picture people. But Caramel adds "action" to his plots in order to sell to the cinema he abhors, and becomes known as one who was "making a great fortune by writing trash for the movies" (422). He perverts his gifts without having the honesty to admit—even to himself—that he is doing so.

Gloria's reaction to the cinema is more complex than that of Anthony or Richard Caramel. In the section, "A Flash-Back in Paradise," when the Voice tells Beauty, who becomes Gloria, that she is going to Earth, he says, "At first it was thought that you would go this time as an actress in the motion-pictures but, after all, it's not advisable" (29). Instead, she becomes a "susciety gurl." The comparison of the two, however, emphasizes the essential falseness which lies behind Gloria's beautiful facade. It is also ironic in that Gloria, when she recognizes that her time as a society girl is ending, that she is moving past the accepted age for such a role, turns to the motion pictures as her own hope of escape. When she is young and courageous in her youth, she speaks in a manner reminiscent of Ardita Farnam. While visiting General Lee's home, which she sees as pathetic because it is denied the decency, the dignity, of abiding by its naturally allotted time, she argues passionately on the value of transiency:

> "Beautiful things grow to a certain height and then they fail and fade off, breathing out memories as they decay. And just as any period decays in our minds, the things of that period should decay too, and in that way they're preserved for a while in the few hearts like mine that react to them. . . . There's no beauty without poignancy and there's no poignancy without the feeling that it's going, men, names, books, houses—bound for dust—mortal——" (166-67).

Yet, when she is faced with her own aging, she—just like Anthony and Richard—turns to the cinema as a means of denying the actual. Offered a screen test by Bloeckman when she was younger, Gloria turned it down. Now, nearing thirty, she sees a certain kind of immortality available to her on film. There she can be fixed, held, in her momentary perfection, not only for herself but for all others who see the film. Also, as an actress, she can escape into what she sees as a very romantic world, unlike that she is now facing with Anthony. But when she first makes the rounds of the motion picture employment agencies, she is appalled by the reality beneath her dream. The first agency smells "as though it had been dead a very long time" (370), a harsh foreshadowing of her own realization of mortality. When she is finally given a screen test, arranged by Bloeckman, she enacts the part of a twenty-year-old girl, but is eventually offered the role of a *"very haughty rich widow"* (403). Ironically, the artificial medium in which she had hoped to preserve her beauty, the means by which she had tried to avoid reality, becomes the very agent which forces her—if only momentarily—to acknowledge the truth. Her brave valediction at Lee's home becomes a pathetic, confused whimper: "Oh, my pretty face! Oh, I don't want to live without my pretty face! Oh, what's *happened?*" (404). And she, too, retreats, "smear[ing] her face with some new unguent which she hoped illogically would give back the glow and freshness to her vanishing beauty" (416).

Against these three failed characters, the coarse, crude Joseph

Bloeckman, the movie magnate, stands out as the most admirable person in the novel. As vice-president of "Films Par Excellence," he is completely out of place among the sophisticates of the Patch crowd. He is the object of their undisguised scorn. Although he loves Gloria, she calls him "Blockhead," and Anthony thinks of him as "a robust and offensive hog" (125). Yet, with everything against him, Bloeckman is, nonetheless, "a dignified man and a proud one" (96), which makes him far superior to Anthony. What he lacks in sophistication, he makes up for in energy, determination, and a sharp sense of reality. From a totally inauspicious beginning, he, alone, of all the characters, is able to realize his dream, and that dream is himself. Quoting subtitles from his own movies, he begins slowly and carefully to recreate himself into his chosen image. Although his rise is clearly meant to emphasize Anthony's decline, it also contrasts the man of action— the man who produces, who directs—with the man who merely poses. By the end of the novel, Bloeckman, whose name is now changed to Black, is obviously the better man in every way. He is also the only true artist in the book and clearly foreshadows both Jay Gatsby and Monroe Stahr.

Gatsby's similarities to Bloeckman are numerous. Both are men of compelling vision, admittedly limited and singleminded, but nonetheless impressive. Both literally create themselves a new personality, a new being, out of less than promising materials. And both, rather than deny the real, are able to organize it in accord with their visions. Yet, Gatsby's devotion to attaining his imagined committed moment is superior to all others. There are two people in *The Great Gatsby* who properly appreciate Gatsby's achievement. Nick Carraway recognizes not only the sheer power of his dream but also its theatrical essence. He sees Gatsby as an actor; to him Gatsby's "very phrases were worn so threadbare that they evoked no image except that of a turbaned 'character' leaking sawdust at every pore. . . ."[7] Yet he also sees the greatness of Gatsby's creation. He shares this opinion with Gatsby's other admirer, the character known as Owl Eyes, whom he meets in the library at Gatsby's first party. The party itself has been carefully directed, carefully prepared for tone and atmosphere; the whole set is staged with the perfect combination of reality and romance. And Owl Eyes recognizes this. "It fooled me," he says in admiring amazement. "This fella's a regular Belasco. It's a triumph. What thoroughness! What realism! Knew when to stop, too . . ." (55). In comparing Gatsby to David Belasco, a famous American actor, playwright, and producer, Owl Eyes has grasped the essence of Gatsby, and it is appropriate that he should be among the few who pay their respects to Gatsby at his funeral. James Gatz is playing the role of Jay Gatsby, but, again, he goes beyond the pose, and in doing so becomes not just the actor, but also the artist, the director. In becoming the artist, as Nick realizes and as Owl Eyes probably suspects, Gatsby successfully creates his own reality. Gatsby's dream is greater than its source, its own *raison d'être*. Nick says:

> There must have been moments . . . when Daisy tumbled short of his dreams—not through her own fault, but because of the colossal vitality of his illusion. It had gone beyond her, beyond everything. He had thrown himself into it with a creative passion, adding to it all the time, decking it out with every bright feather that drifted his way. No amount of fire or freshness can challenge what a man can store up in his ghostly heart (116).

Gatsby's "creative passion" is crystallized by Nick in the image of the actress and the director who are among those celebrities attending Gatsby's parties. Although most of these people are essentially cheap, vulgar, and unworthy of being a part of Gatsby's dream, they emphasize in their cheapness the success of Gatsby's illusion in that he is nonetheless able to transform them into creatures of glorious possibilities. The actress is described as a "gorgeous, scarcely human orchid of a woman who sat in state under a white-plum tree . . . a hitherto ghostly celebrity of the movies" (126-27). As Gatsby and Daisy watch, and Nick reports, she and the director are figuratively framed and filmed as in slow motion: " . . . their faces were touching except for a pale, thin ray of moonlight between. It occurred to me that he had been very slowly bending toward her all evening to attain this proximity, and even while I watched I saw him stoop one ultimate degree and kiss at her cheek" (129). Surely this is what Gatsby himself has been doing, preparing for and creating the situation worthy for that one moment, frozen, captured.

But the moment passes, as Nick, as all but Gatsby, surely know it must. The "satisfactory hint of the unreality of reality, [the] promise that the rock of the world was founded securely on a fairy's wing" (119) is ultimately the stuff of dreams, in Gatsby's case the stuff of great dreams, but, in truth, a dream not unlike that of Gloria Gilbert. But Gatsby is worthy, if only for a short time, as Gloria is not, and he meets his end with a tragic greatness totally alien to any of the beautiful and damned.

At one point in the novel, Nick describes Gatsby in a revealing image:

> Out of the corner of his eye Gatsby saw that the blocks of the sidewalks really formed a ladder and mounted to a secret place above

the trees—he could climb to it, if he climbed alone, and once there he could suck on the pap of life, gulp down the incomparable milk of wonder (134).

As the image suggests, the ladder leads one to a sense of "wonder," but one must first be able, be worthy to make the climb. Such is not the case of Jacob Booth, the protagonist in a short story written in 1927, "Jacob's Ladder," important because it not only re-examines this theme found in *Gatsby,* but because it also foreshadows the theme's further development in *Tender Is the Night.* In 1927 Fitzgerald had made his first trip to Hollywood to work for United Artists on the screenplay "Lipstick." Financially it was not a successful trip. But there Fitzgerald learned, or began to suspect, that in the entertainment industry in general and in Hollywood in particular he had a subject which was worth much more development. In the works already mentioned, the concept of the theater and the cinema did not provide the major themes or images; rather they were used to support ideas which were being expressed in more abstract terms. But in the concrete image of Hollywood and the movie industry he found a rich and rewarding subject which gave him realistic grounds on which to build his stories of dreamers. One might finally question the existence of a Jay Gatsby, but no one who could accept the fact of Hollywood could deny the possibility of a Monroe Stahr.

"Jacob's Ladder" is one of Fitzgerald's first stories to deal seriously with Hollywood. In the earlier story "The Diamond as Big as the Ritz," for example, he had dismissed it as a place run by the kind of person who "was used to playing with an unlimited amount of money, though he did tuck his napkin in his collar and couldn't read or write."[8] Now Fitzgerald began to explore in greater depth Hollywood's metaphorical possibilities in relation to his established themes. In "Jacob's Ladder," Jacob Booth is a man with imagination, but he uses it, like Anthony Patch, as a means of denial of the real. He meets Jenny Delehanty at the sordid murder trial of her sister, who has slain her sailor-paramour with a meat ax. Jacob had gone to this trial out of boredom and curiosity, which reflects the barren state of his existence. The trial is itself a kind of performance, attracting great crowds who have come seeking a "breathless escape from their own private lives."[9]

Jenny is sixteen and very much a girl of the world, quite beautiful but also quite common. Booth is thirty-three and sees her in completely romantic terms; to him she has "the face of a saint" and is "an intense little Madonna" who, in his imagination, is "lifted fragilely out of the mortal dust of the afternoon" (4). He tells her that he has no designs on her, which comes as both a surprise and a disappointment to her, and decides to make her into a movie star by introducing her to a director he knows. He gives her the name Jenny Prince although she prefers Tootsie Defoe. If Jacob fools himself about Jenny, the director, Billy Farrelly, does not. "They're all the same," he tells Jacob. "Shucks! Pick 'em out of the gutter today and they want gold plates tomorrow" (5). But Jacob prefers to idealize her, to perfect her, by making her a star. In doing so, he is also removing her as any kind of sexual threat, for in Jacob's mind, the physical cannot co-exist with the illusionary. Thus, although she offers herself to him, she later tells Farrelly that she "couldn't make" Booth (5); Jacob is much happier in bed alone with his dreams of Jenny:

> His desire recreated her until she lost all vestiges of the old Jenny. . . . Silently, as the night hours went by, he molded her over into an image of love—an image that would endure as long as love itself, or even longer. . . . Slowly he created it with this and that illusion from his youth, this and that sad old yearning, until she stood before him identical with her old self only by name.
> Later, when he drifted off into a few hours' sleep, the image he had made stood near him, lingering in the room, joined in mystic marriage to his heart (63).

Jenny is a success as an actress and goes to Hollywood, immediately becoming a part of that world. Jacob later follows her and finds it increasingly difficult to keep separate this pure illusion he has created about her from the reality of her that he begins to see. Again, ironically, by entering into a world based on illusion, Fitzgerald's character is forced to face the truths which underlie his own dreams. Jacob is disgusted at Jenny's friends; he refers with contempt to her attraction toward Raffino, who is, Jacob sneers, only "an actor" (58), ignoring the fact that that is what he has made Jenny into. Finally she is forced to tell Jacob that she has fallen in love with her director. "It only comes once, Jake, like that . . . if you lose it once, it'll never come like that again and then what do you want to live for?" (63).

Certainly this is a type of love that Jacob is unable to handle, and there must be a certain amount of relief mixed in with his sorrow, as he retreats from the cheapness, and also from the vitality, within Jenny. He returns to the illusion wherein she is perfect and removed. As he walks in his confusion, he sees her name in lights and thinks, with something like ecstasy, "She was there! All of her, the best of her—the effort, the power, the triumph, the beauty"(64). Buying a ticket, he becomes again a part of the crowd, escaping again into the womb-like protection, the "fast-throbbing darkness" of the theater (64).

In 1931 Fitzgerald made a second trip to Hollywood, and although it proved to be even less of an artistic success than the first, it nevertheless gave him new material, which he incorporated into his next novel, *Tender Is the Night*. Although *Tender* takes place in Europe, the movies and Hollywood play an integral role in the action. In the earlier concepts of the novel, Fitzgerald had apparently intended to emphasize the cinema even more. One of the earliest protagonists, Francis Melarkey, was to have been a young motion picture technician, and in another version, the Lew and Nicole Kelly one, Lew Kelly was a brilliant motion picture director. Also, in the writing of the novel, Fitzgerald found himself drawing heavily on earlier short stories, such as the aforementioned "Jacob's Ladder" and another Hollywood story, "Magnetism." From the story of Jacob and Jenny in "Jacob's Ladder" he developed the romance between Dick and Rosemary Hoyt, while he also gave Dick some of Jacob's more unfortunate characteristics. From "Magnetism" Fitzgerald lifted not only character traits, but also whole passages which he included, with apology, into *Tender*.

"Magnetism" is the story of George Hannaford, a "young and extraordinarily handsome" actor in Hollywood.[10] Having entered the movie business by accident, he finds himself constantly adrift in what he recognizes as "the most bizarre community in the rich, wild, bored empire . . ." (76). Hannaford's problem is a comic one; he is too handsome, and he is irresistible to women. Yet, in reality, he is "a straightforward, slow-thinking, romantic man" who has been thrust into an "accidentally glamorous life" (76). When he finds himself in an impossible situation, being blackmailed by a woman who has loved him in secret for years, she tells him:

> "I tried to make love to you, just like the rest, but it was difficult. You drew people right up close to you and held them there, not able to move either way."
> "This is all imaginary," he protests, "and I can't control—"
> "No, I know," she interrupts him. "You can't control charm. It's simply got to be used. You've got to keep your hand in if you have it, and go through life attaching people to you that you don't want" (76).

Hannaford, then, as an actor, has no control over his charm or his life and is swept along in an imaginary "bizarre" world he cannot direct. That Fitzgerald would use both Hannaford and Booth in the creation of Dick Diver tells us much about Diver and about Fitzgerald's attitude toward him. However, in the first part of *Tender*, Dick Diver seems to be very much in control of not only his and Nicole's lives, but also the lives of everyone else who enters his sphere of influence. He is described as a director in connection with his parties. One is set up so as to provoke conflict, and it ends in the serio-comic duel between Albert McKisco and Tommy Barban, which Luis Campion, having brought his movie camera, intends to film. Another party "moved with the speed of a slapstick comedy. . . Everything had been foreseen."[11] Dick keeps everything in control,[12] and this is one of the main things that attracts the actress, Rosemary Hoyt, to him. She is, at this stage of her life, in need of a director, a position previously held by her mother, for Rosemary's life is largely a matter of acting and posing. When she convinces herself that she loves Dick and arranges to throw herself at him, she is "astonished at herself—she had never imagined she could talk like that. She was calling on things she had read, seen, dreamed through a decade of convent hours. Suddenly she knew too that it was one of her greatest rôles and she flung herself into it more passionately" (85). Still, although Rosemary indulges herself in some self-deluding romanticizing, she is far beyond being long fooled by it; she is "In the movies but not at all At them" (39).

Like Anthony Patch and Jacob Booth, Dick has a certain snobbery concerning actors and acting. Yet his adamant refusal to take a screen test which Rosemary has arranged for him reveals a basic weakness of his character:

> "I don't want a test," said Dick firmly. . . . . "The pictures make a fine career for a woman—but my God, they can't photograph me. . . . The strongest guard is placed at the gateway to nothing," he said. "Maybe because the condition of emptiness is too shameful to be divulged" (92).

Dick avoids the prying eye of the camera which had forced Gloria Patch to see herself as she really was. He fears having to look at himself, having to recognize the actor in him, and having to acknowledge the "condition of emptiness" which the mask of the actor disguises. Nor is he as immune to Rosemary and to the romantic aura with which he surrounds her as he would like to think. Like Booth, he at first tries to remove from his idea of her any sort of sexual connotation, hence his obsession with the story related by Collis Clay. Its physical implications tarnish his romantic ideal.

What Fitzgerald quite clearly marks as a "turning point" in Dick's life occurs on the day he goes to the movie studio to meet Rosemary, in effect, to enter into her world of illusion: "He knew that what he was now doing . . . was out of line with everything that had preceded it—even out of line with what effect he might hope to produce upon Rosemary. Rosemary saw him always as a model of correctness—his presence walking around this block was an intrusion" (119). An earlier description of the studio (taken largely from "Magnetism") becomes, at this point, quite important. The studio is portrayed in hellish terms, as a demented land of the damned. As Rosemary had walked through the "half darkness" of the studio:

> Here and there figures spotted the twilight, turning up ashen faces to her like souls in purgatory watching the passage of a mortal through . . . a French actor . . . and an American actress stood motionless face to face. They stared at each other with dogged eyes, as though they had been in the same position for hours; and still for a long time nothing happened, no one moved. A bank of lights went off with a savage hiss, went on again . . . a blue face appeared among the blinding lights above, called something unintelligible into the upper blackness (29).

Going to the studio, Dick enters symbolically into the ghastly hell in which he is caught like the motionless actor awaiting the director's orders. And it is at this point that the motif of the actor rather than the director takes over in Fitzgerald's description of Dick. As he stands outside the studio, which is located in a "melancholy neighborhood," surrounded by signs of "Life and death," he begins to realize that his "necessity of behaving as he did was a projection of some submerged reality: he was compelled to walk there, or stand there. . . . Dick was paying some tribute to things unforgotten, unshriven, unexpurgated" (119).

Rosemary seems immediately to recognize the reversal of her and Dick's roles, for when they are finally alone together in her room, Rosemary "stood up and leaned down and said her most sincere thing to him:

'Oh, we're such *actors*—you and I' " (138).

And when they leave, "Dick clung to the situation; Rosemary was first to return to reality.

'I must go, youngster,' she said" (143).

As her calling him "youngster" indicates, Rosemary has gained, and knows that she has gained, the upper hand in their relationship.

Dick's disintegration follows. He becomes lost in the world of illusions which he is unable to control. It is a cheap world. He "was in love with every pretty woman he saw now, their forms at a distance, their shadows on a wall" (263). Rather than wanting to organize, to help, he now wants "to be admired" (269), the role of an actor. He is incapable of any sustained dream: "He pretended they were this and that . . . falling in with his own plot, and drinking too much to sustain the illusion . . ." (269). By the end, his dream is completely lost. "But you used to want to create things," Nicole tells him, "Now you seem to want to smash them up" (344). One of Dick's last scenes is a prolonged discourse on acting, something at which he has become quite adept.

Between the publication of *Tender* in 1934 and Fitzgerald's third and last venture to Hollywood in 1937, he went through the most nightmarish period of his career. This was the time of the "Crack-Up" essays, when he began to doubt his abilities as a writer, when his wife's illness forced him to put her in an institution, when he was deeply in debt and his whole life was in shambles. He recognized that Hollywood offered him perhaps his only hope of survival. At the same time, he feared Hollywood, because he knew from his own experiences and the experiences of others that, as with Richard Caramel, it had a knack for drawing out the very worst in writers, for destroying whatever talents they might have had before selling themselves to it. And he recognized clearly his own potential susceptibility.

In spite of this foreboding, when Fitzgerald finally realized that he had no choice, he turned toward Hollywood with a certain amount of hope, perhaps his own brand of Ardita Farnam's "faith in the eternal resilience of me." Hollywood disgusted him in many ways, but it also inspired him to attempt some of his best work. He expressed this feeling in a letter to his old friend Gerald Murphy:

> I find, after a long time out here, that one develops new attitudes. It is, for example, such a slack *soft* place—even its pleasure lacking the fierceness or excitement of Provence—that withdrawal is practically a condition of safety. . . . Everywhere there is, after a moment, either corruption or indifference . . . the new Armageddon, far from making everything unimportant, gives me a certain lust for life again. . . . The gloom of all causes does not affect it—I feel a certain rebirth of kinetic impulses—however misdirected. . . .[13]

It would have been easy for Fitzgerald to turn his withering scorn on Hollywood in his fiction as he sometimes did in his letters, and he could fully appreciate Nathanael West's scathing portrayal of the place in *The Day of the Locust* and perhaps even applaud West's solution of having Hollywood erupt in bestial hysteria and purging flames.[14] He seemed to echo West in another of his letters when he wrote, "Isn't Hollywood a dump—in the human sense of the word? A hideous town, pointed up by the insulting gardens of its rich, full of the human spirit at a new low of debasement."[15] And in his own fiction, such as "Discard" and "Last Kiss," both of which remained unpublished at his death, he pointed out that "Hollywood is not a very civilized place."[16]

His bitterness toward and his hatred of certain aspects of

Hollywood were best expressed, however, in the Pat Hobby series, which he wrote during the last two years of his life. Pat is the consummate Hollywood scoundrel; he represents some of the worst it had to offer. Yet, although Pat is a completely incompetent, alcoholic fool, Fitzgerald does not use the series to castigate the entire industry. Unlike West, Fitzgerald could find the potential in the movie industry; he did not feel that it had yet completely betrayed itself. He had earlier predicted, in the "Crack-Up" essays, that the movies might one day supersede the novel as "the strongest and supplest medium for conveying thought and emotion from one human being to another,"[17] and even in the Hobby series he does not reject this possibility.

In Hobby Fitzgerald was able to personify and, to some extent, explain the "softness" of the evil in Hollywood. At the same time, as Thomas Daniels points out, he balanced his "Pat Hobbys" with the "Tycoons" of the industry, who are described as "intelligent, perceptive men,"[18] able and willing to make something out of the system Pat is content merely to feed on. Pat relies on Hollywood's essential phoniness but is unable to see its greatness. And yet greatness is there, as is illustrated in "Two Old Timers." Although the circumstances surrounding the filming of the battle scene in this story are comic and rather disgraceful, the results of the film are powerful and effective; a woman who has laughed at war comes to know its horror and can understand her husband's deepest emotions concerning it.

Certainly not all of the Pat Hobby stories are as good as "Two Old Timers"—some have little redeeming value—but if, as Robert Sklar has suggested,[19] they enabled Fitzgerald to purge himself of the hatred he felt for Hollywood and thus allowed him to look at it in an objective way, then they served an important purpose. Rather than condemn, Fitzgerald was able to examine, and this examination resulted in *The Last Tycoon*.

In what remained of Fitzgerald's career, he set about to explain the enigma of Hollywood through a study of his last and perhaps greatest hero, Monroe Stahr. In "Crazy Sunday," a short story written after Fitzgerald's second visit to Hollywood, he had first attempted such a study. Miles Calman, the "only American-born director with both an interesting temperament and an artistic conscience,"[20] possessed both the strengths and weaknesses which Fitzgerald would give to Stahr. Within the industry Calman is the complete artist, honest to himself and to his profession, but his greatest creation is his wife, Stella. Following Calman's death, however, the tawdriness which his dream transcended becomes clear; Stella is seen as being, in reality, very cheap and pitiful. Still, as Joel Coles, the narrator, recognizes, "Everything he touched he did something magical to. . . . He even brought that little gamin alive and made her a sort of masterpiece" (222).

Monroe Stahr is such an artist, but he works on a much larger scale than Calman. He creates not just one woman but a whole world. In fact, when Stahr is at the height of his power, he imposes his judgment and his imagination on the entire world; he is the man who shapes people's dreams: in his projection room "dreams hung in fragments . . . suffered analysis, passed—to be dreamed in crowds, or else discarded."[21] Cecilia Brady, who has her own romantic fantasies about Stahr, realizes that "I had nothing to offer that he didn't have; some of my more romantic ideas actually stemmed from pictures. . . . It's more than possible that some of the pictures which Stahr himself conceived had shaped me into what I was" (18).

Although Stahr refers to himself as a "merchant," a "chief clerk" (79), he is, as the more perceptive recognize, a creative genius. Boxley, the writer, knows it, and so, in his own way, does Pete Zavras, the cameraman, who grandly tells Stahr, "You are the Aeschylus and the Euripides of the moving picture. . . . Also the Aristophanes and Menander" (61). Despite Stahr's self-effacing denials, he judges himself perhaps even greater than do his admirers, for he sees himself as "the unity" (58), the godhead,of the studio.

The sheer magnitude of Stahr's accomplishments and the impossible daring of his desires are described by Cecilia:

> Beginning at about twelve, probably, with the total rejection common to those of extraordinary mental powers, the "See here: this is all wrong—a mess—all a lie—and a sham—," he swept it all away, everything, as men of his type do; and then instead of being a son-of-a-bitch as most of them are, he looked around at the barrenness that was left and said to himself, "*This* will never do" (97).

Stahr, then, is the final avatar of the Fitzgerald hero. The world is a mess; there is little to work with that is not cheap, tawdry, but there is the imagination and the courage within certain men which allows them to use these materials to create something fine, if only for a moment. This is what Stahr does. The most damning condemnation he can make of any picture is that it is "cheap" or "trash," that it fails to transcend the elements which went into its making. These are the same values by which he judges life.

Stahr fails, as he must, as do all of Fitzgerald's heroes. Despite their efforts, the "fairy's wing" of the imagination can never long support the rock-like world. When this world of reality begins to intrude into Stahr's studio, as it does with Kathleen, the Unions and the Communists, Stahr loses his infallible judgment. Away from the studio he finds himself vulnerable. In an outside world that cannot accept his greatness, he, like Gatsby, is reduced to the level of seeming a fool. If Fitzgerald had gone on to complete the novel as his notes suggest, Stahr's own life would have become a kind of "bad script;" he would have reached a level of debasement before recognizing it and then fighting his way back. Cecilia can imagine him judging his own funeral as "Trash!" (132), but its very trashiness is another indication of the singularity of his achievement, and of the inability of his successors to maintain it or even adequately to conceive of it.

Like Fitzgerald himself, his heroes "hold in balance the sense of the futility of effort and the sense of the necessity to struggle; the conviction of the inevitability of failure and still the determination to 'succeed.' . . ."[22] The good ones, the worthy ones, do succeed, if only for the one fleeting, captured moment. The others—the actors wearing a mask covering nothing—retreat into their dreams.

University of South Carolina

[1]F. Scott Fitzgerald, "The Crack-Up," in *The Crack-Up*, ed. Edmund Wilson (New York: New Directions, 1956), p. 69.

[2]Fitzgerald, "Pasting It Together," *The Crack-Up*, p. 75.

[3]In 1924 Fitzgerald proposed an article for *The Saturday Evening Post* entitled "Why Only Ten Percent of Movies Succeed." Although it was not finished or published, he did write in it that "It is the director not the censor or the poor exhibitor or the star who is absolutely responsible." Quoted in Henry Dan Piper, *F. Scott Fitzgerald: A Critical Portrait* (New York: Holt, Rinehart and Winston, 1965), p. 260.

[4]*This Side of Paradise* (New York: Scribners, 1920), p. 19. All quotes taken from this edition.

[5]"The Offshore Pirate," in *Flappers and Philosophers* (New York: Scribners, 1920), p. 34.

[6]*The Beautiful and Damned* (New York: Scribners, 1922), p. 11. All quotes taken from this edition.

[7]*The Great Gatsby* (New York: Scribners, 1925), p. 79. All quotes taken from this edition.

[8]"The Diamond as Big as the Ritz," *Tales of the Jazz Age* (New York: Scribners, 1922), p. 172.

[9]"Jacob's Ladder," *The Saturday Evening Post*, CC (20 August 1927), 3.

[10]"Magnetism," *The Saturday Evening Post*, CC (3 March 1928), 5.

[11]*Tender Is the Night* (New York: Scribners, 1934), p. 101.

[12]In a letter to Harold Ober a few days after Fitzgerald's death, Zelda Fitzgerald wrote, "I am heart-broken over Scott: he loved people and had dedicated [sic] so much of his life to the moral sustenance of many that I am sure that he must have left many friends. . . . In retrospect it seems as if he was always planning happinesses for Scottie, and for me. . . . Life seemed so promisory always when he was around: and I always believed

that he could take care of anything." Quoted in *As Ever, Scott Fitz—: Letters Between F. Scott Fitzgerald and His Literary Agent Harold Ober 1919-1940*, ed. Matthew J. Bruccoli, with the assistance of Jennifer McCabe Atkinson (Philadelphia and New York: Lippincott, 1972), p. 424.

[13]Letter to Murphy dated September 14, 1940. In *The Letters of F. Scott Fitzgerald*, ed. Andrew Turnbull (New York: Scribners, 1963), pp. 429-30. One should also note two articles which give a more positive view of Fitzgerald's life in Hollywood. See Frances Ring and R. L. Samsell, "Sisyphus in Hollywood: Refocusing F. Scott Fitzgerald,"*Fitzgerald Hemingway Annual 1973*, 93-104; and R. L. Samsell, "Hollywood—It Wasn't All That Bad," *Fitzgerald/Hemingway Annual 1969*, 15-19.

[14]See David D. Galloway, "Nathanael West's Dream Dump,"*Critique*, VI (Winter 1963), 46-64. Of *The Day of the Locust*, Fitzgerald wrote: "The book, though it puts Gorki's 'The Lower Depths' in the class with 'The Tale of Benjamin Bunny,' certainly has scenes of extraordinary power—if that phrase is still in use. Especially I was impressed by the pathological crowd at the premiere, the character and handling of the aspirant actress and the uncanny almost medieval feeling of some of his Hollywood background set off by these vividly drawn grotesques." Quoted in *F. Scott Fitzgerald: In His Own Time: A Miscellany*, ed. Matthew J. Bruccoli and Jackson R. Bryer (Kent State University Press, 1971), p. 160. See also *Letters*, 583-584. The quote is somewhat different here.

[15]Letter to Alice Richardson dated July 29, 1940. In *Letters*, p. 603.

[16]"Discard," *Harper's Bazaar*, LXXXII (January 1948), 103, 143-44, et passim; "Last Kiss," *Collier's*, CXXIII (April 16, 1949), 16, 34, et passim.

[17]"Pasting It Together," *The Crack-Up*, p. 78.

[18]Thomas E. Daniels, "Pat Hobby: Anti-Hero," *Fitzgerald/Hemingway Annual 1973*, 132.

[19]Robert Sklar, *F. Scott Fitzgerald: The Last Laocoon* (Oxford: Oxford University Press, 1967), p. 328.

[20]"Crazy Sunday," *Taps at Reveille* (New York: Scribners, 1935), p. 220. All quotes taken from this edition.

[21]*The Last Tycoon* (New York: Scribners, 1941), p. 56. All quotes taken from this edition.

[22]"The Crack-Up," p. 70.

MICHAEL ADAMS

DICK DIVER AND CONSTANCE TALMADGE

In *Tender Is the Night* Dick Diver is walking around the block of the Films Par Excellence Studio, trying to decide what to do about Rosemary, when he begins to read the signs posted about the neighborhood: "On either side he read: 'Papeterie,' 'Pâtisserie,' 'Solde,' 'Réclame'—and Constance Talmadge in 'Déjeuner de Soleil,' and farther away there were more sombre announcements: 'Vêtements Ecclésiastiques,' 'Déclaration de Décès,' and 'Pompes Funèbres.' Life and death."[1] A problem with this reference to the Constance Talmadge movie is that this scene is taking place in 1925 and *Breakfast at Sunrise* was released in October, 1927.[2] An allusion to Constance Talmadge in *Tender Is the Night* is appropriate since Fitzgerald met Lois Moran, the model for Rosemary Hoyt, while in Hollywood writing the unproduced "Lipstick" for Miss Talmadge in 1927.[3] Perhaps the actress was working on *Breakfast at Sunrise* when Fitzgerald was there. The plot of the movie, based on André Birabeau's 1925 farce, does not seem to have anything to do with the events of *Tender Is the Night*. Constance Talmadge plays a woman who begins a flirtation with one man in order to make another jealous but ends up in love with her co-conspirator. Fitzgerald may have been interested in the movie merely because of the aptness of its title in his "Life and death" contrast.

University of South Carolina

61

¹F. Scott Fitzgerald, *Tender Is the Night* (New York: Scribners, 1934), p. 91.
²*The American Film Institute Catalog of Motion Pictures Produced in the United States: Feature Films, 1921-1930*, ed. Kenneth W. Munden (New York & London: Bowker, 1971), p. 83.
³Andrew Turnbull, *Scott Fitzgerald* (New York: Scribners, 1962), pp. 169-170.

Constance Talmadge.

STEVEN CURRY & PETER L. HAYS

FITZGERALD'S *Vanity Fair*

> *There is a great quantity of eating and drinking, making love and jilting, laughing . . . —women, . . . and yokels— [and] dancers. . . . Yes, this is VANITY FAIR: not a moral place certainly; nor a merry one, though very noisy.*
>
> *—Thackeray*

In his critical biography of Fitzgerald, *The Far Side of Paradise*, Arthur Mizener records an exchange between Fitzgerald and a correspondent of *Hound & Horn* concerning the literary influences on *The Great Gatsby:* when the correspondent "ventured a guess that Thackeray had been an important influence on the book, Fitzgerald replied, 'I never read a French author, except the usual prep-school classics, until I was twenty, but Thackeray I had read over and over by the time I was sixteen, so as far as I am concerned you guessed right.'"[1] It is curious, in light of this comment by Fitzgerald, that no serious attempt has been made to trace and measure the extent of Thackeray's influence on him, especially that of *Vanity Fair* on *The Great Gatsby;* for even a cursory comparison of these two works uncovers a great number of likenesses. To begin with, there is a similarity in narrative technique, parallels between the major characters in both works— though not in a one-to-one correspondence—and parallels between the settings, for both are set essentially in "vanity fairs"; in both works, too, similar elements of the settings are raised to metaphorical significance and function as commentaries on the values and attitudes of the society contemporary to each novel—for example, popular music, modes of transportation, and money; and both make significant thematic use of time, the past, and history, especially war. Each novel, too, contains an indictment of the materialism and superficiality of its respective age, yet each novel lacks a moral center itself; finally, each is, as Thackeray subtitled his work, "A Novel Without a Hero."

Critics have noted that the narrative technique in *Gatsby* is perhaps modelled after, or at least inspired by, Conrad's use of Marlow as a narrator who is a character in his own story, as in *Lord Jim*, for example; but no one, apparently, has yet considered the possibility that one or both of these authors might have been influenced by Thackeray. For Thackeray's narrative technique in *Vanity Fair*—regardless of how unsophisticated it may appear by comparison—is without question a precursor of Conrad's and Fitzgerald's; and it is not simply a matter of the narrator's appearing in the first-person.[2] Mario Praz likens Thackeray's use of a narrator to a photographer, who, when taking a group portrait, directs his camera into a mirror, thus including himself in his own photograph.[3] (And indeed, in his own illustration for the title page of the book, Thackeray showed the Puppet Master depicted examining his face in a mirror; cf. p. 19 of the novel.) The Puppet Master in *Vanity Fair* is as much an actor in his own "show" as are Marlow and Nick in their narratives; and although he never reaches the stature as a character that the latter two achieve, his "situation" in the novel is equally determined by the circumstances he is narrating. Not only that, his reliability is open to question at almost any given moment— he can be as guilty of sentimentality or of rationalization in describing Becky or Amelia or Dobbin as Nick can be in describing Gatsby or Daisy. Thackeray's Puppet Master and Fitzgerald's Nick Carraway also share a similar compulsion to relate their tales for therapeutic reasons.

For each, the "telling" of their respective stories answers not only the authors' desire for social criticism but, concurrently, the narrators' keenly felt need produced by the sordid state of the societies they find themselves in. Telling stories is as old as human life itself; it is the way men have of accounting for themselves in the world—a way of reconciling themselves with the circumstances of their experiences which they find larger than themselves. Thackeray's narrator offers the following apology:

> . . . it is not from mere mercenary motives that the present performer is desirous to show up and trounce his villains; but because he has a sincere hatred of them, which he cannot keep down, and which must find a vent in suitable abuse and bad language. (p. 81)

Similarly, Nick is compelled by his contempt for the society of East and West Egg to tell his story; he must account for it to himself—for it has violated him in every way; he must reconcile himself to his experience of it and set it behind him if he is to recover himself and continue in the "normal" world.

Nick tells us on the first page of his narrative, "I'm inclined to reserve all judgments. . . . Reserving judgments is a matter of infinite hope."[4] Of course, Nick does not reserve his judgments, he cannot; his description of Tom (pp. 7-9), for example, is replete with opinions and editorial comments. He has reached a point beyond which he cannot go without judging—however erroneous or self-deluding those judgments, or his denial of their very existence, may be:

> And, after boasting this way of my tolerance, I come to the admission that it has a limit. Conduct may be founded on the hard rock or the wet marshes, but after a certain point I don't care what it's founded on. (p. 2)

And though Nick's "limit" is grounded in a contradictory experience, he is in every way compelled by a contempt for society, which must, like that of Thackeray's narrator, "find a vent in suitable abuse":

> Only Gatsby, the man who gives his name to this book, was exempt from my reaction—Gatsby, who represented everything for which I have an unaffected scorn. (p. 2)

Nick's scorn is not "unaffected," of course; quite the opposite is true. But even if his contempt is "affected" and extravagant—smacking, as it does, of hypocrisy—given his "limitations," self-delusions, and his circumstances, it is the only means available to him to reconcile himself to what he has experienced. What he has experienced is the "vanity fair" of the "East."

It is the carnival-like setting of *Gatsby*, which Nick describes as "that slender riotous island" in "one of the strangest communities in North America" (p. 5), which gives rise to Nick's contradictory experience, and, too, which provides one of the most striking points of comparison between Fitzgerald and Thackeray. For both novels are set, finally, in "Vanity Fair." And just as Thackeray's novel calls an entire moral structure into question—that is, by asserting the "vanity" of a material structure of ideals and values—the same may be said of Fitzgerald's novel—for Gatsby's "booth" at the "fair" is only slightly more gaudy and extravagant than Daisy's and Tom's. It is interesting to note in this context that the original dust jacket pictures such a carnival; in Mizener's words, the design was "intended to suggest—by two enormous eyes—Daisy brooding over an amusement-park version of New York" (Mizener, p. 184); and that Fitzgerald does liken Gatsby's parties to an amusement park (pp. 49-50).

Thackeray's narrator describes Vanity Fair as ". . . a very vain, wicked, foolish place, full of all sorts of humbugs and falsenesses and pretensions" (p. 80), and he closes the novel with ". . . *Vanitas Vanitatum!* Which of us is happy in this world? Which of us has his desire? or, having it, is satisfied?" (p. 666). If these words were not so transparently Thackeray's, they could easily be claimed as narrative summaries of *Gatsby*, both of the setting and of the title. For Fitzgerald's characters are trapped in a world equally "vain" and "foolish," a world of "humbugs and falsenesses and pretensions." The title itself, *The Great Gatsby*, refers not to any greatness on Gatsby's part—except, perhaps, in Nick's eyes—but to his potential "greatness," the greatness he might have achieved had his tremendous energy and capability been focused on a worthier object and in a less materialistic setting. Gatsby's dream is vain and leads him into "falsenesses and pretensions," because that is the kind of world he lives in; for however platonic and idealistic his dream may be, circumstances dictate that the dream may only be realized in the context of a materialistic world. That is the education he received from James J. Hill, Dan Cody, Ella Kaye, and young Daisy, herself. Thus, the dream is corrupted both by context and circumstance. Nick says of the "colossal vitality of [Gatsby's] illusion," "It had gone beyond [Daisy], beyond everything. He had thrown himself into it with a creative passion, adding to it all the time, decking it out with every bright feather that drifted his way" (p. 116). It is precisely Gatsby's preoccupation with "things" that dooms him to failure, the "bright feathers" he adorns his illusion with in order to make it seem more "real"; and it is the "universe of ineffable gaudiness" that Gatsby creates with "things" of no intrinsic value, for which Nick has his "unaffected scorn." Of course, Daisy too is a mundane, real entity, a thing, not the fabulous creature which Gatsby's love has created. Gatsby's admirable energy is spent in a world unworthy of his "extraordinary gift for hope"; he is led into "falsenesses" (his Oxford pose, "Old Sport," and the dubious source of his wealth) and "pretensions" (his house, his shirts and suits, his cars, and his parties). Thus, Nick's dilemma, as well as ours, is where to center a moral judgment.

The Great Gatsby, like *Vanity Fair*, lacks a moral center. Most novels prior to World War II contain at least the locus of a scale of values: in *Tom Jones*, for example, we at least have Fielding's narrator who affects a moral stance, and, too, there is an assertion of the values represented by the social class that Tom is finally reconciled to; in *Pride and Prejudice,* the Gardiners embody a mediating standard of conduct; in *Moby-Dick,* metaphysical truths are invoked, which—however abstract they may seem—serve as touchstones; and in Hemingway there is always, finally, "the code." But where is that locus in *Vanity Fair* and *Gatsby?* Conduct, Nick correctly asserts, can become outrageous whether it's "founded on the hard rock or the wet marshes"; the Buchanans have all the license and privilege of their position and wealth, yet their conduct is unacceptable; Gatsby's conduct—like Becky Sharp's—exhibits admirable energy and resolve, but is undercut for us because of its untenable ground—ultimately, it is a waste of human potential. Yet given the "moral" frame of the societies in these two novels, the "highest moral good" is exemplified in the strivings of Gatsby and, like Napoleon, of Becky Sharp, but what they are aspiring to is the world of the Buchanans, the Sir Pitt Crawleys, and the Lord Steynes; that is, the "careless," valueless world where, Nick tells us, people ". . . smashed up things and creatures and then retreated back into their money or their vast carelessness, or whatever it was that kept them together, and let other people clean up the mess they had made . . ." (p. 216). Much of what we are to understand about the world—the world in both novels—is contained in the word "care-less-ness"; it is an uncaring world, grounded in a small, vicious and, finally, amoral circle—like a doughnut, where the center is a void: the world of *Gatsby* and *Vanity Fair* is an entity defined by its lack of a substantial center: a world where God is a "puppet master" or a pair of faceless, bespectacled billboard eyes, both of which are products of the world they oversee.

And our narrators, to paraphrase Goethe's observation about poets, are no more moral than the next man, they are only more perceptive; they are talkers, not doers. Granted, Nick stays through to the end, but he is compromised by the world he is so contemptuous of. However romantically we may wish to embroider his actions, he panders for Gatsby. When he shakes hands with Tom at the end of the novel, he rationalizes the act by characterizing Tom as a child, thus making an excuse for him and for everything he represents; in short, Nick acquiesces to the amoral world.[5]

These novels lack a moral center because it is precisely this lack, and the desire to expose it, that is the generating idea behind them—it is, in part, the idea that energy doesn't work in a vacuum. The flaw in the materialistic, middle-class world view that these novels call into question is two-fold: first, such a world view, because it is self-contained, allows for no foundation upon which "higher" moral considerations might be based; and, second, because men like Nick and the Puppet Master persist in searching for "higher" moral values, which are made conspicuous in these novels by their absence, the very idea that a self-contained, self-sufficient world is possible at all is called into question. The idea that men are, or can be, self-sufficient is epitomized and, at the same time, challenged in the figures of Becky and Gatsby.

Both Becky and Gatsby are bent upon transcending their lower-class origins and entering the realms that the *nouveaux riches* have usurped from a decaying aristocracy; their ascent to the higher classes is facilitated by—indeed, encouraged by—the Protestant work-ethic doctrine of faith in the self-made man; in short, what once took generations, the divine rights of kings, and, occasionally, even merit to accomplish, now only takes money. The problem, finally, for Becky, Gatsby, and the entire middle-class system of values is that if the "self" is supreme, where is the moral authority, the metaphysical center, which acts as a check against individual extravagance? There is none, which is why Becky and Gatsby are defeated by the world—or, rather, they are defeated *in* the world and *by* their own sense of morality and values.

Thackeray's narrator says of Becky, "She determined at any rate to get free from the prison in which she found herself, and now began to act for herself, and for the first time to make connected plans for the future" (p. 22); and:

> . . . it became *naturally Rebecca's duty to make herself,* as she said, agreeable to her benefactors, and to gain their confidence *to the utmost of her power.* Who can but admire this quality of gratitude in an unprotected orphan; and, if there entered some degree of selfishness into her calculations, who can say but that her prudence was perfectly justifiable? "I am alone in the world," said the friendless girl. "I have nothing to look for but what my own labour can bring me; . . . Well, let us see if my wits cannot provide me with an honorable maintenance; and if some day or the other I cannot show Miss Amelia my real superiority over her. . . . it will be a fine day when I can take my place above her in the world, as why, indeed, should I not?" *Thus it was that our little romantic friend formed visions of the future for herself.* . . . (p. 88; italics added)

Such lines in Thackeray are conceivably one source, at least, of Fitzgerald's inspiration for Gatsby. For of Gatsby's origins and aspirations, Nick says:

> His parents were shiftless and unsuccessful farm people—his imagination had never really accepted them as his parents at all. The truth was that Jay Gatsby of West Egg, Long Island, sprang from his Platonic conception of himself. He was a son of God—a phrase which, if it means anything, means just that—and he must be about

His Father's business, the service of a vast, vulgar, and meretricious beauty. So he invented just the sort of Jay Gatsby that a seventeen-year-old boy would be likely to invent, and to this conception he was faithful to the end.[6] (p. 118)

It shouldn't be necessary to elaborate further on the similarities, except to point out, perhaps, that just as Becky is motivated, in part, by a desire to upstage Amelia, Gatsby is driven by a similar desire to outdo and supplant Tom—the "have-nots" invariably seem to hold the "haves" in contempt.

And both characters, finally, fall victim to the set of values which obsesses them—as if their obsessions were not victimage enough; but where Becky is the victim of a practical joke when she is lured out of her "cool" pose by the promise of a sum of money which she and Rawdon imagine to be a fortune (and which, when she rushes to collect it, turns out to be a twenty-pound note), Gatsby, on the other hand, is brutally deluded by the promises of wealth and love. Becky and Gatsby may be "self-made," but both, ultimately, are puppets who are made to dance, dangling from the purse-strings of the world. And it may be just this aspect of the quality of life in a middle-class society that led G. K. Chesterton to observe, as Geoffrey and Kathleen Tillotson note in their introduction to the novel, that " 'in *Vanity Fair* the chief character is the World' " (p. ix). This observation would seem to be equally true of both novels.

If the "chief character" in both of these novels is "the World," then, as we have said, Thackeray's subtitle, "A Novel Without a Hero," applies equally to both novels. In the sense that Becky and Gatsby both possess an admirable energy and resolve, they are potentially heroic, but since they never direct that energy and resolve toward accomplishing something for the common good, and because their energy is turned inward upon themselves, in vain, futile and, ultimately, destructive gestures of self-aggrandizement, their potential is never realized. In light of this failure, both novels could easily share the subtitle "Chronicles of Human Waste"; for if this heroic potential consumes itself, as it does, and if this potential epitomizes the best of the world of middle-class values which gives rise to it, where is there hope of salvation? Certainly not in the Nicks and Dobbinses of the world. Their ability to see a bad situation through to the end is an admirable quality, but both are compromised by their situations, both are cowed by circumstances, convention, and other characters, and are shown to be ineffectual when it comes to the significant human action required of a hero.

There is little hope, too, for a hero to emerge from among the ranks of the other characters in either of these works. Amelia and Daisy are of a kind; both are insipid and vain characters, incapable of even fantasizing on the same grand scale with Becky and Gatsby, let alone of acting on it. Tom Buchanan is a vulgar and violent man, who, for all of his wealth, amounts to little more than a common garden variety of Gatsby: ". . . I felt that Tom would drift on forever seeking, a little wistfully, for the dramatic turbulence of some irrecoverable football game" (p. 7); his arrogance and moral blindness—or, perhaps, "ignorance" is a better word for it—leave him only slightly better off than his counterparts in Thackeray's work.

There are Rawdon Crawley and George Osborne. The former, of course, is exiled to Coventry the moment he asserts himself by proposing an alternative to the morality of "Vanity Fair"—he is expelled from the world, because neither the closed system of "Vanity Fair" nor of "East and West Egg" admit an alternative. George Osborne, who is probably closest to Tom in his brashness, is made the object of a lesson which should chasten even the most arrogant—but doesn't. After three-hundred and fifteen pages of the novel, in which he is raised to the stature of a major character, his death is quietly reported, without any preparation of the reader, in a relative clause: "Darkness came down on the field and city: and Amelia was praying for George, who was lying on his face, dead, with a bullet through his heart" (p. 315). The point is, of course, that we are all horribly and always vulnerable—vulnerable to circumstance, the designs of others, or our own weaknesses. Fitzgerald raises the same point.

Gatsby's death is treated almost as unceremoniously as George Osborne's; like George, Gatsby dies "off-stage," and the reader is first informed of it in a parenthesis: "No telephone messages arrived, but the butler went without his sleep and waited for it until four o'clock—until long after there was any one to give it to if it came" (p. 194). Certainly Gatsby is vulnerable, floating in the world on a vision of life as insubstantial as the air-mattress he dies on, but he is not the only character in these novels who suffers from the delusion that ". . . the rock of the world [is] founded securely on a fairy's wing" (p. 119). Both novelists insist on their readers' seeing that the middle-class notion of "reality," grounded as it is in philosophical materialism, is a wisp of a world in which everyone is vulnerable and every*thing* is futile and vain: "and the success or the pleasure of yesterday become of very small account when a certain (albeit uncertain) morrow is in view, about which all of us must some day or other be speculating" (*VF*, p. 180).

There is a "greater reality" which will have its way with us, finally, whether we acknowledge its existence or not. It is a world of necessity that both Fitzgerald and Thackeray allow—according to its nature—to intrude into the dreams and delusions of the inhabitants of their "vanity fairs." So long as the human potential for greatness remains only a potential, and perhaps Fitzgerald learned this from Thackeray, this world-of-necessity will be the only agent of significant change and will remain, as Chesterton observed about *Vanity Fair*, the "central character in our fictions." To use the word "hero" in its broadest sense, all of our novels will be, like *Vanity Fair* and *The Great Gatsby*, novels without heroes.

But the comparison of these two novels doesn't stop here. First, both novels not only feature music as a prime ingredient of entertainment and accompaniment to the dances that occur in each, but both novelists suggest something of the culture of their times, the taste of their characters, and—in addition—use the songs for ironic comment. Thus Becky "sang a French song, which Joseph did not understand in the least,"

> and which George confessed he did not understand, and then a number of those simple ballads which were the fashion forty years ago, and in which British tars, our King, poor Susan, blue-eyed Mary, and the like, were the principal themes. They are not, it is said, very brilliant, in a musical point of view, but contain numberless good-natured, simple appeals to the affections, which people understood better than the milk-and-water *lagrime, sospiri,* and *felicità* of the eternal Donizettian music with which we are favoured now-a-days. (p. 40)

The music of Gatsby, on the other hand, is not forty years behind the time but strives for modernity with "The Sheik of Araby" (p. 94), "The Love Nest" and "Ain't We Got Fun" (p. 115), "Beale Street Blues" (p. 181), and "'Vladimir Tostoff's latest work, which attracted so much attention at Carnegie Hall last May'. . . . 'The Jazz History of the World'" (pp. 60-61). One of the ballads Becky sang made such pathetic reference to the plight of orphans, that "everybody felt the allusion . . . to her hapless orphan state." Jos, in particular, is quite overcome, and the Puppet Master slyly remarks that "if George and Miss Sedley had remained, according to the former's proposal, in the farther room; Joseph Sedley's bachelorhood would have been at an end, and this work would never have been written" (p. 41). Equally ironical is Thackeray's use of the romantic marching song "The Girl I Left Behind Me" as a title for Chapter 30, which depicts both the plight of Amelia and the very unromantic machinations of Becky.

Fitzgerald uses songs in like manner. As Jos was touched by Becky's ballad, so Daisy is moved by "'Three o'Clock in the Morning,' a neat, sad little waltz of that year," that suggested "romantic possibilities totally absent from her world" (p. 131). Ironically, besides composer

Tostoff's name, there are the specific fragments of lyrics which Fitzgerald quotes from two of the songs mentioned above. Gatsby, like the Valentino character in "Sheik of Araby," feels that Daisy's love does belong to him, and he has crept stealthily into the tent of her society; and as the Wilsons and Buchanans demonstrate, from "Ain't We Got Fun,"

> "One thing's sure and nothing's surer
> The rich get richer and the poor get—. . . ."

Finally, during the confrontation scene in the Plaza Hotel, while Daisy announces to her husband that she loves Gatsby, and to Gatsby that while she loved her husband, she loved him too, the strains of Mendelssohn's Wedding March create a striking counterpoint.

Becky and Gatsby both elaborate on their given roles, to fit their platonic conception of themselves, and both—like Napoleon (to whom Becky is several times compared)—do well so long as they can get away with the unusual, the unexpected, and the daring; they advance until society marshalls its collective forces against them. As Becky advances figuratively from mere aid-de-camp to strategist and near commander, so Gatsby rises through the ranks from farm boy to lieutenant, then major (as Dobbin does), then to Wolfsheim's chief general.

Both novels use modes of transportation as metaphors for social mobility and signs of class rank:

Vanity Fair	The Great Gatsby
"My father's a gentleman and keeps his carriage" (p. 45).	". . . he'd brought down a string of polo ponies from Lake Forest. It was hard to realize that a man in my own generation was wealthy enough to do that" (p. 7).
Becky denies Lady Bareacres her horses (p. 307) . . .	. . . just as Tom refuses to sell his car to Wilson (pp. 29-30).
"A title and a coach and four are toys more precious than happiness in Vanity Fair" (p. 83).	"A dead man passed us in a hearse heaped with blooms, followed by two carriages with drawn blinds, and by more cheerful carriages for friends. . . . a limousine passed us, driven by a white chauffeur, in which sat three

> modish negroes. . . . I laughed aloud as the yolks of their eyeballs rolled toward us in haughty rivalry" (pp. 82-83).

Both characters are present at watering places hosting grand society, Becky at Pumpernickel, Gatsby in his home at West Egg. The 400 at both places deserve comparison:

Vanity Fair	*The Great Gatsby*
Lord Tapeworm, Marshall Tiptoff, his Transparency the Duke, the Earl of Bagwig, Zwieback, Madam de Burst, Madam de Schnurrbart, Mmes. Strumpf and Lederlung, and Gräffin Fanny de Butterbrod (Ch. 63).	Leeches, Civet, Hornbeams, Willie Voltaires, "and a whole clan named Blackbuck, who always gathered in a corner and flipped up their noses like goats," Edgar Beaver, Endive, Fishguards, Mrs. Ulysses Swett, the Dancies, Whitebait, Hammerhead, and Beluga (pp. 73-74)[7]

Sir Pitt Crawley suggests bestiality like Wolfsheim, Katspaugh, or James B. ("Rot-Gut") Ferret. Lord Steyne's name makes its own moral comment. Lord Bareacre's name suggests his actual poverty, so that "it was a wonder how my Lord got the ready money to pay. . . . The Hebrew gentleman knew how he got it" (*VF*, p. 596); and Wolfsheim knows—and is like Thackeray's Hebrew gentlemen the source—where Gatsby got his money.

In each novel, war is used as a background, a *diabolus ex machina,* a device to get characters off stage at certain times and then allow certain of them to return. In each, there are characters in love with unworthy women (Dobbin and Gatsby), and characters who seek to achieve their personal goals through social climbing of dubious means (Becky and Gatsby). In each money is the glue that brings together disparate social strata.

Vanity Fair	*The Great Gatsby*
"People in Vanity Fair fasten on to rich folks quite naturally" (p. 196).	". . . East Egg condescending to West Egg . . ." (p. 54).

"These money transactions—
these speculations in life and
death—these silent battles for
reversionary spoil—make brothers very loving towards each
other in Vanity Fair" (p. 95).

"'I picked him for a bootlegger
the first time I saw him, and I
wasn't far wrong.'
"'What about it?' said Gatsby
politely. 'I guess your friend
Walter Chase wasn't too proud
to come in on it. . . . He came
to us dead broke. He was very
glad to pick up some money, old
sport'" (p. 161).

Becky "could be a good woman if . . . [she] had five thousand a
year" (p. 409), and Daisy, whose voice is full of money, "wanted her
life shaped now, immediately—and the decision must be made by
some force—of love, of money . . ." (p. 181).

Structurally, each novel progresses from scenes of apparent
domesticity, flashbacks of the past, to party scenes, strained
domesticity and suppressed violence, to more parties and severely
qualified domesticity again. The differences between these two
novels, finally, are in the use of literary conventions; the worlds
which those conventions are used to describe stay the same—not at
all an encouraging prospect.

University of California, Davis

We are grateful to our colleague, Professor Elliot L. Gilbert, for sharing
with us his insights into *Vanity Fair*.
[1]Arthur Mizener, *The Far Side of Paradise* (Boston: Houghton
Mifflin, 1965); p. 185. Cf. Robert Emmet Long's note, *"Vanity Fair* and
the Guest List in *GG"* in *Fitzgerald Newsletter*, 38 (Summer 1967), 270:
". . . *Vanity Fair* was one of his [Fitzgerald's] favorite novels; he refers to
it often in his letters, . . . even quoting lines from it from memory; and it
was the first work to be read in his reading program for Sheilah Graham."
[2]William Makepeace Thackeray, *Vanity Fair*, ed. Geoffrey and
Kathleen Tillotson (Boston: Houghton Mifflin, 1963), p. 602, for example.
Subsequent quotations from this edition will be cited in our text.
[3]Mario Praz, "Anthony Trollope," *The Victorian Novel: Modern
Essays in Criticism*, ed. Ian Watt (New York: Oxford University Press,
1971), p. 362.

[4]F. Scott Fitzgerald, *The Great Gatsby* (New York: Scribners, 1925), pp. 1-2. Subsequent quotations from this edition will be cited in our text.

[5]Cf. Peter L. Hays, "Fitzgerald and Hemingway," *Hemingway In Our Time* (Corvallis, Oregon: Oregon State University Press, 1974), pp. 87-97.

[6]As a relevant and interesting aside, Taylor Alderman, in a recent note (*Modern Fiction Studies*, 19 [Winter 1973-74], 563-565), suggests that, given Gatsby's origins from within himself, his name is based on a double-pun: "Gatz be-gat Gats-be. Gatsby was begat by-Gatz. . . . the newly-coined surname reflects Gatsby's begetting of his new self out of the self that had been." A "jay," Prof. Alderman goes on to suggest, is "one who is easy to dupe."

[7]Cf. Robert Emmet Long, *op. cit.*

THOMAS E. DANIELS

THE TEXTS OF "WINTER DREAMS"

As many have pointed out, F. Scott Fitzgerald relied entirely on his writing throughout his adult life for earning a living. That has never been a particularly easy method of getting rich, and there is little doubt that Fitzgerald not only wanted to get rich but also had a very difficult time in the attempt. It is also well known that he wrote for most markets available to him—magazines of all sorts, from the most crassly commercial to the very sophisticated; newspapers; the movies on various occasions; the radio, and, of course, for the very respectable publishing house which handled his books in this country, Charles Scribner's Sons. But what isn't known very widely, and an area that has attracted little attention even in this current explosion of Fitzgerald scholarship, is that he also exploited most of the foreign markets that he or perhaps more accurately Harold Ober, could interest in his work.[1] It is even more surprising that the materials Fitzgerald published in England have attracted little attention, since it is often quite instructive to compare the English texts of American writers with the American texts.

The primary concern here is with the short stories which Harold Ober, Fitzgerald's agent, and perhaps others, placed in various English journals after original appearances in American periodicals, and before at least some of them were put together in various collections by Scribners; and more particularly, I will focus on the story "Winter Dreams."[2] Once a story appeared in a collection during Fitzgerald's lifetime, the text used in that collection usually became the text which reprints relied upon. However, as everyone knows who has done any serious work with Fitzgerald's short stories, there are no definitive texts available for them; in fact, even to procure most—let alone all—of the texts of his stories these days in any form is a very difficult task.[3] My concern then is with the texts of stories which first appeared in this country, then appeared in an English journal; in some cases these same stories were later included in a collection—though of the twenty-four stories which can be so categorized fourteen were never collected during Fitzgerald's lifetime.[4]

In the process of collating the above-mentioned group of stories— and particularly "Winter Dreams"—I have found that the English texts of most of these stories are quite different from the American. And in the case of "Winter Dreams" I will argue that many of the differences in the English text make it superior aesthetically to the two American texts which can be considered authoritative.

The question as to the source, or sources, of the difference between the American and English texts of this story, and most of the others for that matter, is not satisfactorily answered yet, and perhaps never will or can be. Matthew J. Bruccoli states to me in a letter of 26 September 1974 that "there is no evidence at all that Fitzgerald ever revised a story for England. None." And indeed I have found no external evidence that gives us any help one way or another here. However, he also states in the same letter, "but the changes in WD ['Winter Dreams']—some at least—clearly go beyond editorial tinkering." That many of the changes do go beyond "editorial tinkering" is about the only evidence we have so far concerning the source(s) of the differences. Prof. Bruccoli does suggest in another letter to me of 13 November 1974 a "working solution. Fitz sent story to Ober. Ober sent one copy of TS to American mag and another copy to English mag. Still 2 copies of Fitz version at this point. American mag sent proofs, which he revised. English mag did not send proofs. So in case like this USA mag text represents Fitz's final intention, but English mag represents original intention. This story works for 'Winter Dreams.' The difference in time between Dec. 1922 and Feb. 1923 did not allow *Royal* to send proofs to Fitz (even if they wanted to) before airmail. I cling to idea that Fitz did not customarily (if at all) revise stories for English re-publication. No evidence. But quite possibly probable that some English story republications actually derive from Fitz's unrevised text." He states further that if a manuscript or typescript can be found for "Winter Dreams" this theory could be checked out "by collating MS or TS against *Royal*." Unfortunately, neither exists in the Princeton collection, and I have been unable to find either anywhere else. In the one reference Fitzgerald makes to "Winter Dreams" in his published correspondence, however, he states that the story should reach the Reynolds agency on the 13th or 14th of September 1923.[5] Actually, then, if Fitzgerald were not overly optimistic in his estimated time of completion of the story, the agency had the story from mid-September; it was one of five stories Fitzgerald submitted to *Metropolitan* under a contract he signed with them in May 1920. Though I am not arguing that Fitzgerald did in fact receive proofs from the *Royal,* it was possible in terms of time. There were at least three full months from the time the Reynolds agency received the story and the time the *Royal* published it, and possibly four.

There is one story which is substantially different in the English edition, for which I have been able to find a typescript. That story is "Flight and Pursuit." The English publication of that story does include Fitzgerald's hand-written corrections which appear on the typescript, so at least in this particular instance Prof. Bruccoli's theory does not apply. In collating the corrected typescript of "Flight and Pursuit" with the English edition which appeared in the June 1932 issue of *Britannia and Eve,* it became readily apparent that the English version is closer in most ways to the authorially corrected typescript than is the *Post* text. I have not been able to locate proofs of this story; and since Fitzgerald did not usually even see proofs of stories while he was in Europe (he was in Paris when he wrote this story, though he had returned to this country by the time it appeared in *Post*), it appears likely that in this instance a corrected typescript was sent to *Britannia and Eve,* and the *Post* then "house styled" the story to fit their own editorial desires. This theory would indicate that the English editors of *Britannia and Eve* were more concerned with the authority of Fitzgerald's text than the editors of *Post.* We know that Ober, and at least some magazine editors in this country, were willing to make substantial changes in Fitzgerald's short stories without consulting him. In one memo, for instance, Ober states, "Mr. Aley called up and said that he had to cut about two hundred words in Scott Fitzgerald story. They changed the type of the magazine to larger type and they cut all their stories. He said he would do it very carefully. I don't think we need to say anything to Fitzgerald about it because I don't think he ever reads his stories."[6] If my theory is correct in this instance, then a case could be made for using the English text as the most authoritative, or the "copy-text" for "Flight and Pursuit." And, if we could apply that theory to "Winter Dreams," then the *Royal* text of that story would become the most authoritative. That leap, however, may be too long in the absence of further external evidence regarding "Winter Dreams." About textual problems in *Gatsby* Bruccoli states that the difficult part for the textual critic of Fitzgerald's work is not to determine what Fitzgerald wrote but to determine "how he wanted what he wrote to be printed."[7] He is referring to *Gatsby* here, but in most instances I believe this assertion even more applicable to the stories. Fitzgerald always relied heavily on "house styling" for his novels and other work, and evidence suggests he relied on many magazine editors, and Ober's office, for editorial help especially with the later stories.

All of these problems must be taken into account whenever one tries to establish a copy-text for anything like a definitive edition. There is not space here to go into all of the intricacies and guidelines now established concerning the methods for selecting a copy-text— that problem vis-à-vis Fitzgerald's short stories is the subject of a longer work I am preparing concerning all of the stories—but it is necessary to consider at least some of the difficulties as they relate to "Winter Dreams." Probably the most helpful work on the subject now, since it is the most comprehensive and is also well documented with an annotated bibliography, is the revised edition of the *Statement of Editorial Principles and Procedures: A Working Manual for Editing Nineteenth-Century American Texts.*[8] I assume that the *Statement of Editorial Principles* can be applied to twentieth-century texts as well as nineteenth. The authors of this work begin by stating that

> It is the editor's first obligation to make sure that he examines all the available forms of the text which could conceivably contain changes made by the author. "Form" means holograph manuscript, author-corrected proof, printed copy, or printed copy with the author's holograph revisions. It is a large part of the editorial job to distinguish relevant forms from potentially relevant forms: to determine relevance is a matter which must be decided by actual collations rather than by tradition or mere assumption of probability. . . . Potentially relevant forms consist of all forms dating from the author's lifetime (excluding those with which the author had no connection, such as pirated editions) and often include posthumous editions as well. . . .[9]

Following these guidelines, then, there are at least three printed texts of "Winter Dreams," to my knowledge, which must be considered in carrying out this "first obligation": the original text which appeared in the December 1922 edition of *Metropolitan;* the English text, which appeared in the February 1923 edition of *Royal;* and the text which appeared in the *ASYM* collection in 1926. All three texts are substantially different; all three contain changes which "conceivably" could have been made by Fitzgerald; and, as mentioned, so far as I know there is no extant holograph manuscript, author-corrected proof, or typescript for consideration so that a definitive text will have to be built from the printed forms of the story in this case. There is no question that the *Metropolitan* text was originally prepared by Fitzgerald—though certainly it is impossible at this point to divine how much "editorial tinkering" is there—and there is little question that Fitzgerald had a lot to do with the *ASYM* text;[10] the only question then is the "relevance" of the *Royal* text. It can't have been a "pirated" edition since Fitzgerald lists it as sold in his *Ledger;* and if we take Prof. Bruccoli's proposed explanation, in his letter to me of 13 November 1974, we would have to argue that the *Royal* text is indeed the "original intention" of the story, and would, therefore, carry with it primary authority concerning matters of accidentals—as argued by Greg; though, one would have to consider the fact that it was styled for the English audience. If, as is the case with "Flight and Pursuit," we could show that the *Royal* text has less house-styling than the *Metropolitan,* we could then argue that it too is closer to Fitzgerald's intentions. Given the lack of evidence for support of these theories, however, probably the best way to proceed, at least here, is to consider all three texts, since again, all three "conceivably" contain changes made by Fitzgerald himself. Therefore, I am assuming that the *Metropolitan* text and the *Royal* text are authoritative—each with varying degrees of house-styling—since it seems impossible to ascertain, given the evidence we have, the precise degree of Fitzgerald's involvement with either. Then, the *ASYM* becomes the "final intentio" text.*

---

*Of help here is the distinction that G. Thomas Tanselle makes between the "creative" and the "scholarly" editor, and it will probably be well to keep in mind the reliance they both must have on "critical" judgments. Tanselle says, in part: "The scholarly study of literature is historical and the aim of scholarly editing must be the reconstruction of the exact words which a particular author used. But it is an obvious absurdity to suppose that the 'best' reading, from an artistic point of view, is always the author's; and it is equally obvious that an editor could conceivably produce a version of a work aesthetically superior to the original. In such a case the editor would in effect become a collaborator of the author, in the way that publisher's editors or literary executors sometimes are. So long as one is concerned only with individual aesthetic objects, there can be no objection to the procedure; but if one is interested in a work as part of an author's total career, one must insist on having the words which the author actually wrote. The scholarly editor, though he may be equally as capable of producing a superior work as the creative editor, puts his critical abilities to the service of understanding *what the author* (given his turn of mind and his habits of expression) would have preferred at any particular point. I belabor this distinction in order to emphasize the fact that 'scholarly' or 'scientific' editing does not preclude literary judgment; rather, it relies on such judgment—but, for the scholarly editor as well as the scholarly critic, *the judgment is effective to the extent that it reflects an insight into the author's thought and expression*" ("Textual Study and Literary Judgment," *The Papers of the Bibliographical Society of America,* 65 [2nd quarter 1971], 113-114). Italics mine.

In the case of a study of the three texts available to us, then, and
given the general lack of evidence as to the relevance of the English
text involved, for this paper it will probably be most instructive to
approach all three texts from the point of view of "what would
Fitzgerald have preferred at any particular point." From there we
can make some decisions as to whether or not those judgments
reflect particular "insight into the author's thought and
expression."

In the process of collating the three texts I have found that the
Metropolitan text has 9600 words, and the *Royal* 9200. The *ASYM*
text, however, has only 8350 words. It may be argued that Fitzgerald
thought the story too long in the original version and consequently
set out to cut it, or that he wanted to cut the sections he did for solely
aesthetic reasons. He obviously cut part of the description of the
Jones house because he used it in *The Great Gatsby*. I have no
historical evidence which would help us out here. At close to 10,000
words in the *Royal* and *Metropolitan* versions, it is one of
Fitzgerald's longer stories; but unlike many of his longer short
works this story does not suffer greatly from unnecessary verbiage
and long authorial attempts to justify action. Indeed "Winter
Dreams" has often been seen as important apprentice work for *The
Great Gatsby* since it explores the same kind of character types
which were developed so well in that novel.[11] The story, in my
judgment, is intrinsically important too; I believe it is one of
Fitzgerald's best stories. It was written at a time when he was
maturing very rapidly as an artist—that is, those years from the
publication of *The Beautiful and Damned* (1922) to *The Great
Gatsby* (1925).

According to my count, there are 208 differences between the
Royal text and the *Metropolitan* text. That figure is a bit misleading
however, since I count a change, even if it involves a number of
words rewritten, added, or left out, as only one difference. Of those
208 changes, though, forty-five are substantive. Obviously the most
common type of difference is with the accidentals which were
usually altered to conform with British standards of spelling,
punctuation, and the like. The setting of this story was not moved to
England, as was the case with seven of the twenty-one English
versions of Fitzgerald's stories I have located. My major concern here
is, of course, with substantive differences; and it is important that
given the total effect of the changes in the *Royal* text, I find it the
most aesthetically pleasing of the three texts.

The first change made, unfortunately, seems to belie that
contention. To have shifted the very good and appropriate title from
"Winter Dreams" to the very prosaic and sentimental "Dream Girl
of Spring"—which the *Royal* did—can only be justified on the

grounds that someone wanted a title that would appeal to a more sentimental and less sophisticated audience. However, the most common substantive differences in the story are what may be called changes in "cute" language or mere word play. With such revisions also occur, of course, changes in tone—usually from a rather overdone feeling to a much more controlled and even understated level of irony. (This is not true in the case of the characterization of Judy Jones, however. That is discussed below when dealing with the changes between the *Metropolitan* and the *ASYM* text.) The first sentence is a good example. The *Metropolitan* text reads: "Some of the caddies were poor as sin and lived in one-room houses with a neurasthenic cow in the front yard, but Dexter Green's father owned the second best grocery store in Dillard—the best one was The Hub, patronized by the wealthy people from Lake Erminie—and Dexter caddied only for pocket-money" (*Metropolitan*, p. 11). The *Royal* version reads, "Some of the caddies were poor as sin; but Dexter Green's father owned the second best grocery store in Dillard—the best one was The Hub, patronized by the wealthy people from Lake Erminie—and Dexter caddied only for pocket-money" (*Royal*, p. 538). The *Royal* version, then, leaves in the material essential for the introduction—Dexter's economic background, the fact that he would never encounter the rich Judy Jones in his store, and the general setting—but cuts the cute and superficial "and lived in one-room houses with a neurasthenic cow in the front yard."

In the second paragraph we are told in the *Metropolitan* version that the golf course Dexter caddied at lay in "enforced fallowness" during the winter; the *Royal* version changes that awkward locution to "enforced idleness." When Dexter first meets Miss Judy Jones, the *femme fatale* of the story, she is with her nurse at the golf course, and Judy is most petulant and spoiled. Interestingly, though, the nurse, Hilda, is portrayed as a well-starched, proper woman who tries diligently to maintain her composure even when threatened by Judy with a golf club. The *Metropolitan* version has this woman tell Dexter that "Mrs. Mortimer Jones [Judy's mother] sent us out to play golf and we don't know how without we get a caddy." Surely the *Royal* reading is much more consistent with Hilda's characterization in its simple reading that they can't play golf "without a caddy." There is no justification, as far as I can tell, for the colloquial American reading. Years later, Dexter becomes rich, and he and Judy have dinner together. (Fitzgerald had a tendency in early stories to move characters from poverty to wealth very quickly in a Gatsby-like way in order to place them in the position of being "poor boys with money." George Rollins in "'The Sensible Thing'" is another good example of this.) During dinner she tells Dexter that she just that day rejected a man she liked

very much because she suddenly discovered he was poor. Then, in
the *Metropolitan* version, she asks Dexter "Does this sound horribly
mundane?" The *Royal* text reads "horribly mean?" "Mean" in the
sense of unkind, or causing pain, makes better sense here than
"mundane"—or trite and meaningless. Both characters agree that
being honest with each other concerning backgrounds and the like
is very important and such information, therefore, could not be
mundane. (Dexter proceeds to tell Judy that he has more money
than anyone in the area his age). Her rejection of her former lover,
however, could well be "mean." In aggregate, this concern for more
precise language does affect the story, and I strongly suspect that a
more careful editor would have caught many of these problems.

The other major difference between the *Royal* text and the
Metropolitan text is that the direct authorial voice is diminished in
the *Royal*. On two occasions in the story, Fitzgerald injects himself
in order to instruct the reader as to where the story is going and the
major themes involved. The first occurs after Dexter has quit his job
as a caddy at the country club where Judy Jones's father was a
member—he quit rather than caddy for Judy and her nurse. He
certainly was not in their social or economic class, but to act as
"servant" for Judy was to demean himself too much. Fitzgerald's
problem at this point is to move Dexter from his position of
inferiority on every scale, to at least a position of equality on the
economic scale. He does so by telling us directly that Dexter strove
for the best, even though it was more difficult, and even given the
difficulty of the struggle he managed to make a great deal of money
very quickly in the laundry business. The *Metropolitan* version
reads, "Often he reached out for the best without knowing why he
wanted it—and sometimes he ran up against the mysterious denials
and prohibitions in which life indulges. It is with one of those
denials and not with his career as a whole that this story deals"
(*Metropolitan*, p. 12). The *Royal* version of the story does not have
the last sentence of the above, which is direct instruction on
Fitzgerald's part as to the particular concern of the story. It is
obvious, or at least it should be by this time, that the story is about a
"mysterious denial," and that Dexter cannot have Judy Jones no
matter how much money he makes because, like Jay Gatsby, merely
obtaining money does not provide him the social position necessary
to join the Joneses (his case is interestingly different from Gatsby's,
though, since in the end Dexter is only melancholic not dead).
That's why, surely, his is a "winter dream" and not a "dream of
spring." It is apparent that the sentence cut from the *Royal* version
is of little value to the story in general and is quite heavy-handed.

Another such difference occurs near the end of the story, and
again at a transitional point. By this time in the narrative Dexter is

fully aware that he can never have Judy Jones, even though he has fulfilled the economic requirement. He hears from a man named Devlin, from Detroit, that Judy has married someone who treats her badly and that she has faded "just like that!" Leading into this final scene in the *Metropolitan* version, Fitzgerald tells us: "This story is not his biography, remember, although things creep into it which have nothing to do with those dreams he had when he was young. We are almost done with them and with him now. There is only one more incident to be related here and it happens seven years farther on" (*Metropolitan*, p. 106). The *Royal* version includes only the last sentence, which certainly is not the smoothest transition, but again we do not have in the English version Fitzgerald's direct instructions as to the major concerns of the story. He had difficulty throughout his career in forcing himself to dramatize scenes rather than giving long descriptions and interpretations, and one of the important achievements of *Gatsby* was that the narrator's point of view helped to keep the authorial voice out of the story—an effect Fitzgerald wanted very much to duplicate later in *The Last Tycoon*.[12]

Unlike the *Royal* text of the story, the *ASYM* version is different from the *Metropolitan* in ways that suggest that at least one major concern Fitzgerald had was to cut it—most likely for aesthetic reasons, though, since space is usually not a problem in books. As previously mentioned, the *ASYM* version is roughly a thousand words shorter than either of the magazine versions, and one of the major cuts is made in two consecutive scenes. Also, evidence suggests that when preparing the *ASYM* version Fitzgerald worked from the *Metropolitan* text and not from the *Royal*. It is possible that Fitzgerald had a copy of the *Royal* text and could have worked from that, since he obviously knew of its existence;[13] but since there is no extant manuscript, typescript, or revised tearsheets of the story, it is impossible to tell whether or not he personally revised from a manuscript, typescript, tearsheet, or the printed copy of the story itself when preparing the text for the collected volume. However, two of the place-names were changed for the first time for the *ASYM* text. And, there is no consistency that I have been able to determine in the revisions of the accidentals between the *Royal* and the *ASYM* versions; most importantly, perhaps, none of the major substantive changes in the *Royal* text are included in the *ASYM* text; therefore I conclude that the *ASYM* text came from the *Metropolitan* text. If, then, Fitzgerald were involved with the revisions for the English text of this particular story, he must have either considered the revisions pertinent and salutary for just the English version, or he could have lost any copy he may have had of the English text and not had one available to work from when preparing the *ASYM* text. The other possibility is of course, that he had nothing to do with the English version; but, as previously mentioned concerning "Flight and Pursuit," it is possible that the English editors for "Dream Girl of Spring" adhered more closely to Fitzgerald's original intention than did the American. It is quite possible that when he went to work revising all of the stories he planned to include in the *ASYM* volume, he did not have all of the manuscripts with him, especially since he was abroad in 1925 when he revised the stories for the collection. It appears that he was willing to accept the changes in "Winter Dreams" in the *Metropolitan* text, whether or not he had anything to do with them. And he may not have been aware, by 1925, that there were many differences.

According to my count there are 262 differences between the *Metropolitan* text and the *ASYM* text. There are, though, 328 differences between the *Royal* text and the *ASYM* text. So, the *Royal* text is more different from the *ASYM* but less different from the *Metropolitan*. It is important to keep in mind, however, that I count an entirely re-written scene which may involve a number of paragraphs as only one substantive change as long as the differences are consecutive.

Again, for some reason Fitzgerald, or someone, decided to change some of the place-names for the *ASYM* text. The "Dillard" and "Lake Erminie" of the *Metropolitan* texts are changed to "Black Bear" and "Sherry Island" in the *ASYM* text. The Fitzgeralds moved to Minnesota during Zelda's pregnancy in 1921, and they lived in a resort town named White Bear Lake, Minnesota. Place-name changes account for a good many of the accidental variants in *ASYM*. He did, though, leave these two resorts in Minnesota.

The major substantive change between the *Metropolitan* text and the *ASYM* text occurs in about the middle of the story when Dexter meets Judy Jones as an adult, after he has made his money, and he and Judy fall in love—or at least come as close to it as possible given their "different stations" in life. An extensive cut is made just when Dexter meets Judy on a raft at the country club where they had met when she was a petulant little girl and he was a caddy, and in the following scene at the Jones house. This time he is at the country club as a successful young businessman—still only as a guest, however—and she drives her boat up to the dock on which he is sitting. She asks him to drive for her while she rides the surf-board, and while doing that invites him to her home for dinner the following evening. The *Metropolitan* version of these two scenes reads:

> "It's awful cold, kiddo," she shouted, "What's your name anyways."

"The name is Dexter Green. Would it amuse you to know how good you look back there?"

"Yes," she shouted, "It would amuse me. Except that I'm too cold. Come to dinner tomorrow night."

He kept thinking how glad he was that he had never caddied for this girl. The damp gingham clinging made her like a statue and turned her intense mobility to immobility at last.

"—At seven o'clock," she shouted, "Judy Jones, Girl who hit man in stomach. Better write it down,"—and then, "Faster—oh, faster!"

Had he been as calm inwardly as he was in appearance, Dexter would have had time to examine his surroundings in detail. He received, however, an enduring impression that the house was the most elaborate he had ever seen. He had known for a long time that it was the finest on Lake Erminine, with a Pompeiian swimming pool and twelve acres of lawn and gardens. But what gave it an air of breathless intensity was the sense that it was inhabited by Judy Jones—that it was as casual a thing to her as the little house in the village had once been to Dexter. There was a feeling of mystery in it, of bedrooms upstairs more beautiful and strange than other bedrooms, of gay and radiant activities taking place through these deep corridors and of romances that were not musty and laid already in lavender, but were fresh and breathing and set forth in rich motor cars and in great dances whose flowers were scarcely withered. They were more real because he could feel them all about him, pervading the air with the shades and echoes of still vibrant emotions.

And so while he waited for her to appear he peopled the soft deep summer room and the sun porch that opened from it with the men who had already loved Judy Jones. He knew the sort of men they were—the men who when he first went to college had entered from the great prep-schools with graceful clothes and the deep tan of healthy summers who did nothing or anything with the same debonaire ease.

Dexter had seen that, in one sense, he was better than these men. He was newer and stronger (*Metropolitan*, pp. 15, 98, 100).

The *ASYM* version of the same scene reads:

"It's awful cold," she shouted. "What's your name?"

He told her.

"Well, why don't you come to dinner tomorrow night?"

His heart turned over like the fly-wheel of the boat, and, for the second time, her casual whim gave a new direction to his life.

Next evening while he waited for her to come down-stairs, Dexter peopled the soft deep summer room and the sun-porch that opened from it with the men who had already loved Judy Jones. He knew what sort of men they were—the men who when he first went to college had entered from the great prep schools with graceful clothes and the deep tan of healthy summers. He had seen that, in one sense, he was better than these men. He was newer and stronger (*ASYM*, pp. 69-70).

The major difference between the two versions of this first "serious" meeting of Dexter and Judy is, of course, that the original version is much longer—by over two hundred and fifty words. There are a number of arguments which could be used to support the longer version: there is greater emphasis placed on the Jones's house as it relates to Judy herself, her boyfriends, and all of those romantic indulgences of her class; the fact that Dexter is awed not by the physical size or splendor of the structure but by the type of people who inhabit it is significant for the over-all concerns of the story since it does become possible for Dexter to acquire the same kind of physical things as the Jones's house represents but given his background he can never have Judy—even when "faded"; in the first part of the scene when Judy is surf-boarding, she, in the *Metropolitan,* is more "mod" and "rakish," and she often refers to people as "kiddo," which are all cut or changed in the *ASYM* text; her beauty is emphasized in the *Metropolitan* text, and she is more extravagant; the *Metropolitan* version repeats the fact that Judy is cold and that she has become frozen "like a statue" with "intense immobility" which heightens Fitzgerald's major point that Judy is indeed a "winter dream" for Dexter; and the extremely trite metaphor of "His heart turned over like the fly-wheel of the boat," is not in the earlier text.

Probably the best case to be made for the excision of the material from an aesthetic point of view is that the longer scene is over-done or redundant; and, Judy's "hip speech" is too much for someone in her class so that she becomes a parody of the flapper type. It is interesting that the English version of the story does not cut this scene, though in other places that edition toned down the language and cut some things which were obviously irrelevant. However, it is in this scene that Dexter and Judy are placed together for the first time in any sort of "equal and adult" position, so that to indicate in some detail Judy's house, her language and her general outlook is justified as it contrasts with Dexter's. The greater brevity of the *ASYM* text does eliminate quite a bit of "telling" about Dexter's reaction to the Jones's house, but it also cuts a good deal out of the dramatized scene on the raft, and the "telling" involved is strictly related as Dexter's feelings, not Fitzgerald's.[14]

Throughout the *ASYM* text of the story much of the stronger or more colloquial language is changed to more "acceptable" usage particularly in the scenes dealing with Judy, so that the total effect of her characterization between the two texts is quite different.

Fitzgerald must have been quite pleased with the characterization of Dexter and he must have felt the plot of the story adequate since they are almost exactly the same in both the *ASYM* and *Metropolitan* texts.

Of the three texts considered it seems apparent to me that if one were selecting a copy-text at this point in time it would most probably have to be the *Metropolitan* version. Although there is apparently no evidence available to us as to the extent of housestyling which was involved in preparing that text, it is likely that subsequent editions have become more and more corrupt as they have appeared—a general rule which seems irrefutable—unless the attempt is made somewhere along the way to recover the original. But to argue that is not to suggest that the reprints of the story should be taken strictly from the *Metropolitan* text. Emendations should most probably be made into that text though. And, the authority for accidentals should also rest with that version. It is probable that the *Metropolitan* text is as close as we can come right now to recovering "what the author wrote," lacking any further evidence. There is no question that Fitzgerald himself revised the story for the *ASYM* collection and would have to be considered authoritative in matters of substantives unless other evidence intervenes.

In selecting the *Metropolitan* text as the copy-text for "Winter Dreams" I am not suggesting that it represents Fitzgerald's "final intention." Obviously the *ASYM* text is that. I do believe, however, that the *Metropolitan* text is aesthetically superior to the *ASYM* version, and therefore a definitive edition built from that version would be, in my judgment, the best story. As is the case with *Tender Is the Night*, I don't believe editors should be bound to "final intention," but must take all relevant factors into consideration— including aesthetic ones. Ideally, we would print the story in at least two different versions—the *Metropolitan* and the *ASYM*—since they are in a way two different stories. But given the unlikelihood of that, I would argue that the *Metropolitan* version would be the better place to begin, all things considered.

In most critical analyses of Fitzgerald's short stories, it is usually pointed out that Fitzgerald had difficulty with his plot constructions. Consequently, he was much better off when able to dramatize action rather than falling into the necessity of lengthy explanation. He was always much better off when he used structures which kept him from long explanatory indulgences. The major structural flaw of "Winter Dreams" is precisely the difficulty Fitzgerald had in transforming Dexter from one point of his development to another. In terms of time, the story covers quite a period. It begins when Dexter is fourteen and a caddy at the local country club in Minnesota, and ends when he is thirty-two, and a successful, sophisticated man of the world in New York. The most severe problems occur in the *Metropolitan* version at the transition points in the story, but the *Royal* version handles them much more smoothly simply by cutting some of the authorial instructions. When uncertain, the usual tendency is always to overdo, it seems, and I believe that was the trap Fitzgerald fell into here. The other major shift in the *Royal* text is to more precise diction and an elimination of some unnecessary and trite language. Interestingly, though, it is not stripped of colloquial usage—especially in the characterization of Judy Jones.

The *Royal* text has to be considered somewhere along the way, since it is possible that the changes made for that edition are authorial, and in some ways it is aesthetically the best text available to us. It cannot be considered bogus in the sense that it was pirated; and I have found no evidence that Fitzgerald did not approve of the revisions made. Whether or not he was aware, or became aware, of what that text looked like in every detail cannot be answered by me at this time. Certainly, however, he could have seen the text and I presume one could argue that since there is no evidence that he objected to the editing done to the story, even if he had nothing to do with it—or any of the twenty-four stories so published by English journals—surely he did not object to the English "editorial tinkering." And, as ascertained regarding the "Flight and Pursuit" text, it is possible that in some cases the English versions are actually more authorial than the American.

It is difficult to argue in a general way as to the aesthetic superiority of the *ASYM* text of the story. The only way finally to make sound judgments is to consider each substantive variant and emend or not emend according to the validity of the individual case. In total, and considering the over-all effect of the story, the *ASYM* version has the awkward transitional passages in it that are in the *Metropolitan* version, and the shift in Judy's characterization does not enhance the story to my mind, so consequently I prefer either of the magazine versions to the *ASYM* text. There seem to be fewer aesthetic reasons, at least, for accepting the book version over the other two. If I am correct in this judgment, it is quite sad that all subsequent collections of this story, including the English *Bodley Head Scott Fitzgerald*, have used *ASYM* for their reprints.

---

[1]The very special kind of relationship that developed between Ober and Fitzgerald, both personal and professional, is best seen in the collection of letters, *As Ever, Scott Fitz—*, ed. Matthew J. Bruccoli and Jennifer Atkinson (New York & Philadelphia: Lippincott, 1972). All subsequent references to this collection will read, *As Ever*.

[2]"Winter Dreams" originally appeared in the December 1922 issue of *Metropolitan Magazine*. It then appeared in England under the title of "Dream Girl of Spring," in the February 1923 issue of *The Royal Magazine*. It was later included under the original title in the collection titled *All The Sad Young Men* which Scribners published in 1926. The *All The Sad Young Men* text is the one used in all reprints of the story that I have seen. All subsequent references to the *Metropolitan Magazine* will read *Metropolitan*. Subsequent references to *The Royal Magazine* will read *Royal;* and subsequent references to the *All The Sad Young Men* collection will read *ASYM*.

[3]See my "Bibliographical Problems with the Materials of F. Scott (and Zelda) Fitzgerald" (*Midwest Modern Language Association Proceedings,* 1972) and Matthew J. Bruccoli's *F. Scott Fitzgerald: A Descriptive Bibliography* (Pittsburgh: University of Pittsburgh Press, 1972). All subsequent references to the *Fitzgerald Bibliography* are to Prof. Bruccoli's compilation.

[4]The following is a list of the twenty-four stories so published in England. An asterisk indicates that I have been unable to locate the English text of the story. There are three such "missing" stories. For a thorough discussion of the bibliographical problem involved with these stories see my "English Periodical Publications of the Short Stories of F. Scott Fitzgerald: A Correction of the Record" in the *Fitzgerald/Hemingway Annual 1976*. The following list is in alphabetical order and uses the American titles: "The Adolescent Marriage," "Bernice Bobs Her Hair,"* "The Camel's Back," "The Fiend," "Flight and Pursuit," "Gretchen's Forty Winks,"* "Head and Shoulders," "Image on the Heart," "Last Kiss," "Love in the Night," "Magnetism," "Myra Meets his Family," "A New Leaf,"* "The Offshore Pirate," "One of My Oldest Friends," "A Penny Spent," "Presumption," "Rags Martin-Jones and the Pr-nce of W-les," "'The Sensible Thing'," "Shaggy's Morning," "The Third Casket," "Two for a Cent," "Winter Dreams," "Zone of Accident."

[5]*As Ever.,* p. 48.

[6]*As Ever.,* p. 80. The story referred to here is in question. Bruccoli and Atkinson state "probably 'Not in the Guidebook.'" If they are correct, then Mr. Aley would most likely be an editor for *Woman's Home Companion*. "Not in the Guidebook" was published by that magazine in its May 1925 issue and has not been collected.

[7]Matthew J. Bruccoli, *Apparatus for F. Scott Fitzgerald's The Great Gatsby* (Columbia: University of South Carolina Press, 1974), p. 23.

[8]This work relies heavily on W. W. Greg's very important essay, "The Rationale of Copy-Text," *Studies in Bibliography, 3 (1950-51), 374-91.*

[9]*Statement of Editorial Principles and Procedures,* Revised Edition (New York: MLA, 1972), p. 1.

[10]For instance, while in Paris he wrote to Perkins concerning the *ASYM* volume "The stories (now under revision) will reach you by July 15 (1925). No proofs need be sent over here.

It will be fully up to the other collections and will contain only one of those *Post* stories that people are so snooty about. (You have read only one of the stories (Absolution)—all the others were so good that I had difficulty in selling them, except two" (*Dear Scott/Dear Max,* ed. John Kuehl and Jackson Bryer [New York: Scribners, 1971], p. 112). Fitzgerald seldom corrected proof for stories while he was abroad, but this is the only instance I know of when he didn't correct proof for one of his books. And, given his usual nonchalance about accidentals I suspect that the *Metropolitan* version is closer to his original intentions than is the *ASYM* text. By the time Scribners set the type for the collection they were working from a revised text. I've not been able to discover for certain from which text or texts Fitzgerald revised, though the supposition is very strong that he worked from the *Metropolitan*—which had been "styled" by *Metropolitan* editors; Scribners undoubtedly also "styled" the revised version Fitzgerald sent to them. I would agree, then, with the *Statement of Editorial Principles and Procedures* that states that very often writers are not particularly concerned with accidentals when revising materials, so that one is usually better off to accept the earlier texts for copy-texts—an argument W. W. Greg made a number of years earlier. This of course is not to argue that all substantive readings need or should, come from the *Metropolitan* text.

¹¹See John A. Higgins, *F. Scott Fitzgerald: A Study of the Stories*)N.Y.: St. John's University Press, 1971), pp. 36-37.

¹²One of the typical comments he made about his work on *The Last Tycoon* appears in a letter he wrote to Zelda on October 23, 1940: "I am deep in the novel, living in it, and it makes me happy. It is a *constructed* novel like *Gatsby*, with passages of poetic prose when it fits the action, but no ruminations or side-shows like *Tender*. Everything must contribute to the dramatic movement" (*The Letters of F. Scott Fitzgerald*, ed. Andrew Turnbull [New York: Scribners, 1963], p. 128).

¹³On 16 August 1921, Fitzgerald wrote to Ober and told him that "The Sovereign Magazine hasn't arrived yet" (*As Ever*, p. 25). *Sovereign* was an English publication and its July 1921 issue included Fitzgerald's "Myra Meets His Family." Apparently Fitzgerald wanted a copy of that publication. Moreover, on a number of other occasions in his letters to Ober he asks Ober to provide him with precise information regarding the sales of stories in English magazines so he can keep his records straight— his "records" being the *Ledger*. This amount of evidence suggests he probably received at least a copy of the English version of "Myra," and possibly others, and that throughout most of his career he did indeed keep quite close account of the sales of his stories to British publishers; there are, however, a number of errors in his *Ledger* entries. See my "English Periodical Publications of the Short Stories of F. Scott Fitzgerald: A Correction of the Record" in the *Fitzgerald/Hemingway Annual 1976*.

¹⁴Professor Bruccoli pointed out to me in a letter of 14 January 1976 the obvious similarity between the description of Judy Jones's house in "Winter Dreams" and that of the house in which Daisy Buchanan grew up and was living in when Gatsby met her; it reads as follows: "But what gave it [Daisy's house] an air of breathless intensity, was that Daisy lived there— it was as casual a thing to her as his tent out at camp was to him. There was a ripe mystery about it, a hint of bedrooms up-stairs more beautiful and cool than other bedrooms, of gay and radiant activities taking place through its corridors, and of romances that were not musty and laid away already in lavender but fresh and breathing and redolent of this year's shining motor-cars and of dances whose flowers were scarcely withered. It excited him, too, that many men had already loved Daisy—it increased her value in his eyes. He felt their presence all about the house, pervading the air with the shades and echoes of still vibrant emotions" (*The Great Gatsby* [New York: Scribners, 1925], pp. 177-178). Fitzgerald commonly "mined" his stories for novel material, and very often he would "kill" a story that he had used extensively in some other place—which simply meant he wouldn't let the story be reprinted in any form. He must have felt that his

use of Daisy's house description was not a serious enough "borrowing" to kill the story, but he probably also felt he then had to cut the description of Judy's house in the *ASYM* version of the story which was published after *The Great Gatsby* appeared. It is important to note, however, that the scene in the *ASYM* version is changed much more thoroughly than merely cutting the above quoted one hundred and twenty-five words.

One could also use the argument in selecting the *Metropolitan* text as the superior text aesthetically, that Fitzgerald used the description of the house in *The Great Gatsby* because he liked it so much; and, the only reason he cut it from the *ASYM* was because he would not allow materials he used in his novels to appear elsewhere. To use the *ASYM* version as the copy-text would be choosing a version which leaves out some material which Fitzgerald liked a great deal.

COLLATION

The following is a collation of substantive variants in the relevant three texts of "Winter Dreams": *Metropolitan; Royal;* and *ASYM.* The numbers which appear indicate the page and line numbers for the *Metropolitan* reading; the first number in the series refers to the page(s) and the following number(s) refers to the line(s). I do not indicate columns. The *Metropolitan* reading is always first; the *Royal* second; and the *ASYM* third. A caret indicates absence of punctuation as shown in the other readings. I have not considered any variants in paragraphing substantive.

Substantive Variants: *Metro*   [*Royal*   [*ASYM*

11.1-2   sin and lived in one-room houses with a neurasthenic cow in the front yard, but   [sin; but   [*same as Metro.*
11.12-13   gallowness   [idleness   [fallowness
12.11-12   played over a hundred times in the fairways   [*same as Metro.*   [played a hundred times over the fair-ways
12.19   springboard of the Erminie Club raft.... Among   [spring-board of the Erminie Club raft. Among   [spring-board of the club raft .... Among
12.20   those most impressed was Mr.   [*same as Metro.*   [those who watched him in open-mouthed wonder was Mr.
12.23   Dexter, almost with tears   [*same as Metro.*   [Dexter with tears
12.30   "You're—why, you're not more   [*same as Metro.*   ["You're not more
12.30-31   Why did you   [*same as Metro.*   [Why the devil did you
12.36   and caught the train for Dillard.   [*same as Metro.*   [and walked home to Black Bear Village.
12.51   the course   [the golf course   [*same as Metro.*
12.56   illumined   [*same as Metro.*   [graced

12.57   smiles [*same as Metro.* [grimaces
12.59   say, then she drew [say; then she drew [say. She drew
12.63   I guess [*omitted* [*same as Metro.*
12.68   right"—the smile—"I'll [*same as Metro.* [right. I'll
12.69   faintly [*same as Metro.* [slightly
12.83   least half‸a‸dozen men [least half-a-dozen men [least a dozen men
12.83-84   carry to the grave. [*same as Metro.* [carry into middle age.
12.85   teacher [professional [*same as Metro.*
12.94   we get [*omitted* [*same as Metro.*
12.102   conversation. The conversation was [*same as Metro.* [conversation, which was
12.107   "You darn *fool!*" cried [*same as Metro.* ["You damn little mean old *thing!*" cried
12.110   smile‸ [*same as Metro.* [laugh,
12.110-111   time slew the smile before it reached maturity. [*same as Metro.* [time restrained the laugh before it reached audibility.
12.131   elsewhere in Dillard. [*same as Metro.* [elsewhere around the lake.
12.139   to pass up [to give up [*same as Metro.*
12.146   anything shoddy in the [*same as Metro.* [anything merely snobbish in the
12.151-152   It is with one of those denials and not with his career as a whole that this story deals. [*omitted* [*same as Metro.*
12.160   canned rubbish in [*same as Metro.* [*omitted*
14.2   steady eyes [*same as Metro.* [confident mouth
14.4   it. Dexter [*same as Metro.* [it but Dexter
14.5   how the English washed fine woolen golf stockings [how to wash fine woollen golf stockings [*same as Metro.*
14.6   them. Inside of a year [them. Inside a year [them, and within a year
14.8   *omitted* [should [*omitted*
14.15   here [*same as Metro.* [*omitted*
14.15   *omitted* [*omitted* [the day
14.19   over [*omitted* [*omitted*
14.39-42   Hedrick rather neatly in the stomach. ¶ Mr. T. A. Hedrick grunted and cursed. ¶ "By Gad!" [Hedrick rather neatly in the stomach. ¶ Mr. T. A. Hedrick grunted and cursed. ¶ "My God!" [Hedrick in the abdomen. ¶ "By Gad!"
14.47   *omitted* [*omitted* [wildly
14.50-51   men. She nodded to Sandwood and then [*same as Metro.* [men—then
14.58-59   green except that I hit something." [green if I hadn't hit something." [*same as Metro.*
14.82   "Gosh, she's good- looking!" ["She's good-looking," ["My God, she's good-looking!"
14.86   young [*same as Metro.* [*omitted*
14.94-95   "Better thank the Lord she ["You'd better thank heaven she [*same as Metro.*

14.98   "Come on. Let's go."   [*same as Metro.*   [*omitted*
15.2-3   "The Pink Lady" and "The Chocolate Soldier" and "Mlle. Modiste"   [*The Pink Lady* and *The Chocolate Soldier* and *Mlle. Modiste* ["Chin-Chin" and "The Count of Luxemburg" and "The Chocolate Soldier"
15.8   once and because he could   [*same as Metro.*   [once when he could
15.9   proms in those days he had   [*same as Metro.*   [proms, and he had
15.11   and the splash of the fish jumping   [*same as Metro.*   [*omitted*
15.13   now   [*omitted*   [*same as Metro.*
15.13-14   him now. The ecstacy was a gorgeous appreciation. It was his sense that   [him. The ecstacy was a gorgeous appreciation. It was his sense that   [him now. It was a mood of intense appreciation, a sense that
15.19   peninsula   [*same as Metro.*   [Island
15.31   which consisted apparently of pink rompers.   [*omitted*   [*same as Metro.*
15.32-33   "Oh—you're one of the men I hit in the stomach."   [*same as Metro.*   [*omitted*
15.34-61   raft. After an inexpert struggle, Dexter managed to twist the line around a two-by-four. Then the raft tilted rakishly as she sprung on. ¶ "Well, kiddo," she said huskily "do you"—she broke off. She had sat herself upon the springboard, found it damp and jumped up quickly,—"do you want to go surf-board riding? ¶ He indicated that he would be delighted. ¶ "The name is Judy Jones. Ghastly reputation but enormously popular." She favored   [raft. After an inexpert struggle, Dexter managed to twist the line round a two-by-four. Then the raft tilted rakishly as she sprung on. ¶ "Well, kiddo," she said huskily. "Do you"—she broke off. She had sat herself upon the spring-board, found it damp and jumped up quickly—"do you want to go surf-board riding?" ¶ He indicated that he would be delighted. ¶ "The name is Judy Jones. Ghastly reputation but enormously popular." She favoured   [raft, and as the latter tilted rakishly he was precipitated towards her. With different degrees of interest they recognized each other. ¶ "Aren't you one of those men we played through this afternoon?" she demanded. ¶ He was. ¶ "Well, do you know how to drive a motor-boat? Because if you do I wish you'd drive this one so I can ride on the surf-board behind. My name is Judy Jones"—she favored
15.48-54   beautiful. "See that house over on the peninsula?" ¶ "No." ¶ "Well, there's a house there that I live in only you can't see it because it's too dark. And in   [beautiful. "See that house over on the peninsula?" "No." "Well, there's a house there that I live in, only you can't see it because it's too dark. And in   [beautiful—"and I live in a house over there on the Island, and in
15.55   fella   [feller   [man
15.58-61   out by the dock because he has watery eyes and asks me if I have an ideal."   [*same as Metro.*   [out of the dock because he says I'm his ideal."
15.71-72   with exquisite crawl.   [with an exquisite crawl.   [with a sinuous crawl.
15.90   ecstatically   [*same as Metro.*   [wide
15.91   kiddo   [*same as Metro.*   [*omitted*
15.91-96, 98.1-39, 100.1   name anyways." ¶ "The name is Dexter Green.

Would it amuse you to know how good you look back there?" ¶ "Yes," she shouted, "It would amuse me. Except that I'm too cold. Come to dinner tomorrow night." ¶ He kept thinking how glad he was that he had never caddied for this girl. The damp gingham clinging made her like a statue and turned her intense mobility to immobility at last. ¶ "—At seven o'clock," she shouted, "Judy Jones, Girl who hit man in stomach. Better write it down,"—and then, "Faster—oh, faster!" ¶ Had he been as calm inwardly as he was in appearance, Dexter, would have had time to examine his surroundings in detail. He received, however, an enduring impression that the house was the most elaborate he had ever seen. He had known for a long time that it was the finest on Lake Erminie, with a Pompeiian swimming pool and twelve acres of lawn and garden. But what gave it an air of breathless intensity was the sense that it was inhabited by Judy Jones—that it was as casual a thing to her as the little house in the village had once been to Dexter. There was a feeling of mystery in it, of bedrooms upstairs more beautiful and strange than other bedrooms, of gay and radiant activities taking place through these deep corridors and of romances that were not musty and laid already in lavender, but were fresh and breathing and set forth in rich motor cars and in great dances whose flowers were scarcely withered. They were more real because he could feel them all about him, pervading the air with the shades and echoes of still vibrant emotion. ¶ And so while he waited for her to appear he peopled   [name anyway?" ¶ "The name is Dexter Green. Would it amuse you to know how good you look back there?" ¶ "Yes," she shouted, "it would amuse me, except that I'm too cold. Come to dinner to-morrow night." ¶ He kept thinking how glad he was that he had never caddied for this girl. The damp bathing suit clinging made her like a statue and turned her intense mobility to immobility at last. ¶ "—At seven o'clock," she shouted, "Judy Jones, girl who hit man in stomach. Better write it down,"—then, "Faster—oh faster!" ¶ Had he been as calm inwardly as he was in appearance, Dexter would have had plenty of time to examine his surroundings in detail. He received, however, an enduring impression that the house was the most elaborate he had ever seen. He had known for a long time that it was the finest on Lake Erminie, with a Pompeiian swimming pool and twelve acres of lawn and garden. But what gave it an air of breathless intensity was the sense that it was inhabited by Judy Jones—that it was as casual a thing to her as the little house in the village had once been to Dexter. ¶ There was a feeling of mystery in it, of bedrooms upstairs more beautiful and strange than other bedrooms, of gay and radiant activities taking place through these deep corridors and of romances that were not musty and laid already in lavender, but were fresh and breathing and set forth in rich motor-cars and in great dances whose flowers were scarcely withered. They were more real because he could feel them all about him, pervading the shades and echoes of still vibrant emotion. ¶ And so while he waited for her to appear he peopled   [name?" He told her. ¶ "Well, why don't you come to dinner to-morrow night?" ¶ His heart turned over like the fly-wheel of the boat, and, for the second time, her casual whim gave a new direction to his life. ¶ Next evening while he waited for her to come down-stairs, Dexter peopled
100.7   prep-schools   [schools   [prep schools

100.9-11   summer, who did nothing or anything with the same debonair ease. ¶ Dexter had   [*same as Metro.*   [summers. He had

100.17-18   which this graceful aristocracy eternally   [*same as Metro.* [which they eternally

100.18-19   sprang. ¶ When, a year before, the   [*same as Metro.*   [sprang. ¶ When the

100.38-42   He waited for Judy Jones in her house, and he saw these other young men around him. It excited him that many men had loved her. It increased her value in his eyes.   [*same as Metro.*   [*omitted*

100.51   have   [serve   [serve

100.54-56   cocktail perhaps. It even offended him that she should know the maids name.   [*same as Metro.*   [cocktail.

100.57-60   down together on a chintz-covered lounge.   [*same as Metro.* [down side by side on a lounge and looked at each other.

100.61   *omitted*   [*omitted*   [thoughtfully

100.62-67   ¶ "Ought I to be sorry?" ¶ "They're really quite nice," she confessed, as if it had just occurred to her. "I think my father's the best looking man of his age I've ever seen. And mother looks about thirty." [¶ "Ought I to be sorry?" ¶ "They're really quite nice," she confessed. I think my father's the best-looking man of his age I've ever seen. And mother looks about thirty."   [*omitted*

100.70   tonight. They would wonder   [to-night. They would wonder [to-night—they might wonder

100.78-88   lakes. ¶ Before dinner he found the conversation unsatisfactory. The beautiful Judy seemed faintly irritable—as much so as it was possible to be with a comparative stranger. They discussed Lake Erminie and its golf course, the surf-board riding of the night before and the cold she had caught, which made her voice more husky and charming than ever. They talked   [*same as Metro.*   [lakes. ¶ They talked

101.8   guilt   [*same as Metro.*   [uneasiness

101.11   at a silver fork, at   [*same as Metro.*   [at a chicken liver, at

101.19   ¶ "Do I seem gloomy?" she demanded. ¶ "No, but I'm afraid [*same as Metro.*   [¶ "Do you mind if I weep a little?" she said. ¶ "I'm afraid

101.21-23   you," he answered quickly. ¶ "You're   [you." ¶ "You're [you," he responded quickly. ¶ "You're

101.24   rather an unpleasant   [*same as Metro.*   [a terrible

101.26   about. He told me   [*same as Metro.*   [about, and this afternoon he told me

101.29   mundane   [mean   [*same as Metro.*

101.31   I   [*same as Metro.*   [*omitted*

101.32   thoughtfully   [*same as Metro.*   [*omitted*

101.44   suggested suddenly.   [*same as Metro.*   [interrupted herself suddenly.

101.47-51   hesitated. There were two versions of his life that he could tell.

There was Dillard and his caddying and his struggle through college, or—
¶ "I'm nobody,"   [*same as Metro.*   [hesitated. Then: ¶ "I'm nobody,"
101.59-83   She smiled, and with a touch of amusement. ¶ "You sound like
a man in a play." ¶ "It's your fault, you tempted me into being assertive."
¶ Suddenly she turned her dark eyes directly upon him and the corners of her
mouth drooped until her face seemed to open like a flower. He dared scarcely
to breathe, he had the sense that she was exerting some force upon him;
making him overwhelmingly conscious of the youth and mystery that
wealth imprisons and preserves, the freshness of many clothes, of cool rooms
and gleaming things, safe and proud above the hot struggles of the poor.
¶ The porch was bright with the bought luxury of starshine. The wicker of
the settee squeaked fashionably when he put his arm around her,
commanded by her eyes. He kissed her curious and lovely mouth and
committed himself to the following of a grail. ¶ It began   [She smiled,
with a touch of amusement. ¶ "You sound like a man in a play." ¶ "It's
your fault. You tempted me into being assertive." ¶ Suddenly she turned her
dark eyes directly upon him, and the corners of her mouth drooped until her
face seemed to open like a flower. He dared scarcely to breathe; he had the
sense that she was exerting some force upon him, making him
overwhelmingly conscious of the youth and mystery that wealth imprisons
and preserves, the freshness of many clothes, of cool rooms and gleaming
things, safe and proud above the hot struggles of the poor. ¶ The porch was
bright with the bought luxury of starshine. The wicker of the settee
squeaked fashionably when he put his arm round her, commanded by her
eyes. He kissed her curious and lovely mouth, and committed himself to the
following of a grail. ¶ It began   [Then she smiled and the corners of her
mouth drooped and an almost imperceptible sway brought her closer to
him, looking up into his eyes. A lump rose in Dexter's throat, and he waited
breathless for the experiment, facing the unpredictable compound that
would form mysteriously from the elements of their lips. Then he saw—she
communicated her excitement to him, lavishly, deeply, with kisses that were
not a promise but a fulfilment. They aroused in him not hunger demanding
renewal but surfeit that would demand more surfeit . . . kisses that were like
charity, creating want by holding back nothing at all. ¶ It did not take him
many hours to decide that he had wanted Judy Jones ever since he was a
proud, desirous little boy. ¶ ·It began
101.90-91   Whatever the beautiful Judy Jones desired, she   [What-ever
the beautiful Judy Jones desired she   [Whatever Judy wanted, she
101.96   mental quality in any   [*same as Metro.*   [mental side to any
101.129   ended, one of a dozen, a varying dozen, who   [*same as
Metro.*   [ended, one of a varying dozen who
101.149   in the kinetic sense   [*omitted*   [*same as Metro.*
101.167   her charm was a powerful opiate rathen than a tonic.   [her
charm was a powerful opiate rather than a tonic.   [her was opiate rather
than tonic.

102.22   with an old beau   [with an old lover   [with a local beau
102.25   old beau   [old lover   [local beau
102.36   the stag-lines at   [*omitted*   [*same as Metro.*
102.41   downtown   [*omitted*   [down-town
102.65   beaus   [lovers   [suitors
104.2   curved   [*same as Metro.*   [incorrigible
104.43   and cut in on her once.   [and danced with her once.   [*same as Metro.*
104.84-85   He ceased to be an authority on her.   [*omitted*   [*same as Metro.*
105.1   *omitted*   [came   [*omitted*
105.17-19   of night the hushed wonder of the hours and seasons . . . Slender   [of night the hushed wonder of the hours and the seasons; slender   [of nights the wonder of the varying hours and seasons . . . Slender
105.20   lips like poppy petals, bearing   [lips like poppy petals; bearing   [lips and bearing
105.21-22   eyes . . . a haunting gesture, light of a warm lamp on her hair. The thing   [eyes; a haunting gesture, light of a warm lamp on her hair. The thing   [eyes . . . The thing
105.24-25   strong, too alive   [*same as Metro.*   [strong and alive
105.37-38   intensely a "good egg." ¶ He   [*same as Metro.*   [intensely "great." ¶ He
105.64   "Hello, kiddo."   ["Hullo, kiddo!"   ["Hello, darling."
105.86   young   [*same as Metro.*   [*omitted*
105.87   plaintive   [*same as Metro.*   [provocative
105.92-93   If you haven't I have."   [*omitted*   [*same as Metro.*
105.102   but these things were all her own outpouring.   [*same as Metro.*   [but this was her own self outpouring.
105.105-106   and avoiding her surprised glance backed into   [*same as Metro.*   [and back into
105.110   slashed   [*same as Metro.*   [crossed
105.111-112   downtown and affecting a disinterested abstraction traversed   [down town and affecting a disinterested abstraction traversed   [down-town and, affecting abstraction, traversed
105.138   for a moment   [*same as Metro.*   [*omitted*
105.144   sophomores. Yet it   [undergraduates, yet it   [*same as Metro.*
105.147   kiddo   [*same as Metro.*   [darling
105.147   kiddo   [*same as Metro.*   [darling
105.148   obsolete slang   [*same as Metro.*   [endearment
106.21   fine   [*same as Metro.*   [*omitted*
106.56   It seems strange to say that neither   [*same as Metro.*   [It was strange that neither
106.91-93   Irene, that it was on her conscience—did not   [*same as Metro.*   [Irene—Judy, who had wanted nothing else—did not

106.108-113   This story is not his biography, remember, although things creep into it which have nothing to do with those dreams he had when he was young. We are almost done with them and with him now.   [*omitted* [*same as Metro.*

106.114-115   related here and it happens   [related and it happened [*same as Metro.*

106.130   and raised on Wall   [and brought up in Wall   [*same as Metro.*

106.133   was an usher at   [was best man at   [*same as Metro.*

106.136-144   coming. There was a magic that his city would never lose for him. Just as Judy's house had always seemed to him more mysterious and gay than other houses, so his dream of the city itself, now that he had gone from   it,   was   pervaded   with   a   melancholy   beauty. ¶ "Judy Simms,"   [*same as Metro.*   [coming. ¶ "Judy Simms,"

106.158-160   he beats her, you understand, or anything like that. But he [*same as Metro.*   [he ill-uses her, but he

106.164   him," said Devlin. ¶ "Too   [him." ¶ "Too   [*same as Metro.*

106.166   Dexter, "why man, she's   [Dexter, "why, God! man, she's [Dexter. "Why man, she's

106.171   felt,   spasmodically,   involuntarily. ¶ "I   [*same   as Metro.*   [felt spasmodically. ¶ "I

107.53   on his lounge   [*omitted*   [*same as Metro.*

107.75   morning.   Why   these   [morning. These   [morning. Why, these

University of Wisconsin—Green Bay

FITZGERALD FILMOGRAPHY

This filmography lists the directors, screenwriters, producers, and casts for all the theatrical movies made from the works of F. Scott Fitzgerald. Of the twelve Fitzgerald films made between 1920 and 1976, six are silent. *Pusher-in-the-Face,* the first sound adaptation of a Fitzgerald story, is not a feature but a two-reel short. The names of its director and screenwriter are not available. Many of the character names in several of the movies have been changed by the filmmakers.[1]

The Chorus Girl's Romance

Based on "Head and Shoulders"
Metro; 1920
Director: William C. Dowlan
Screenwriter: Percy Heath
Cast:

Marcia Meadows	Viola Dana
Horace Tarbox	Gareth Hughes
Steve Reynolds	Phil Ainsworth
P. P. Anderson	William Quinn
Betty Darrell	Jere Sundin
Fred Ward	Sidney De Grey
Jose Brasswine	Lawrence Grant
Charlie Moon	Tom Gallery
Dr. Tarbox	Edward Jobson

The Husband Hunter

Based on "Myra Meets His Family"
Fox; 1920
Director: Howard M. Mitchell
Screenwriter: Joseph F. Poland
Cast:

Myra Hastings	Eileen Percy
Kent Whitney	Emory Johnson
Lilah Elkins	Jane Miller
Arthur Elkins	Harry Dunkinson
Bob Harkness	Evans Kirk
Charles Mack	Edward McWade
Kelly	John Stepling

The Offshore Pirate

Metro; 1921
Director: Dallas M. Fitzgerald
Screenwriter: Waldemar Young
Producer: Bayard Veiller
Cast:

Ardita Farnam	Viola Dana
Toby Moreland	Jack Mulhall
Uncle John Farnam	Edward Jobson
Ivan Nevkova	Edward Cecil

The Beautiful and Damned

Warner Brothers; 1922
Director: William A. Seiter
Screenwriter: Olga Printzlau
Cast:

Anthony Patch	Kenneth Harlan
Gloria	Marie Prevost
Adam Patch	Tully Marshall
Dick	Harry Myers
Muriel	Louise Fazenda
Dot	Cleo Ridgely
Mr. Gilbert	Emmett King
Hull	Walter Long
Bloeckman	Clarence Burton
Maury	Parker McConnell
Shuttlesworth	Charles McHugh
Rachel	Kathleen Key
Tanner	George Kuwa

Grit

Based on an original story by Fitzgerald
Film Guild; 1924
Director: Frank Tuttle
Screenwriter: James Ashmore Creelman
Cast:

"Kid"Hart	Glenn Hunter
Annie Hart	Helenka Adamowska
Houdini Hart	Roland Young
Boris Giovanni Smith	Osgood Perkins
Flashy Joe	Townsend Martin
Orchid McGonigle	Clara Bow
Pop Finkel	Dore Davidson
Bennie Finkel	Martin Broder
Tony O'Cohen	Joseph Depew

The Great Gatsby

Based on Fitzgerald's novel and Owen Davis' play
Famous Players-Lasky-Paramount; 1926
Director: Herbert Brenon
Screenwriters: Becky Gardiner and Elizabeth Meehan
Producers: Adolph Zukor and Jesse L. Lasky
Cast:

Jay Gatsby	Warner Baxter
Daisy Buchanan	Lois Wilson
Tom Buchanan	Hale Hamilton
Nick Carraway	Neil Hamilton
Jordan Baker	Carmelita Geraghty
Myrtle Wilson	Georgia Hale
George Wilson	William Powell
Charles Wolf	George Nash
Lord Digby	Eric Blore
Bert	"Gunboat" Smith
Catherine	Claire Whitney

Pusher-in-the-Face

Paramount; 1929
Producer: Daniel Frohman
Cast:

Charles David Stewart	Lester Allen
Edna	Estelle Taylor
Cafe owner	Raymond Hitchcock
One who is pushed	Carroll McComas
Other waitress	Lillian Walker

Viola Dana and Jack Mulhall in *The Offshore Pirate* (1921).

Party scene in *The Beautiful and Damned* (1922).

Warner Baxter, Lois Wilson, and Hale Hamilton in *The Great Gatsby* (1926).

The Great Gatsby

Based on Fitzgerald's novel and Owen Davis' play
Paramount; 1949
Director: Elliot Nugent
Screenwriters: Cyril Hume and Richard Maibaum
Producer: Richard Maibaum
Cast:

Jay Gatsby	Alan Ladd
Daisy Buchanan	Betty Field
Tom Buchanan	Barry Sullivan
Nick Carraway	Macdonald Carey
Jordan Baker	Ruth Hussey
Myrtle Wilson	Shelley Winters
George Wilson	Howard da Silva
Klipspringer	Elisha Cook Jr.
Myron Lupus	Ed Begley
Dan Cody	Henry Hull
Ella Cody	Carole Mathews
Owl Man	Nicholas Joy
Mavromichaelis	Tito Vuolo

The Last Time I Saw Paris

Based on "Babylon Revisited"
MGM; 1954
Director: Richard Brooks
Screenwriters: Julius J. and Philip G. Epstein
Producer: Jack Cummings
Cast:

Helen Ellswirth	Elizabeth Taylor
Charles Wills	Van Johnson
James Ellswirth	Walter Pidgeon
Marion Ellswirth	Donna Reed
Lorraine Quarl	Eva Gabor
Maurice	Kurt Kaszner
Claude Matine	George Dolenz
Paul	Roger Moore
Vicki	Sandra Descher
Mama	Celia Lovsky
Barney	Peter Leeds
Campbell	John Doucette
Singer	Odetta

Tender Is the Night

20th Century-Fox; 1962
Director: Henry King
Screenwriter: Ivan Moffat
Producer: Henry T. Weinstein
Cast:

Dick Diver	Jason Robards Jr.
Nicole Diver	Jennifer Jones
Baby Warren	Joan Fontaine
Abe North	Tom Ewell
Rosemary Hoyt	Jill St. John
Tommy Barban	Cesare Danova
Dr. Dohmler	Paul Lukas
Dr. Gregorovius	Sanford Meisner
McKisco	Charles Fredericks
Mrs. McKisco	Bea Benaderet
Mrs. Hoyt	Carole Mathews
Collis Clay	Mac McWhorter
Louis	Albert Carrier
Francisco	Richard de Combray
Pardo	Alan Napier
Lanier Diver	Michael Crisalli
Topsy Diver	Leslie Farrell
Governess	Arlette Clark
Sir Charles Golding	Maurice Dallimore
Mrs. Dunphrey	Carol Veazie
Piano player	Earl Grant

The Great Gatsby

Paramount; 1974
Director: Jack Clayton
Screenwriter: Francis Ford Coppola
Producer: David Merrick
Cast:

Jay Gatsby	Robert Redford
Daisy Buchanan	Mia Farrow
Tom Buchanan	Bruce Dern
Nick Carraway	Sam Waterson
Jordan Baker	Lois Chiles
Myrtle Wilson	Karen Black
George Wilson	Scott Wilson
Klipspringer	Edward Herrmann
Meyer Wolfsheim	Howard da Silva

Mr. Gatz	Roberts Blossom
Wilson's friend	Elliot Sullivan
Gatsby's bodyguard	John Devlin
Twins	Janet and Louise Arters
Mourner	Tom Ewell

The Last Tycoon

Paramount; 1976
Director: Elia Kazan
Screenwriter: Harold Pinter
Producer: Sam Spiegel
Cast:

Monroe Stahr	Robert DeNiro
Kathleen	Ingrid Boulting
Cecilia	Theresa Russell
Pat Brady	Robert Mitchum
Brimmer	Jack Nicholson
Wylie	Peter Strauss
Boxley	Donald Pleasence
Ridingwood	Dana Andrews
Fleishacker	Ray Milland
Didi	Jeanne Moreau
Rodriguez	Tony Curtis
Popolos	Tige Andrews
Marcus	Morgan Farley
Edna	Angelica Huston
Stahr's secretary	Diane Shalet
Guide	John Carradine
Doctor	Jeff Corey
Seal trainer	Seymour Cassell

University of South Carolina

---

[1]The sources for these film credits are *The American Film Institute Catalog of Motion Pictures Produced in the United States: Feature Films, 1921-1930*, ed. Kenneth W. Munden (New York & London: R. R. Bowker Company, 1971); *The New York Times Film Reviews, 1913-1968* (New York: New York Times & Arno Press, 1970); *Motion Picture News; Variety; Filmfacts*. Patrick J. Sheehan, reference librarian of the motion picture section of the Library of Congress, was helpful in locating some material.

ERNEST HEMINGWAY

AUTHOR'S PREFACE.

   Many critics commenting on a book of stories
written by myself and published last fall remarked on how
much whatever excellencies they detected in these stories
resembled the excellencies of Mr. Sherwood Anderson. Having
just read a novel by Mr. Anderson which was called, I believe,
Dark Laughter and which is, I believe, generally acknowledged
to be a masterpiece and being exceedingly impressed by
what these critics had written I resolved to write henceforth
exclusively in the manner of Mr. Anderson. The careful
reader will see that in my attempt to write as Mr. Anderson
writes I have failed most signally. It is therefore to his
indulgence that I commend myself most diffidently.

ERNEST HEMINGWAY

THE "AUTHOR'S PREFACE"
FOR The Torrents of
Spring

The F. Scott Fitzgerald Papers at Princeton include the carbon typescript of *The Torrents of Spring* that Ernest Hemingway presented to F. Scott and Zelda Fitzgerald (see rear endpaper, *Fitzgerald/Hemingway Annual 1972*). This typescript includes the crossed-out "Author's Preface" which was omitted from the book. It is published here with the generous permission of Mrs. Ernest Hemingway.

It is not difficult to see why Hemingway killed this preface: apart from its cumbersome facetiousness, it admits that the impetus for the parody was that "many critics" had noted resemblances between the stories in *In Our Time* and Sherwood Anderson's work.

HANS-JOACHIM KANN

PERPETUAL CONFUSION IN "A CLEAN, WELL-LIGHTED PLACE": THE MANUSCRIPT EVIDENCE

Ever since the appearance of the first articles by F. P. Kroeger and William E. Colburn in 1959,[1] it has been clear that, apart from the apparent ambiguity in the first dialogue, the third dialogue section of "A Clean, Well-Lighted Place" is obscure (or even messy) at the end. Numerous attempts have been made[2] to explain the contradiction and to restore order in the two waiters' dialogue. Otto Reinert wanted to have two indented and quotation-marked lines read as one line of dialogue; Josef F. Gabriel saw the confusion as an intended literary device; John V. Hagopian pleaded for splitting the line, "I know. You said she cut him down." and redistributing the two sentences (the 1965 Scribners edition of the stories followed this advice); in 1973, Scott MacDonald[3] argued in favor of reverting to the original text; in between, Warren Bennet[4] suggested as a solution the assumption that a slug of type was misplaced[5] and Nathaniel M. Ewell[6] saw two slugs of type lost.

The tearsheets from the first publication in *Scribner's Magazine*[7] do not offer any assistance—the proofreading marks do not affect the lines in question.

More can be learned from the manuscript[8] (an interpretative investigation of what, how, and why Hemingway altered or deleted—for instance, the last twenty-nine words of the original draft—is a rewarding undertaking, but it would go beyond the limited scope of this note).

Hemingway began with an undifferentiated "boys," changed his mind on page 2, between line 2 and line 15, crossed out "boys"/"boys," and put in "waiter"/"waiters" instead.

He must have felt the need of a differentiation beyond "one waiter"/"the other waiter"; thus, on page 2, "One of the waiters" is changed to "The younger waiter," although this must have happened when Hemingway had already been writing for some time because the correction is written with a thicker, worked-down pencil. Hemingway obviously saw the danger of ambiguity in other parts, too, as is demonstrated by the alterations "the waiters came over"/"the waiter who was in a hurry came over" (p. 4), "the waiter"/"the unhurried waiter" (p. 5), "the waiter"/"the waiter who was in a hurry" (p. 6).

The separation of "with his colleague again" and " 'He's drunk now,' he said" (p. 3) through paragraphing and indentation made the identification of the "he" somewhat difficult—Hemingway connected the two lines with a run-in indication. Unfortunately the printed version disregarded his proof-reading mark.

Another printing mistake was the deletion[9] of the period after "Anyway" in "Anyway I should say he was eighty." Here, the manuscript supports Edward Stone's[10] theory that "Anyway" is supposed to be a literal translation from the Spanish dialogue and that it functions as an affirmative.

In two places, Hemingway was confused himself. In the first instance when he had already written the younger waiter's utterance ". . . three o'clock."/"He should have killed himself . . ." as two separate lines, he corrected himself by a simple run-in mark (p. 3). In the second instance he saw that the alternating line count attributed "His niece looks after him." to the younger waiter positionally, just as the next line, "I wouldn't want to be that old. An old man is a nasty thing." (p. 4) was the younger waiter's line. To restore the alternating count Hemingway inserted a line,[11] however with the wrong semantics: the older waiter might say "I know." but not "I know. You said she cut him down." Hemingway must not have recognized the mistake either at the time of writing or later— otherwise he would not have written in 1956 that the dialog "made perfect sense to him."[12]

Thus, although the passage does not make sense, it is still Hemingway's original—the teacher, however, may, for his students' sake, point out that, since the whole line is "filling material," the second sentence might be quietly disregarded.

Trier, Germany

(4)

"Anyway, I should say he was eighty."

"I wish he would go home. I never get to bed before three o'clock. What kind of hour is that to go to bed."

"He stays up because he likes it."

"He's lonely, I'm not lonely. I have a wife waiting in the bed for me."

"He had a wife once too."

"A wife would be no good to him now."

"You can't tell. He might be better with a wife."

"His niece looks after him."

"I know. You said she cut him down."

"I wouldn't want to be that old. An old man is a nasty thing."

"Not always. This old man is clean. He drinks without spilling. Even now, drunk. Look at him."

"I don't want to look at him. I wish he would go home. He has no regard for those who must work."

The old man looked from his glass across the square then over at the waiters.

"Another brandy," he said pointing to his glass. The waiter who was in a hurry came over.

[1]Both in *College English*, XX (February 1959), 240-2.

[2]For a discussion of Kroeger, Colburn, Reinert, Stone, Gabriel, Hagopian, and Hagopian/Dolch see Hans-Joachim Kann, *Übersetzungsprobleme in den deutschen Übersetzungen von drei anglo-amerikanischen Kurzgeschichten: Aldous Huxleys "Green Tunnels", Ernest Hemingways "The Killers" und "A Clean, Well-Lighted Place"* (München, 1968), Mainzer Amerikanistische Beitrage, X, pp. 59-61. Most of these articles are reprinted in Morris Friedman and David B. Davis, eds. *Controversy in Literature: Fiction, Drama and Poetry with Related Criticism* (New York: Scribners, 1968), pp. 121-141. More recent items are listed in Nathaniel M. Ewell, "Dialogue in Hemingway's 'A Clean, Well-Lighted Place,'" *Fitzgerald/Hemingway Annual 1971*, 306, n. 1, and in Audre Hanneman, *Supplement to Ernest Hemingway: A Comprehensive Bibliography* (Princeton: Princeton University Press, 1975), pp. 9-10.

[3]"The Confusing Dialogue in Hemingway's 'A Clean, Well-Lighted Place': A Final Word?" *Studies in Short Fiction*, 1 (Spring 1973), 93-101.

[4]"Character, Irony, and Resolution in 'A Clean, Well-Lighted Place,'" *American Literature*, 42 (March 1970), 70-79.

[5]*Ibid.*, 70.

[6]*Ibid.*, 305.

[7]# 222, Hemingway Collection, John F. Kennedy Library, Waltham, Massachusetts.

[8]#337, Hemingway Collection. The author is indebted to Mrs. Ernest Hemingway for her permission to quote from the MS.

[9]Except for one instance of a stylistic change, the printed version differs from the manuscript only in unimportant details of spelling, punctuation and grammar (definite article deleted twice), besides the two important changes mentioned above.

[10]"Hemingway's Waiters Yet Once More," *American Speech*, 37 (October 1962), 240. For Hemingway's repeated attempts to have the speech in this story sound like a literal translation from Spanish, see Kann, pp. 62-64.

[11]The line is squeezed in and even slightly indented to fit.

[12]George Monteiro, "Hemingway on Dialogue in 'A Clean, Well-Lighted Place,'"*Fitzgerald/Hemingway Annual 1974*, p. 243.

ANTHONY HUNT

ANOTHER TURN FOR HEMINGWAY'S "THE REVOLUTIONIST": SOURCES AND MEANINGS

The eighteen miniatures that eventually made up Ernest Hemingway's second book, *in our time* (Paris, 1924), were written in two distinct units.[1] Hemingway wrote one third of them at the invitation of Jane Heap for a contribution to the "Exiles" number (Spring 1923) of *The Little Review* which she was then editing.[2] The remaining twelve sketches were written, according to Carlos Baker, sometime during the "late July and early August" of 1923, and "most of the sketches were done by the hot Sunday afternoon of August 5th . . . ."[3]

In his description of this second group of minatures, Carlos Baker alludes to the sources for several of them. Some, he indicates, are obviously adapted from Hemingway's personal experiences, such as the wounding of Nick Adams at Fossalta-di-Piave, or the love affair with Agnes von Kurowsky that served as the basis for "A Very Short Story." Other cameos were adapted from anecdotes, factual or otherwise, related to Hemingway by others, such as Shorty Wornall's interview with the King of Greece that now serves as "L'Envoi" to *In Our Time*. However, Prof. Baker's allusion to the source of "The Revolutionist" appears vague, if not potentially misleading: "There was another sketch about a chance meeting with a young Hungarian Communist in Italy in 1919."[4] The sentence implies that Hemingway himself had a chance meeting with a young Hungarian Communist in Italy in 1919, but, of course, Hemingway was not in Italy or even Europe for eleven and a half months of the entire year. He had sailed from Genoa in early

January, arriving in the United States on January 21, 1919. Roughly a year later, in January 1920, he was on his way to Toronto, Canada, where he would soon begin work on the *Toronto Star*. He did not return to Europe until December 1921.[5] An even more precise chronology is possible since, according to the internal evidence of the story, the time of the "chance meeting" must have been after September 1919 by which time Admiral Nicholas Horthy had taken control fo the Hungarian government and severely suppressed all the elements of the population that he considered radical, including, as the story makes clear, the Communists who had briefly ruled the country from March to August of 1919.[6] The conclusion is obvious: Hemingway never met any Hungarian Communist in Italy in September of 1919; moreover, although a meeting in Canada is not impossible, it seems quite unlikely that Hemingway ever did meet—from September of 1919 to the "late July and early August" of 1923 when Carlos Baker speculates the minature was completed—an actual Hungarian Communist who had suffered under Horthy, passed through Italy, and found himself, as the events of the story relate, in jail in Sion. Neither Professor Baker, nor anyone else that I am aware of, including Hemingway himself, has ever alluded to—and demonstrated proof of—Hemingway's meeting with an Hungarian Communist, or even with someone, like Shorty Wornall, who might have told Hemingway about such a Communist and his problems.

On the other hand, since Hemingway constantly wrote from what he called "practical experience," one looks for some actual experiences to fill in the background for "The Revolutionist." More importantly, as with all source-hunting, one hopes that the discovery of plausible sources will reveal basic information as to how the author, consciously or unconsciously, goes about the business of fictional composition. I would like to suggest that "The Revolutionist" is not only not based on an actual meeting with an Hungarian Communist —certainly not in September of 1919—but that it is the result of Hemingway's transformation of several discrete, even apparently unconnected, mental and physical experiences that occurred in a different context and time period into a single, composite, fictional cameo. Further, the story's composition is also strongly influenced by its contextual position as a coherent entity in the sequence of sketches first published as the Paris *in our time*. Finally, the compositional "glue" that binds these various elements together in Hemingway's mind, it seems to me, is a sense of what I would call "spatial continuity."

A theory based on the importance of places to Hemingway is hardly new, except in its application to "The Revolutionist," for Philip Young, among others, has clearly demonstrated that certain

locations had an almost magnetic fascination for Hemingway's
creative imagination; some of these places assumed the importance
of personal, archetypical images in his mind and work as he
returned time after time to build his literary creations on the same
spatial configurations.[7] The significance of a particular fictional
location may often be best appreciated when the reader situates
himself in the biographical and historical contexts in which
Hemingway lived during the writing of that story. Admittedly,
biographical approaches to criticism have often been viewed as
outmoded since the advent of "New Criticism," but the true test of
any critical findings should be the integrity and plausibility of the
conclusions as they are weighed against existing interpretations.
The approach of this paper should at least be on equal, if not firmer,
footing with those made by Barbara S. Groseclose and Kenneth G.
Johnston who depend primarily on an analysis of the painters
mentioned in the story: Mantegna, Giotto, Masaccio, and Piero
della Francesca.[8] Is it more plausible to believe that Hemingway,
writing in the early 1920s to a contemporary audience, logically
expected from his readers a knowledge of art history and techniques
going back to the Italian Renaissance, or is it more believable that
he counted on their knowledge of significant contemporary places
and situations in the political and cultural life of Europe, especially
that of Italy? Both expectations may have some validity, but the
immediate impact of the story on its contemporary readers would
seem to depend on situations that were making headlines each day
in 1922 and 1923 when Hemingway was actually composing the
story, rather than on fine and subtle distinctions among art
historians as to the relative realism or classicism of various
Renaissance artists. This thesis gains strength, of course, when one
considers that Hemingway himself was a professional journalist
reporting the European headlines of those days for the *Toronto
Star.*

   As a prelude to a discussion of the significance of the four Italian
artists mentioned in the story, it is important to consider first the
proper fictional context of "The Revolutionist." Its matrix is not
only that of the 1925 *In Our Time*—and of editions subsequent to
it—where the sketch has been "promoted" to a full-fledged story
with a title (instead of a chapter number), and where it is preceded by
the sketch of the Irish policemen responsible for the death of two
Hungarians. Although the link provided by the use of the word
"Hungarian" in these two sketches may be intentional,
nevertheless, the first context of "The Revolutionist" remains the
Paris *in our time* where the story is preceded even more significantly
by the brief tale—now known as "A Very Short Story"—of Ag, a
young man, and their unsuccessful love affair.

In the 1924 *in our time* the story opens on "one hot evening in Milan" and proceeds to its first emotional climax when the lovers quarrel:

> On the train from Padova to Milan they quarrelled about her not being willing to come home at once. When they had to say good-bye in the station at Padova they kissed good-bye, but were not finished with the quarrel. He felt sick about saying good-bye like that.[9]

When Hemingway revised the story for the first American edition of 1925, he still began the story on a "hot evening in Milan," but he clarified some of the geographical contradictions inherent in the first version. If then they had somehow quarrelled on the train from "Padova to Milan" and yet also said good-bye "in the station at Padova," Hemingway now wrote:

> On the train from Padua to Milan they quarrelled about her not being willing to come home at once. When they had to say good-bye, in the station at Milan, they kissed good-bye, but were not finished with the quarrel. He felt sick about saying good-bye like that.[10]

By the time of the second American edition, published by Scribners in 1930, Hemingway completed the fictionalizing of his original sketch by switching the opening locale to "One hot evening in Padua . . . ."[11] In sum, then, Milan has become the city of good-byes as it progressively relinquishes its symbolic function as a city of growing love.

Carlos Baker argues that Hemingway made the change "from fear of libel" and the strength of his argument is underscored by two additional changes in the sketch as Hemingway revised it for subsequent editions.[12] In the Paris edition the story concludes when the young man "contracted gonorrhea from a sales girl from The Fair riding in a taxicab through Lincoln Park."[13] By 1925 Hemingway has changed the specific place name of the store in Chicago to a more generalized version: "A short time after he contracted gonorrhea from a sales girl in a loop department store riding in a taxicab through Lincoln Park."[14] Later editions merely change the last clause to "while riding in . . . Park" in order to clear up the grammatical ambiguity of the former version. If fear of libel was Hemingway's major concern, it is strange that he waited until the fifth American printing (the first Scribners publication) to make what is, perhaps, the most significant change. Both the Three Mountains edition and the four Boni & Liveright printings use the name "Ag" for the woman who serves, through her unfaithfulness, as a destroyer of the young man's illusions about love. The reference to the real-life Agnes von Kurowsky is unmistakable. By 1930 Hemingway's fictional imagination, perhaps acting more along the lines of creating a symbolical figure of "enlightenment" for the young man rather than "from fear of libel," changed the nurse's name from "Ag" to "Luz."

Regardless of Hemingway's reasons, the effect of these changes is to emphasize the area "from Padua to Milan," with special stress given to Milan in the later editions, as a locational symbol for something a young man finds distasteful, some shattering of his verities. Since "The Revolutionist"—the cameo immediately following "A Very Short Story" in the 1924 edition—also contains disagreeable feelings about the area of Northern Italy, specifically Milan, we are drawn into the complex problem of whether these two miniatures were originally intended to be seen as creatively interwoven entities. The young man of "A Very Short Story" leaves Padua/Milan feeling "sick" about the unresolved quarrel, but he blindly clings to his faith in Ag/Luz and their ideal love. When he later learns of her affair with an Italian major, and consequently contracts venereal disease from a sales girl, the story may be seen to end on a note of failure and entrapment similar to that of "The Revolutionist." Shortly after the young revolutionist passes through the Milan that contains Mantegna's disliked paintings, the older narrator says: "The last I heard of him the Swiss had him in jail near Sion" (p. 106). Although the two miniatures were no longer contiguous by the time of the 1925 *In Our Time* a further, and perhaps fortuitous, link was created between them as Hemingway changed "The Fair" to a "loop department store" at the same moment that he created the title "The Revolutionist" for the former "Chapter 11." Always attuned to the magic of names and the significance of places, Hemingway seems to be pointing from Loops to Revolutions, both going around in an eternal uselessness of faith, in the one case faith in love itself, in the other faith in a political movement. These two miniatures clearly reflect each other as well as they convey the pervasive theme of *in our time*, a book about the loss of faith in a context of either violence or indifference to personal emotional belief. "A Very Short Story" and "The Revolutionist" describe two similar turnings of this wheel of loss.

Thus the usual interpretation of the young revolutionist's dislike for Mantegna as symbolic of his refusal to face bitter reality is, in general terms, a valid one. Emily Watts puts it this way:

In "The Revolutionist," Hemingway is demonstrating the foolishness of idealistic causes such as the revolutionist advocated. The young man's dislike of Mantegna reflects his inability to see the reality of the world in which his schemes of revolution will not work.

As the story ends, the young idealist is eventually forced to face the immediate reality of jail.[15]

While I agree with Professor Watts that "Hemingway is demonstrating the foolishness of idealistic causes," I am not at all sure that the young revolutionist is as idealistic as he appears to be. Moreover, I believe that the references to Mantegna are capable of a double perspective that exactly pinpoints the overlapping of biography and fiction. For Hemingway it is the city of Milan, as well as the Mantegna paintings in the Museum, that serves as the true symbolic touchstone. In 1918 Hemingway experienced a profound disappointment when Agnes von Kurowsky "told him quietly that she would not be in Milano to celebrate their first Christmas."[16] This was, of course, the beginning of the end of their affair; he would not see her again before he left for the States. Eventually, like the young man of "A Very Short Story," Hemingway was told that she had fallen in love with someone else. Milano, then, is a biographical place of loss. The city also serves as a fictional symbol of disappointment. In "The Revolutionist" when the narrator speaks to the young Communist about the "Mantegnas in Milano," the answer he receives indicates that the younger man is equally indifferent to the city itself as to the painter:

> "No," he said, very shyly, he did not like Mantegna. I wrote out for him where to eat in Milano and the addresses of comrades. He thanked me very much, but his mind was already looking forward to walking over the pass. (p. 106).

It is, therefore, not just one of its chief painters that brings out the young man's dislike; Milan itself is to be passed through quickly, if not avoided altogether.

It is significant, I believe, that Hemingway has chosen in this story not to give us clues to the particular painting by Mantegna that the young revolutionist would find so distasteful. In retrospect, Kenneth Johnston's identification of Mantegna's *The Dead Christ*, with its bitterly realistic details of plainly obvious nail holes in Christ's body, is correct. Furthermore, as he makes clear, there are indeed connections to be made between the character of the young revolutionist and that of Frederic Henry, the American ambulance driver of *A Farewell to Arms*. Both characters are involved in "revolutions," both make a "separate peace," both eventually "escape" Italy by way of Switzerland, and both mention the artist Mantegna with dislike.[17] However, Professor Johnston does not concern himself either with the three remaining artists named in "The Revolutionist"—Giotto, Masaccio, and Piero della

Francesca—or with several other allusions, primarily political and geographical, that have a bearing on the interpretation of the story. Thus, while one can remain in essential agreement with Professor Johnston's conclusions, two puzzling questions about the references to artists remain: why didn't Hemingway provide us with a clue—as he does in *A Farewell to Arms*—as to the identity of the Mantegna painting, and what are we to make of the other allusions to Italian painters. Both questions, it seems to me, are answered by considering the locale of the artist rather than either his specific works or his use of certain techniques and styles. The tenuousness of an interpretation based on the stylistic difference among the artists is pointed up by the qualifying phrases Professor Barbara Groseclose is forced to use in her article on "The Revolutionist":

> In addition to a similar locale (Florence), Masaccio and Piero share a direct lineage from Giotto based upon the depiction of man as a massive, rock-like form situated in an acutely observed physical world. How Hemingway perceived the art of the three *cannot be definitely ascertained,* but one may postulate the recognition of kinship through this comparable style—a style of monumental simplicity and humanistic concern which depends upon the creation of an ideal, restrained world in which the spectator does not enter.
>
> A demonstration of the validity of this assertion, *admittedly generalized,* is possible through a comparison of the treatment of each artist of a subject similar to *The Dead Christ.*[18]

Thus Professor Groseclose identifies the Mantegna painting as *The Dead Christ,* an identification that I consider correct but misleading in the context of this particular story. Like Professor Johnston she relies on the later Mantegna references in *A Farewell to Arms* to make the identification. However, it is her "admittedly generalized" approach through comparisons with works of a similar subject that does the most harm to Hemingway's intentions. Surely it is only speculative to mention that Mantegna's work demonstrates classical idealism punctured full of realistic holes while ignoring the same fact about Piero della Francesca whose *Flagellation of Christ* may be said to carry the same message of indifference, violence, and bitter reality as the world goes on about its business while Christ is being whipped. Yet the young revolutionist does not dislike the work of della Francesca! It seems that the subtler we become in our artistic distinctions, the sooner we shall become confused by the similarities among the four named artists. Trying to resolve such comparative issues as those of relative monumentality, perspective, and archaeological interest appearing in the work of any two or more artists will only lead us into a swamp of critical opinions. It is not finally important for an interpretation of "The Revolutionist" whether Giotto was the first "modern" painter, or that Masaccio picked up where Giotto left off in his portrayal of human figures, or that Mantegna was a monumental painter, or that della Francesca was a brilliant theoretician on the subject of perspective. All of them were "revolutionary" painters, and all of them were concerned with "realism" in one sense of the word or another; each contributed to a new turn of the artistic wheel, urging the Renaissance onwards.

The distinctions among the painters, then, are not primarily aesthetic; instead, Hemingway returns to a geographical classification, a locational symbology. As we have already indicated, Mantegna is connected with northern Italy, especially with the cities of Mantua, Padua, and Milan. All three cities are located in the same geographical area of the young man's dawning bitterness in "A Very Short Story," as well as, we may imagine, being reminiscent of Hemingway's own personal disillusionment with love and war in 1918. As Barbara Groseclose pointed out in passing, the other three artists share a "similar locale." Giotto is generally linked with Florence, being born near there and dying there. Masaccio, who lived only twenty-seven years, is clearly associated with Tuscany and especially Florence. Finally, Piero della Francesca, for all his greatness, seems to have been something of a provincial in preferring the small towns of Arezzo, Ferrara, Rimini, Urbino, Ravenna, etc., to larger metropolitan centers. Any standard encyclopedia will provide these immediately ascertainable *facts*, and it seems most likely that Hemingway's "iceberg theory" of composition would rely more on his readers' ready knowledge of simple large-scale geographical classifications rather than on their intellectualized view of art history, values, and aesthetics. In sum, Mantegna was a Northern Italian painter and thus associated with Hemingway's city of disappointments, Milan; Giotto, Masaccio, and della Francesca all summon up the sunny rolling hills of Tuscany and the Romagna. The aptness of the young revolutionist's pleasant walk "up into the Romagna" with the narrative "I" of the story becomes immediately apparent. As with his preference in painters, the young revolutionist prefers the more hospitable climates of Central Tuscany and the Romagna to that of the darker industrial metropolis of Milan.

These symbolic locations in "The Revolutionist" seem to indicate a preference on the young man's part for country over city, nature over civilization, and, by implication, easy generalities and idealism over the specific details of harsh reality. Certainly the boy's love of nature and the outdoors is stressed. He is "delighted with Italy. It was a beautiful country. . . . The people were all kind. He had been in many towns, walked much, and seen many pictures" (p. 105). He and the narrator "had a good trip together. It was early September and the country was pleasant" (p. 105). Yet his choice of country over city is slightly too intense, too fragile, to be an easy, simplistic, romantic preference. Unlike Emily Watts who calls the young Communist "starry-eyed," or Joseph DeFalco who calls him an "innocent untouched by experience," or Barbara Groseclose who sees the young man as a symbol of "youth," "idealism," "optimism," and "innocence," Kenneth Johnston is certainly correct when he asserts that the young revolutionist is

> a young man whose idealism has been tested in the crucible of pain, one of Hemingway's initiated who has suffered much. The youth's reluctance to talk or think about his past fits the familiar pattern of the Hemingway protagonist who attempts to neutralize painful and disturbing thoughts by 'nonthinking.'[19]

Yet, once again, like his neglect to discuss the significance of the remaining three Italian painters, Professor Johnston fails to go further than this undiscussed assertion. It is not enough to characterize the young revolutionist as a familiar Hemingway protagonist who solves his problems by "nonthinking," for, if we agree that he is not merely a "starry-eyed" optimist, we must ask ourselves why he says the idealistic things he says.

Hemingway's struggle to create a character whose personal experiences would call forth sympathy while yet allowing the reader to condemn the blatantly idealistic views stated by that character is revealed in a startling change the author made as he revised this sketch for the 1925 edition. In the Paris original the narrator says that the boy "in spite of Italy, . . . believed altogether in the world revolution."[20] Later editions read: "In spite of Hungary, he believed altogether in the world revolution" (pp. 105-106). The effect of the change is subtle, yet important. If Hemingway had retained "Italy" our attitude toward the revolutionist, like the narrator's, would display no small measure of disbelief at the boy's refusal to see the failure of the world revolution, not only in Hungary but also in Italy. His insistence that the movement "will go better," in spite of two examples of failure, would constitute nothing less than stubborn blindness, and such bold ideological faith would strike the reader as stupidity in the face of reason. As a result the boy would wholly lose our sympathies. On the other hand, changing the word to "Hungary" heightens our sense of the boy's single, personal, physical experience of suffering, an ordeal that our sympathies fix on as we search for a way to excuse the boy's statements even as we simultaneously condemn them. We conclude that the boy's mind is not reasonable, but that it is in a state of shock, numbed by the "bad things" done in Hungary.

When the narrator realistically insists that the "movement" is going "very badly" in Italy, the younger man replies rather categorically that Italy "is the one country that everyone is sure of. It will be the starting point of everything" (p. 106). The narrator remains silent: "I did not say anything" (p. 106). Again, reference to the original version in the Paris edition is instructive for there the phrase "I did not say anything" does not appear. Instead, the boy completes his statement about Italy as "the starting point of everything" and, after a paragraph break, the narrator resumes his indirect reportage with "At Bologna he said good-bye to us . . . ."[21] The effect of adding the phrase in later editions, while underscoring the narrator's implicit cynicism toward the boy's idealism, is also to characterize the narrator's protective feelings toward this "shy" young man whom he calls "a very nice boy." He refuses to challenge the boy's idealistic words in any direct manner. He prefers to let the subject silently drop in deference to what he senses to be a fragile state of mind in the boy. After all, the boy has revealed to him, although not to the readers, "a little" of the "bad things" that Horthy's men had done to him. The boy may seem "innocent," but he is hardly "untouched by experience."

Nor is the boy merely "starry-eyed." At the end of the sketch "his mind" is "already looking forward to walking over the pass. He was very eager to walk over the pass while the weather held good. He loved the mountains in the autumn" (p. 106). Clearly, his eagerness to walk over the pass now, while "the weather held good," is an indication that he knows the weather will turn. Moreover, loving "the mountains in the autumn," in addition to emphasizing the contrast between the mountains and the industrial plain in which Milan/Padua is located, also underscores the coming reality of a bitter symbolical winter. That Hemingway intends this traditional use of seasonal symbology seems evident when we learn that this line—"He loved the mountains in the autumn"—was not in the original Paris edition and was first added with the 1925 American edition. The revolutionist's faith in the world revolution may not be as monolithic as it seems. Why, then, does he persist in making such idealistic statements?

Part of the answer comes, again, from an examination of the story's original context, the Paris *in our time*, where an attentive reader will perceive an instructive comparison with the Nick Adams sketch designated as "Chapter 7."[22] Here Nick Adams is described as severely wounded and we find him, in the middle of the sketch, looking "straight ahead brilliantly." In other words, the young revolutionist, like Nick Adams, has been sufficiently hurt by the "bad things" done to him in the service of some cause. Also, like the young man of "A Very Short Story," whose enlightenment comes at the hands of a woman who will eventually be called "Luz," the young revolutionist's "faith" has been thoroughly shaken: he is disoriented, on the verge of lucidity through despair; he turns shy, afraid to talk too much, and he becomes a lover of peaceful quiet things like the natural surroundings of the Romagna and the high passes of the Alps in autumn. Although disengaged and seemingly having made a "separate peace" after his Hungarian experience, he nevertheless clings to his ideas of "world revolution" in a numbed fashion, much as Nick Adams will do later, in the 1925 *In Our Time,* when he desperately clings to his ritualistic fishing in the Big Two-Hearted River. Like Nick and his onion sandwiches, his knowledge of nature and its rituals, the young revolutionist hangs on to his statements about the "movement" while he travels with deliberation, almost sensuousness, through the Italian countryside. He savors its art, its country, and its people. As we, the readers, quickly become aware that something is wrong with Nick Adams' attitude toward fishing, that he is too intense, too sincere, too simplistic in his desires, indeed, too idealistic when it comes to the whole idea of nature and fishing—after all, it is his last hope as he struggles to calm himself down, to remain vitally alive, although caught between the ruined civilization represented by a World War and a burned-over country and, on the other side, the tragedy of nature represented by the swamp that he is unable to face yet—so we are also aware that the young revolutionist is quietly clinging to a last month of freedom (significantly autumn, of course) that exists between poles of impressment: he has been imprisoned in Hungary under Horthy, he will soon be in jail in Sion. In the interval he savors the simple pleasures of Italy without either the complications of positive participation in the Communist movement or the actively negative stance represented by an admission to bitterness, despair, and cynicism. He is neither blind to reality nor a simplistic believer in ideal causes; instead, he is engaged in an intense and fevered struggle to hold on to something he finds slipping from the grasp of his convictions. His very calmness, his "niceness," is a sign of sickness. He cannot admit his illness openly; yet he knows it is there, lurking within himself.

Hemingway's ironic attitude toward idealism in "The Revolutionist" is thus a complex one. On the one hand we are sympathetic with this young man who has suffered so much for his beliefs and who will ultimately be imprisoned in Sion, presumably because he is a Communist. In fact, unless we do not accept the idealistic side of the boy's character there will be no ironic effect possible when we are informed by the narrator of the boy's jailing.

That Hemingway intends this ironic touch at the end of the story is clear from the place name he uses: "Sion," clearly a deliberately chosen pun on the Biblical Zion, the earthly paradise. Yet we cannot overlook the inherent contradictions in the boy's character as Hemingway has drawn him. If the revolutionist is so sure that Italy is the "one country" that "will be the starting point of everything," then we must ask ourselves why doesn't he stay in Italy and work for the movement there? Why exactly is he escaping to Switzerland, the traditional country of refuge? Moreover, if we, the readers, find ourselves suspicious of the young man's attitudes and statements, so, it might be added, do the Italian Communists. He is living off his comrades and they know it. Although he has what passes for an open ticket for food, transportation, and lodging in his square of oilcloth with its ironically "indelible" message written on it, in general he seems to be treated more as an object than a person by his "comrades." The train men "passed him on from one crew to another. He had no money, and they fed him behind the counter in railway eating houses" (p. 105). When they aren't passing him on, they are keeping him behind the counter, and while they reluctantly support him he is busy saving his money to buy reproductions of Renaissance painters, a bourgeois endeavor at best. This is hardly the picture of a true believer in the Communist "world revolution."

This ideological confusion, finally, is at the heart of Hemingway's attitudes in the story, for the fictional ironies underlying the miniatures of *in our time* are based as much on the biographical and historical events of 1922-1923 when Hemingway was writing these sketches, as they are on his original experiences of 1918. And if geography is one touchstone for interpretation in "The Revolutionist," then politics must be the other. In 1934, writing for *Esquire* magazine, Hemingway reminisced about those early years immediately following World War I when many people— Hemingway among them—hoped for an Italian, if not world-wide, Communist revolution:

> For instance the world was much closer to revolution in the years after the war than it is now. In those days we who believed in it looked for it at any time, expected it, hoped for it—for it was the logical thing. But everywhere it came it was aborted. For a long time I could not understand it but finally I figured it out. If you study history you will see that there can never be a Communist revolution without, first, a complete military debacle. You have to see what happens in a military debacle to understand this. It is something so utterly complete in its delusion about the system that has put them into this, in its destruction and purging away of all the existing standards, faiths and loyalties, when the war is being fought by a conscript army, that it is the necessary catharsis before revolution. No country

was ever riper for revolution than Italy after the war but the revolution was doomed to fail because her defeat was not complete; because after Caporetto she fought and won in June and July of 1918 on the Piave. From the Piave, by way of the Banca Commerciale, the Credito Italiano, the merchants of Milan who wanted the prosperous socialist co-operative societies and the socialist municipal government of that city smashed, came fascism.[23]

From the war, the mercantile interests of Milan, and, most ironically, from socialism itself, came fascism. The Fascist movement, significantly enough, was officially founded by Benito Mussolini in our symbolic city of Milan on March 23, 1919.[24] It is with this information that the political undercurrents of "The Revolutionist" begin to be truly felt. Not only does our idealistic young Communist seem less than strictly hewing to the party line by buying reproductions of Renaissance painters when his comrades are struggling to support him, but Hemingway ironically has him wrap them up in a copy of *Avanti,* the official paper of the Italian Socialist Party.[25] Moreover, the full subtlety of this political allusion is not revealed until we know that *Avanti* was, at one time, edited by the soon to be Facist dictator of Italy, Benito Mussolini. Thus, our young revolutionist becomes, for Hemingway, a standing emblem of the inherent contradictions within the movement to bring about a Communist revolution. Thus the "revolution" indicated by the title of this sketch will not result in a linear progression toward an earthly Marxist paradise, but rather it will eventuate in a continual turning of the wheel as mankind supplants one absolutist concept by another, none of them absolutely successful or worthy of absolute belief. For Hemingway, imprisonment in "Zion" begins with a belief in its possibility.

Hemingway has set up a complex chain of connections leading from Mantegna to Milan to the idea of a socialist revolution to the actual experience of Benito Mussolini's Fascism, a movement that Hemingway once called a "brood of dragons' teeth" in an article for the *Toronto Star* on April 13, 1922, just a little over a year away from the time that Carlos Baker says Hemingway was writing his miniatures—August 1923.[26] Interestingly enough, this article, written to cover the Genoa Conference—Conferenza Internazionale Economica di Genova—was almost entirely devoted to Hemingway's description of a hypothetical clash between Communists and Fascists in which the Fascists clearly are the conquerors. "The Revolutionist," then, may be seen as the fictional counterpart of Hemingway's journalistic representation of contemporary Italian history. The revolution was indeed going "very badly."

Further biographical information about the years 1922 and 1923 only confirms such "facts" as the most obvious political and personal sources for the story. Shortly after the Genoa Conference, Ernest, his wife Hadley, and Chink Smith (the man who had told Ernest the two Mons stories used as Chapters 4 and 5 in *in our time*) spent the last two weeks of May at the Gangwisch pension at Chamby in Switzerland. Many days were also spent reading and fishing in or around the inn at Aigle. The closeness of these two Swiss towns to that of Sion only underscores the uncanny ability Hemingway demonstrates as he discovers the symbolic possibilities of factual reality. Such speculation is not fanciful for Carlos Baker relates how, on the last day of May 1922, the three friends began a two day trip that took them on foot across the Pass of St. Bernard to the Italian town of Aosta where they eventually took a train to Milan.[27] These travels are, of course, the exact reverse of the young revolutionist's trip. Milan's symbolic significance is again brought forward when we realize that Hemingway was then deliberately trying to recapture some of the events of his original experiences in Italy in 1918. Reality, memory, and fiction soon cross paths again, for when they reached Milan it was not long before they heard of the

> Facisist attack on Bologna, where 15,000 arrogant young nationalists had seized the city and held it for a day in a "counter-campaign of terrorism" against the Communist working classes. When Ernest heard that Mussolini, the emergent leader of the Black Shirts, was actually in Milan, he used his press card to arrange an interview.[28]

By mid-June of 1922 Ernest and Hadley (Chink Smith had left them) had retraced Ernest's steps of 1918 all the way back to Fossalta-di-Piave where Ernest Hemingway—alias Nick Adams, alias the young revolutionist—as a young boy of eighteen had had some "bad things" done to him. Now, in 1922, according to Professor Baker, he suffered new disillusionment in all the old places: "He had tried and failed to re-create a former actuality for his wife's benefit and perhaps for his own."[29] Thus the events of 1918 flow into those of 1922, and all of them flow into "The Revolutionist." Is it merely a strange coincidence that the fictionalized places of "The Revolutionist"—Bologna, Milan, Aosta, the "walk over the pass" between Italy and Switzerland, and the Swiss district of Sion— should also occur as actual events and locations of personal and historical importance to the author, especially in such a concentrated sequence of months in 1922 just before he should begin-work on composing "The Revolutionist"?

A final surprising link between experience and fiction remains: the trip up through the Romagna. In November of 1922, largely at the prompting of Ezra Pound, Bill Bird of the Three Mountains Press asked Hemingway to contribute a small book for publication in his series.[30] The book would be, of course, the Paris *in our time*. However, the next month brought sheer disaster for Hemingway when his wife Hadley lost almost all the material, including carbons, that he had ever written.[31] Yet, by February of 1923, Hemingway found himself hiking through the Romagna with Hadley and the Pounds who had invited them to Rapallo for this explicit purpose. While staying with the Pounds he was introduced to Robert McAlmon who would soon offer to publish Hemingway's *Three Stories and Ten Poems;* moreover, by April he had his first six vignettes published in the Exiles number of *The Little Review.*[32] Within a few short months all of Hemingway's fortunes revolved: at the end of 1922 he had nothing but disillusionment and despair over his memories of the past, the current world economic and political situation, and his personal literary future; yet by the time the first three months of 1923 had passed he had the promise of two book publications and at least one periodical publication. No wonder then that the few pleasant moments in "The Revolutionist" should occur while walking "up into the Romagna"; this place must have become the spatial symbol for all that seemed good to Ernest Hemingway in those few months of 1922-1923. It was the good place for him just as surely as Milan became spatial evil. The Romagna is "up"; Milan is located on a plain. Giotto, Masaccio, and Piero della Francesca are associated with these sunny hills; Mantegna is part of the Milan-Mantua-Padua industrial plain. The Communists are strongly organized in the vicinity of Bologna, a part of the Romagna; the Fascists are concentrated in Milan. Finally, Hemingway's personal fortunes and emotions seem "up" in the Romagna, yet "down" when he travels the Milan-to-Fossalta plain.

Speculation about the sources for a literary composition is, at best, a dubious business. Whether or not these biographical and historical facts are indeed the proper sources for "The Revolutionist" must be left to the reader's judgment. Although literary criticism may be, at times, a science that establishes facts, more often than not it is marvelously imprecise, bringing more wonder than accuracy about the nature of art and of how life experiences are transfigured into the permanence of artistic images. "The Revolutionist," seen in the contextual matrix of the Paris *in our time* and with its background of geographical and political movements, is certainly no still life. The story fairly pulsates with the complex energy of ironical forces juxtaposed to set up sympathetic vibrations among the characters of the story, the movements of the era depicted by it, Hemingway's own personal feelings, and the reader. Like so many of his "iceberg" stories, "The Revolutionist," in its very brevity, merely provokes more wonder at the massiveness of the material lying under the surface of Ernest Hemingway's laconic writing.

University of Puerto Rico

[1] Critical confusion about the text of *In Our Time* sometimes exists because there are actually three major stages to its composition. The first is the Paris *in our time* published by William Bird's Three Mountains Press in 1924; it consisted of the eighteen miniatures referred to above. The second stage was published by Boni & Liveright in October 1925 as *In Our Time* with capitalized initial letters for each word in the title. This book was substantially altered by the addition of stories and by a change in the arrangement of some of the original sketches; significant textual variations were introduced and Hemingway also designated some of the Paris miniatures as full "stories" merely by changing their "chapter" numbers to worded titles. Thus "Chapter 10" became "A Very Short Story"; "Chapter 11" became "The Revolutionist." A third stage in the evolution of the book is the revised fifth printing of the 1925 edition published by Scribners in 1930 to which Hemingway added "On the Quai at Smyrna" as an introductory story. Page references in the text of this paper, unless otherwise noted, will be to the first American edition: *In Our Time* (New York: Boni & Liveright, 1925).

I should like to thank my good friend and trusted colleague, Professor Donald H. Squire, for his most valuable assistance in the final revision of my manuscript.

[2] Carlos Baker, *Ernest Hemingway: A Life Story* (New York: Scribners, 1969), p. 108.

[3] Ibid., pp. 113-114.

[4] Ibid., p. 113.

[5] Ibid., pp. 56-83 *passim*.

[6] Felix Gilbert, *The End of the European Era, 1890 to the Present,* The Norton History of Modern Europe, Vol. VI, (New York: Norton, 1970), p. 163.

[7] Philip Young, *Ernest Hemingway, A Reconsideration* (University Park: Pennsylvania State University Press, 1966).

[8] Kenneth G. Johnston, "Hemingway and Mantegna: The Bitter Nail Holes," *Journal of Narrative Technique,* 1 (May 1971), 86-94; and Barbara S. Groseclose, "Hemingway's 'The Revolutionist': An Aid to Interpretation," *Modern Fiction Studies,* 17 (1971-1972), 565-570.

[9] *in our time* (Paris 1924), p. 19.

[10] *In Our Time* (New York: Boni & Liveright, 1925), p. 84. Subsequent quotes from this printing are noted in the text.

[11] *In Our Time* (New York: Scribners, 1930), p. 83.

[12] *Ernest Hemingway: A Life Story*, p. 574. "As first printed (Sketch No. 10, *in our time*, Paris, 1924), the story used the locale of Milan and the name of 'Ag.' Later from fear of libel, EH changed the locale to Padua and the name to Luz."

[13] *in our time* (Paris, 1924), p. 19.

[14] *In Our Time* (New York, 1925), p. 85.

[15]*Ernest Hemingway and the Arts* (Urbana: University of Illinois Press, 1971), pp. 135, 137.

[16]*Ernest Hemingway: A Life Story*, p. 55.

[17]Johnston, 91-92.

[18]Groseclose, 568-569; italics are added for emphasis.

[19]*Ernest Hemingway and the Arts*, p. 135; *The Hero in Hemingway's Short Stories* (Pittsburgh: University of Pittsburgh Press, 1963), pp. 88-89; Groseclose, 570; Johnston, 90.

[20]*in our time* (Paris, 1924), p. 20.

[21]Ibid., p. 21.

[22]Ibid., p. 15.

[23]*By-Line: Ernest Hemingway*, ed. William White (New York: Scribners, 1967), pp. 180-181.

[24]*The End of the European Era*, p. 185.

[25]Ibid., p. 63.

[26]*By-Line: Ernest Hemingway*, p. 27.

[27]*Ernest Hemingway: A Life Story*, p. 92.

[28]Ibid.

[29]Ibid., p. 94.

[30]Ibid., p. 100.

[31]Ibid., p. 103.

[32]Ibid., pp. 105-114 *passim*.

ROBERT O. STEPHENS

MACOMBER AND THAT SOMALI PROVERB: THE MATRIX OF KNOWLEDGE

In "The Short Happy Life of Francis Macomber," when he wakes in the middle of the night to hear "the lion roaring somewhere up along the river," Macomber is afraid and, in a significant way, alone. At this crucial point, Hemingway makes it clear that Macomber's fear derives from two failures: he lacks a specific kind of knowledge and he lacks a community of feeling about that kind of knowledge: "There was no one to tell he was afraid, nor to be afraid with him, and, lying alone, he did not know the Somali proverb that says a brave man is always frightened three times by a lion; when he first sees his track, when he first hears him roar and when he first confronts him."[1] During the next day's hunt that failure of knowledge haunts Macomber as he goes through his ordeal to Hemingway's accompanying chant that "he had not thought," "he did not know."

The motif of knowkedge runs even more pervasively in the story, however. For if Macomber lacks one kind of knowledge, he has another. Lying awake again the night after the lion incident and with the knowledge his wife is in Wilson's bed, Macomber surveys what he does know: "He was very wealthy, and would be much wealthier, and he knew she would not leave him ever now. That was one of the few things that he really knew. He knew about that, about motor cycles—that was earliest—about motor cars, about duckshooting, about fishing, trout, salmon and big-sea, about sex in books, many books, too many books, about all court games, about dogs, not much about horses, about hanging on to his money,

about most of the other things his world dealt in, and about his wife
not leaving him" (p. 120/21). The key phrase here, I suggest, is the
"things his world dealt in," for Francis Macomber is caught
between two worlds: the mechanized, dilettantish, and cruel
metropolitan world of the fast international sporting set and the
primitively fierce, traditional, male-cult world of Somali
gunbearers and British professional hunters.

That "The Short Happy Life of Francis Macomber" chronicles a
rite of passage into maturity has, of course, been recognized since the
story was first read. Most criticism, however, has centered on the way
in which Robert Wilson serves as guide and tutor during the action
or on Margot's intent as killer or protectress.[2] Other comment has
emphasized the existential, archetypal, or mythic elements in
Macomber's experience.[3] But to accept Macomber's moment of
elation as the otherwise unaccounted for point of transformation is
to leave unanswered the crucial question of how he is prepared for
that moment and what it means. What these studies have failed to
take into account, as I believe Hemingway's citation of the Somali
proverb calls for, is that Francis Macomber's emergence into
manhood is a conversion from one order of cultural belief to
another— from that of a decadent, industrial, and commercial
system of economic individualism to one of traditional and organic
values in which the individual is not alone but part of a sustaining
communal understanding, embodied in the Somali proverb.

That the new order of belief is stated in terms of the hunter's code
is consistent with Hemingway's experience, thought, and reading at
the time he wrote the story in 1935-36. Most readers are familiar with
his statement in *Green Hills of Africa* that industrial civilization in
America had worn out the continent and that the time had come to
turn to Africa as the new home for men to live in organic
relationships with the land and each other.[4] Even more indicative of
Hemingway's thinking at the time was his recognition that the story
was for him part of a conversion to social consciousness. As Carlos
Baker has shown, in 1937 Hemingway wanted to include
"Macomber" and "The Snows of Kilimanjaro" in a new volume to
be published by Scribners that would document his recent turn to
social awareness. The African stories, then, would be linked with
To Have and Have Not (still unfinished), "The Capital of the
World," the Spanish Civil War dispatches to the North American
Newspaper Alliance, his piece in *New Masses* on the exploited
veterans at Matecumba Key, and his Carnegie Hall speech on the
necessity of writers' involvement in collective resistance to Fascism.[5]

At his moment of transformation, then, Macomber comes into
awareness of a formal and ritual code of feeling and conduct
analogous to that glimpsed by Jake Barnes in Pedro Romero's

behavior. That the gun-bearers and Wilson, as a type of the professional hunter who builds on their values, have a strict traditional code is a matter of record, attested to by other writers whom Hemingway cites in *Green Hills of Africa*. Fellow Michigan writer Stewart Edward White, who made his first safari to East Africa in 1910 and wrote of his findings in *The Land of Footprints* (1912), *African Camp Fires* (1913), and *Lions in the Path* (1926), notes, for example, that the Somali gun-bearers live by a conservative code of belief based on a thousand years of unquestioned acceptance.[6] That belief, translated into action, becomes through the hunter a code of honor. Concerning the hunter's choice whether to accept confrontation with the lion, for example, White says:

> For, and here is the point, up to the moment he pulls the trigger, the decision is his; but after that, if he is a true sportsman and not a welsher, the decision has been made and he must abide by it. He must play the cards as they lie. He did not need to start this thing; but having started it, he is bound in honour to use his very best efforts to finish it. . . . The man who hits his lucky lion stone dead, but who then leaves his unlucky lion in cover without having done everything possible, is not playing the game. He should not even be permitted to hold cards.[7]

That the code has a mystique, particularly for the hunter on foot, is apparent in White's further explanation:

> This necessity of the foot-hunter carries with it a rather beautiful mystical by-product. Such a forced emptying of the mind, not only of all thought, all introspection but also of all imaginings, all daydreams, even the most ephemeral; such a projecting of one's real self outward from one's physical shell into one's surroundings ends by putting one into a curious unity and harmony with those surroundings. One is no longer a sort of self-contained separate unit. One is an integral part of the whole.[8]

Other suggestive links between White's account and Hemingway's story include Kongoni as the name of the chief gun-bearer and White's and Wilson's discussions of the value of whippings, however illegal, to keep discipline among the gun-bearers and other camp workers.

Chicago Tribune cartoonist John T. McCutcheon also went on safari in East Africa in 1908-09, meeting vacationing ex-President Theodore Roosevelt and his son Kermit in safari country. His book *In Africa: Hunting Adventures in the Big Game Country* (1909) notes the code of the Somali gun-bearers in a way that points directly to Macomber's violation: "They are avaricious and money loving to a deplorable degree, but there is one thing that can be said for the Somali. He will never desert in time of danger and will cheerfully sacrifice himself for his master. He has the stamina of a higher type of civilization and in comparison to him the lately reclaimed savage is not nearly so dependable in a crisis."[9]

A major part of the Somali hunter's formal system of knowledge is centered on the lion. Howell and Lawler have observed that the lion is part of the metaphysics of "Macomber" in much the same way that the leopard is for "The Snows of Kilimanjaro."[10] Uninitiated into that metaphysic, Macomber is terrorized by the lion's roar, which seems to be one of the key elements of the mystique. Although I have been unable to identify the exact Somali proverb Hemingway cites, one proverb identified as Swahili asks, "Who will dance to a lion's roaring?"[11] White describes the terrorizing quality of the lion's roar, notably in terms parallel to those experienced by Macomber:

> The peculiar questioning cough of early evening is resonant and deep in vibration, but it is a call rather than a roar. . . . But when seven or eight lions roar merely to see how much noise they can make, as when driving game, or trying to stampede your oxen on a wagon trip, the effect is something tremendous. The very substance of the ground vibrates; the air shakes. . . . There is something genuinely awe-inspiring about it; and when repeated volleys rumble into silence, one can imagine the veldt crouched in a rigid terror that shall endure.[12]

In camp at breakfast before the lion hunt, Macomber listens as "the lion roared in a deep-chested moaning, suddenly guttural, ascending vibration that seemed to shake the air and ended in a sigh and a heavy, deep-chested grunt" (p. 112/13). That such is the stuff deep terrors are made from is indicated not only by the Somali proverb but also by Macomber's waking the next night, "frightened in a dream of the bloody-headed lion standing over him," and he listens with his heart pounding (p. 121/22).

These are some elements of the world into which Macomber is inducted. What has been lacking in analysis of the story to this point has been a set of concepts and the vocabulary necessary for tracing Macomber's movement from one system of cultural assumptions to another. The paradigm of formal, informal, and technical awareness proposed by the anthropologist Edward Hall in *The Silent Language* provides a useful method of analysis.

Formal learning, he says, is a cultural binary system taught by precept and admonition; it assumes that any other way of feeling, speaking, or acting than that of one's own culture is unthinkable. It is the method of traditional inculcation of values. Thus, "formal patterns are almost always learned when a mistake is made and someone corrects it. . . . The details of formal learning are *binary*, of a yes-no, right-wrong character. You either break a taboo or you don't, you steal your neighbor's coconut or you don't, you say 'boyses' for boys or you don't. Hundreds of little details add up until they amount to a formal system which nobody questions."[13] The system is associated with deep emotions and becomes equivalent in the mind of the subscriber to the processes of nature so that "alternative ways of behavior are thought of as unnatural—if not impossible." Persons going from one culture to another find formal learning least apparent but most fundamental and find that subscribers to a formal way of feeling and thinking are least able to explain what the system is in general or rational terms. They know only that particular actions are consistent or inconsistent with "the way things are" (Hall, pp. 91-104).

In informal learning "the principal agent is a *model* used for imitation." One learns informally when he is told to look around him and see what others are doing. One may learn the formal system of a culture by learning informally through the example of the model; the model shows the learner what leeway is available in adherence to formal custom or technical law. When the technical laws of a culture are not identical to cultural understanding, the model can teach, for example, how strictly a speed law is to be observed. Like formal awareness, however, informal awareness involves a high degree of emotional commitment to unstated law (Hall, pp. 92-107).

Technical learning, by contrast, is explicit, systematic, rational, and discussible. It is fully conscious and can be written down, debated, and taught directly. It typically involves suppression of feeling and is the manner of the professional rather than the amateur. Technical learning is associated with authority on the basis of specific expertise. Success in technical learning depends less on the aptitude of the learner than on the intelligence with which materials and models are selected, analyzed, and presented (Hall, pp. 94-111).

To illustrate his system Hall uses the technique and mystique of skiing. He explains how people who live in snow areas learn the formal system from childhood and never question that another way of skiing is possible. Occasional visitors to snow areas may learn the rudiments of skiing, including its lore, by imitating models—that is, informally. Their instruction is random and empirical: "You bend your knees and take off. Eventually you'll get the hang of it" (Hall, p. 88). Those who learn technically are taught by instructors who have analyzed all of the separate elements of the skill and can present them systematically. Hall further observes that the three systems are discrete: "It is extremely difficult to practice more than one element of the formal, informal, technical triad at the same time without paralyzing results" (Hall, p. 89).

When this system of analysis is applied to "The Short Happy Life of Francis Macomber," we become aware of the nature of the inner conflict that first paralyzes and then frees Macomber. His problem is that he has not been made aware of the formal system of belief and action by which Robert Wilson and the Somali gun-bearers live. To that extent, Wilson fails initially as guide and tutor. He has related to Macomber only on the technical level of expert hunter who tells his client how to shoot for bone to break down the lion (p. 111/12). When, soon after, Macomber begins to break the silent, formal code by which the hunters live and of which he is unaware, Wilson begins to look at him "quickly" and "appraisingly" (pp. 111/12, 116/17). When Macomber asks why not leave the wounded lion in the grass, Wilson's thinking suddenly shifts from cool, impersonal technical preoccupations to his unspoken, emotionally-loaded hunter's code: "Robert Wilson, whose entire occupation had been with the lion and the problem he presented, and who had not been thinking about Macomber except to note that he was rather windy, suddenly felt as though he had opened the wrong door in a hotel and seen something shameful" (p. 116/17).

The movement in the story of Macomber's conversion, then, begins with a full dramatization of his disgrace, partly through technical failure, to act by the formal code of Wilson and the Somali gun-bearers. Macomber then recovers partially by reverting to a strictly technical level of knowledge and action, which is confirmed and codified by Wilson's informal instruction. Macomber's full recovery and initiation into the formal code are achieved inductively, with his near-professional technical accomplishment opening the way to larger insight into the formal code.

The opening scene with its loaded silences and Hemingway's statements of things that did not happen, of words not said, is a demonstration of binary formal awareness in operation. The rhetoric of negative statement is his way of conveying the deep chagrin of those whose formal expectations have been violated. Wilson, Margot, and Francis sit in the dining tent after the lion episode "pretending that nothing had happened" (p. 102/3). The personal boys, skinners, and porters (typically of different tribes from those of the Somali gun-bearers, according to White) have carried Macomber into camp on their shoulders, but "the **gun-bearers had taken no part in the demonstration**" (p. 102/3). Wilson and Macomber drink gimlets in the dining tent and "avoided one another's eyes" (p. 105/6. Margot, sensitive to the feelings of others if not knowledgeable about their code, "had not looked at him nor he at her" in the car (p. 119/20), and she "did not speak to him" when she came into the tent (p. 102/3).

That such a failure of knowledge and nerve like Macomber's has occurred before and is provided for in the hunter's formal code is evident in the code language used by professionals to indicate a safari has gone bad. "I'm still drinking their whisky" and "distinguished consideration" say, essentially, that relationships have reverted to the impersonally technical. That the formal code and the facts are not always the same is indicated ironically by Wilson when he says, "You know in Africa no woman ever misses her lion and no white man ever bolts" (p. 106/7). It is, he points out, the difference between the professional, impersonal view and that of formal expectation. He will not talk about his clients, though it is "bad form" to ask him not to. "I'm a professional hunter . . . . I have a living to make" (p. 106/7).

During the lion hunt, Wilson, having assumed for himself and his client the formal system, concentrates on technical actions. As he finds Macomber violating the formal assumptions, he is jerked from the technical to the formal and reacts emotionally. When Macomber asks about the necessity of getting closer than a hundred yards to the lion and when he wants to send beaters into the short grass cover rather than go himself, Wilson reacts with his quick and appraising glances. When they discover the lion at seventy-five yards and Macomber wants to shoot from the shelter of the car, Wilson is jolted again as he is recalled to formal awareness: "You don't shoot them from cars . . ." (p. 113/14). At that point Macomber fails technically by not realizing he still has the safety lock on his rifle, and in the time it takes him to release and re-aim, the lion is moving. Macomber hits him in the flank, not shoulder bone (p. 114/15). His most egregious violation of formal expectations occurs, however, when he wants to leave the lion unkilled; then Wilson's response reaches beyond outrage to a view of something obscene (p. 116/17).

By that time Wilson is "furious" that he has not earlier noted Macomber's unreadiness, his lack of knowledge (p. 117/18). He realizes he must rely on the knowers of the code and begins speaking in Swahili to the two gun-bearers, who, as Macomber can see, are "suffering too with fear" (p. 118/19). But what Macomber does not know is that they share their knowledge of that fear and that he is disgracing them as well as himself when he violates the pieties of men who hunt. After he bolts, he sees that "two black men and a white man looked back at him in contempt . . ." (p. 119/20).

Though all the principals know the formal code of the hunter, equated with manhood in Wilson's and the Somalis' minds, has been violated, Macomber will not accept the verdict of silence ordinarily imposed. He talks, he wants to "fix it up on buffalo," and almost against his commitment to a settled pattern of response, Wilson is drawn again to risk his sense of order. "He was all for Macomber again. If you could forget the morning. But, of course, you couldn't. The morning had been about as bad as they come" (p. 107/8). Wilson apparently recognizes that he has served his client only on the technical level but has judged him for things he did not know. He almost invokes the Somali proverb as the missing clue: "I wouldn't think about that [lion] any more. Any one could be upset by his first lion" (p. 110/11).

Hall observes that "the formal and technical are often confused. For one thing, the formal is supported by the technical. It is the technical that people resort to when all else fails" (Hall, p. 100). This is the process to which Macomber resorts as he works his way out of formal disgrace. Wilson too reverts to the technical problem at hand; he studies the terrain for signs of buffalo that may have fed onto open country during the night and directs the driver through terrain marked by wart-hog holes and ant castles (pp. 125-26/26-27). When they sight the three buffalo and begin chase, it seems for a moment that the formal code will again be violated: "Not from the car, you fool!" he shouts when Macomber raises his rifle. But Macomber at the moment is hunting technically; he has concentrated on "the gray, hairless, scabby look of one huge bull" and jumping from the car, "he was shooting at the bull as he moved away, hearing the bullets whunk into him, emptying his rifle at him as he moved steadily away, finally remembering to get his shots forward into the shoulder . . ." (pp. 126-27/27-28). Wilson recognizes the technical success as he congratulates Macomber on his shooting. When they stop to assess the situation, Wilson continues his technical instruction: "Watch he doesn't get up. . . . Get a little broadside and take him in the neck just behind the ear" (p. 128/29).

With his technical success, Macomber is ready to learn the moral values behind technique. At that point Wilson acts according to the informal system. He is the model who can tell the differences between essential values and legal definitions. He has earlier demonstrated the role when he distinguished between the fairness of whipping the laggard tent boy and fining him (p. 105/6). Similarly, though it is illegal to chase buffalo with cars, he knows the essential principle is the risk involved: "Taking more chance driving that way across the plain full of holes and one thing and another than hunting on foot. Buffalo could have charged us each time we shot if he liked. Gave him every chance" (p. 129/30). When he defends the principle to Margot and thinks of her as a five-letter woman as he had earlier thought of Francis as a four-letter man, he echoes Hemingway's earlier definition of a four-letter man as one who does not know the difference between the essentials and the rules of sportsmanship.[14]

In his informal instruction Wilson also provides his substitute for the Somali proverb. His personal equivalent of the cultural wisdom embodied in the proverb, the quotation from Shakespeare is the same that Hemingway cites in *Men at War* as talismanic wisdom for men who will go into battle. However suspect may be the quotation in its original context, the passage had for Hemingway the effect of protective magic from the first time he learned it from Eric Dorman-Smith in the hospital at Milan.[15] The meaning of that wisdom, he said, was that it assured young men they would not have to suffer more than had others before them. They were part of a continuum of men's experience in war. Like Robert Wilson, he thought it essential knowledge for men who live in danger. But as knower of the formal code, Wilson realizes it must remain silent lore. He is embarrassed at having brought such secret assumptions into consciousness and warns Macomber, "Doesn't do to talk too much about all this. Talk the whole thing away. No pleasure in anything if you mouth it up too much" (pp. 131, 132/32, 33).

Still Wilson recognizes that formal and informal learning are supported by technical knowledge and are best expressed in technical language. Before they go into the thicket for the wounded buffalo, he reverts again to technical instruction: "Now let me tell you about them. . . . When a buff comes he comes with his head high and thrust straight out. The boss of the horns covers any sort of brain shot. The only shot is straight into the nose. The only other shot is into his chest or, if you are to one side, into the neck or the shoulders" (p. 133/34). As the buffalo charges, Macomber again concentrates on the technical problem, shooting for the head and hitting the boss of the horns, but now he acts as a man supported by insight into the code of hunters, induced through his skill. He continues in that state of knowledge and feeling until Margot's bullet explodes "a sudden white-hot, blinding flash" inside his head "and that was all he ever felt" (p. 135/36).

Whether Margot's intent had been to shoot Macomber, it is clear that she has repeated Macomber's earlier pattern. She has failed to understand the formal system of awareness that Macomber has entered with Wilson. "You're both talking rot," she says to the two hunters as they celebrate the mystique behind the action (p. 132/33). Shooting from the car at the buffalo, she recapitulates Macomber's violation, complete with technical failure. As with Macomber during the lion episode, Wilson feels outrage at her violation and then reverts to his professional manner, instructing Kongoni to bring Abdullah to "witness the manner of the accident" (p. 135/36).

But Wilson knows Macomber has experienced that felt knowledge of the true hunter. He knows, as Hemingway too was learning at the time, that men belong in community and gain their sustaining belief—out of which grows their courage—from knowing themselves part of a continuity of human experience. They find their place not by age or exploit but by their recognition of men's interdependence and responsibility. If that recognition is shown in "Macomber" through the metaphor of hunting, it will be shown again in Harry Morgan's death statement and in Robert Jordan's insight that no man is an island in time of war. What "Macomber" shows, however, in a way that the less successful performances of 1937 and 1938 do not, is that Hemingway could dramatize that conversation subtly and convincingly before he added the Marxist dimension. The problem is how to find the knowledge that opens the way into a sense of community. Coming by his own way from isolating fear into communal knowledge, Francis Macomber was, during his short happy life, no longer afraid or alone.

University of North Carolina—Greensboro

[1]*The Fifth Column and the First Forty-Nine Stories* (New York: Scribners, 1938), p. 110; *The Short Stories of Ernest Hemingway*, Modern Standard Authors Edition (New York: Scribners, 1956), p. 11. Subsequent references to the story will be to these editions jointly and will appear within the text, the original first, then the popular edition.

[2]See Earl Rovit, *Ernest Hemingway* (New York: Twayne, 1963), pp. 73-74; Jackson Benson, *Hemingway: The Writer's Art of Self-Defense* (Minneapolis: University of Minnesota Press, 1969), pp. 146-148; Arthur Mizener, *The Sense of Life in the Modern Novel* (Boston: Houghton Mifflin, 1964), pp. 223-226; Warren Beck, "The Shorter Happy Life of Mrs. Macomber," *Modern Fiction Studies*, 1 (November 1955), 28-37; Virgil Hutton, "The Short Happy Life of Macomber," *University Review*, 30 (June 1964), 253-263; John Howell and Charles Lawler, "From Abercrombie and Fitch to *The First Forty-Nine Stories:* The Text of Ernest Hemingway's 'Francis Macomber,'" *Proof*, 2 (1972), 221-225; Philip Young, *Ernest Hemingway: A Reconsideration* (University Park: Pennsylvania State University Press, 1966), p. 73; John Killinger, *Hemingway and the Dead Gods* (Lexington: University of Kentucky Press, 1960), pp. 44-46; R. S. Crane, *The Idea of the Humanities and Other Essays Critical and Historical* (Chicago: University of Chicago Press, 1967), II, 315-326.

[3]See Killinger, p. 44; Robert W. Lewis, *Hemingway on Love* (Austin: University of Texas Press, 1965), 88-89; Joseph DeFalco, *The Hero in Hemingway's Short Stories* (Pittsburgh: University of Pittsburgh Press, 1963), pp. 202-207.

[4]New York: Scribners, 1935, pp. 284-285.

[5]*Ernest Hemingway: A Life Story* (New York: Scribners, 1969), p. 314.

[6]*Land of Footprints* (London: Thomas Nelson, 1912), pp. 186-187.

[7]*Lions in the Path* (Garden City: Doubleday, Page, 1926), p. 128.

[8]*Lions in the Path*, pp. 142-143.

[9]Indianapolis: Bobbs-Merrill, 1909, p. 350.

[10]Howell and Lawler, 218.

[11]Selwyn Gurney Champion, *Racial Proverbs: A Selection of the World's Proverbs Arranged Linguistically* (New York: Macmillan, 1938), p. 584.

[12]*Land of Footprints*, pp. 120-121.

[13]Garden City: Doubleday, 1959, pp. 87-89. Subsequent references will be to this edition and will appear within the text.

[14]"He Who Gets Slap Happy," *Esquire*, 4 (August 1935), 19.

[15]New York: Crown, 1942, p. xiv.

KENNETH G. JOHNSTON

THE BULL AND THE LION: HEMINGWAY'S FABLES FOR CRITICS

"The world is old? I agree; but to hold its attention One resorts, as with a child, to fascination."
—*Jean de La Fontaine, "The Power of Fable"*

In 1950 Ernest Hemingway wrote a pair of fables for the delight of two Venetian children. Entitled "The Faithful Bull" and "The Good Lion," they were published in *Holiday* magazine the following year. Hemingway no doubt enjoyed competing on the fabulous terrain of James Thurber, who was on his list of heroes.[1] But he was seeking more than his own enjoyment or the amusement of children, and from behind the mask of Aesop and La Fontaine, he commented freely, not on the human condition, but on his own.

"If he wrote it he could get rid of it," Nick Adams assured himself in "Fathers and Sons" published in 1933. For Nick, writing was a form of therapy, and he was sure that he could purge himself of the haunting memories of his father's suicide if he would only write them out. "He had gotten rid of many things by writing them."[2] Now at mid-century, the creator of Nick Adams was apparently trying to get rid of some things, and the evidence strongly suggests that Hemingway's anxieties at the time are faithfully mirrored in his Venetian fables. They are thinly disguised, flattering selfportraits, tales of self-justification, probably intended to disarm, forestall and/or anticipate domestic and literary criticism. In fact, they may be read as fables for critics, past, present, and future.

The central idea for "The Faithful Bull" is found in *Death in the Afternoon*. Hemingway's discourse on fighting bulls is interrupted by the little old lady who wants "to know about their love life." Hemingway complies and tells her the fact of ranch life in "a straightforward Christian way." "Their love lives are tremendous," he tells her. As a rule, one seed bull services fifty cows. But then he proceeds to tell the old lady of "an odd occurrence":

> Sometimes a bull on the range will come to so care for one of the fifty cows that he is with that he will make no case of all the others and will only have to do with her and she will refuse to leave his side on the range. When this occurs they take the cow from the herd and if the bull does not then return to polygamy he is sent with the other bulls that are for the ring.
>
> I find that a sad story, sir.
>
> Madame, all stories, if continued far enough, end in death, and he is no true-story teller who would keep that from you.[3]

The conversation, quite naturally, then turns to love and marriage. Only fools, he declares, fall in love many times. "I would sooner have the pox than to fall in love with another woman loving the one I have."[4]

At the time he composed "The Faithful Bull," Hemingway was struggling to dominate his infatuation for Adriana Ivancich, the beautiful nineteen-year-old Venetian girl who served as the model for Renata in *Across the River and into the Trees*. He met her in December, 1948; lunched with her in April, 1949; and wrote his first of many letters to her in October of that year, signing it "With much love, Mr. Papa."[5] "In evolving the figure of Renata, the fifty-year-old Colonel's nineteen-year-old inamorata," writes Carlos Baker, "Ernest followed a line not unlike that of the mythical sculptor Pygmalion, who fashioned the image of woman so beautiful that he promptly fell in love with his creation."[6] The real-life relationship, Baker maintains, was "sentimentally Platonic," but at a luncheon given by the Hemingways in January, 1950, Ernest displayed more serious symptoms:

> Although Ernest called her "daughter" and strove to keep the relationship politely paternalistic, he continued to confuse her with the Renata of his novel, and his gaze in her direction was often moony. Mary [Hemingway's wife] recognized his problem and spoke of it sympathetically, but she was not overjoyed, and believed that Venetian society was filled with predatory females.[7]

Later that same month Hemingway wrote his fable of the faithful bull. The typescript·is dated "Venezia, 26/1/50."[8]

The fable tells the story of "a strange bull" who falls in love with one of the breeding cows, "young and beautiful and slimmer and better muscled and shinier and more lovely than all the others." "He only wanted to be with her, and the others meant nothing to him at all."[9] So the owner of the bull ranch sends the monogamous bull to the ring where he is killed.

The story line strongly intimates that the fable is a disguised reaffirmation of his love for Mary, a declaration that she is his one and only true love and that he will remain faithful until death do them part. Very likely, it was intended to disarm or forestall Mary's criticism of his flirtation, and at the same time to convey to Adriana the true nature of his relationship with her. Presumably, he wrote the story for Adriana's small nephew, but he signed the typescript "For Adriana with love from Mr. Papa,"[10] as though he wanted to make certain she understood that the fable's message was for her. "Mr. Papa," which combines a touch of formality with a reminder of age, is not the sobriquet of a passionate lover, but a suitable one for a fifty-year-old man who wants to maintain a fatherly relationship with an attractive young girl. Although Adriana might at first be taken for the young, beautiful, slim female in the fable, the description applies equally well to the slender, thirty-six-year-old Mary Welsh whom Hemingway met in London during the war. "My own true love is Mary Welsh," he declared in a poem written in September, 1944.[11] Still, the description adds an element of ambiguity to the fable, and Hemingway may have intended it so, for he was reluctant to give up his daydreams of recaptured youth. When he returned to Cuba in the spring, Baker tells us, he sank "almost daily into sentimental daydreams of Venice. He said that it was no sin to love both Mary and Adriana, but merely a form of hard luck."[12] But he dedicated *Across the River* to only one—"To Mary with Love."

But there is still another dimension to the fable. The courageous, noble, faithful bull is apparently Hemingway's idealized conception of himself as a writer. The bull's horns are described as "solid as wood" and "as sharply pointed as the quill of a porcupine." Hemingway's weapon was also a "wooden quill"; his working habit was to always begin a writing project using a pencil.[13] Like the bull, who is "a champion" fighter, Hemingway also fought for, and repeatedly defended his championship. "'It is sort of fun to be fifty and feel you are going to defend the title again,'" he told Lillian Ross in the fall of 1949, when he was working on *Across the River and into the Trees*. "'I won it in the twenties and defended it in the thirties and the forties, and I don't mind at all defending it in the fifties.' "[14] The bull's love of, and serious dedication to, fighting is also reminiscent of Hemingway's. The bull fought "with deadly seriousness"; "each time he fought to kill"; "fighting was his obligation and his duty and his joy." For Hemingway, writing was " 'a damned serious subject.'"[15] "Once writing has become your major vice and greatest pleasure," he told an interviewer, "only death can stop it."[16]

The object of the bull's affections in the fable is "young and beautiful and slimmer and better muscled and shinier and more lovely than all the others." This is a fairly accurate description of the famous Hemingway style, taut, lean, and muscular. Thus Hemingway may well be saying in the fable that his latest novel will once again exhibit his constancy, to style and, by implication, subject matter, though he be slain by the critics who, as he envisions it, will with great reluctance and even greater admiration, put him to the sword when he steps into the ring to defend his title. The fable, then, becomes a kind of fantasy in which Hemingway anticipates the critical failure of *Across the River*. But, as he would have it, the moral victory is his. For he fights "wonderfully," and at the moment of truth dies bravely. " '*Que toro mas bravo*,' " the matador exclaimed. " 'Perhaps we should all be faithful.' "

Across the River and into the Trees was to be Hemingway's first defense of his title since the publication of *For Whom the Bell Tolls* in 1940. Although he boasted of his work in progress to Charles Scribner, his publisher, there were signs of wavering confidence beneath the brag: " 'Jeezoo Chrise,' he wrote, 'you have to have confidence to be a champion and that is the only thing I ever wished to be,' " " 'Am trying to knock Mr. Shakespeare on his ass,' he told Scribner. 'Very difficult.' "[17] When he came to New York in November of 1949, with the unfinished manuscript of *Across the River* under his arm, he told Lillian Ross that, of all the people he did not wish to see in that "phony" town, "the people he wished least to see were the critics." "'I am not worried about what anybody I do not like might do.'" he maintained. "'What the hell! If they can do you harm, let them do it.'"[18] But he was worried and appeared to be in training, psychologically, for the upcoming bout with the critics. " 'Never ran as no genius,' " he said to Scribner as he signed the contract for *Across the River*, " 'but I'll defend the title again against all the good young new ones.' He lowered his head, put his left foot forward, and jabbed at the air with a left and a right. 'Never let them hit you solid,' he said."[19]

In the past the critics had dealt him some bruising critical blows—Aldous Huxley in "Foreheads Villainous Low," Max Eastman in "Bull in the Afternoon," Wyndham Lewis in "The Dumb Ox," and Bernard DeVoto in "Tiger, Tiger!" just to name a few. Huxley had chided him for feigning stupidity in his writing and helping to make "highbrow" a "term of contemptuous abuse." Eastman had objected to the "unconscionable quality of bull—to put it as decorously as possible—" in *Death in the Afternoon* and complained that his romanticism resulted in "child's fairy-story writing." Lewis, conceding that Hemingway's work possessed "a penetrating quality, like an animal speaking," had viciously attacked his first-person narrator as invariably "a dull-witted, bovine, monosyllabic simpleton"; "the expression of the soul of the dumb ox," Lewis had concluded, "would have a penetrating beauty of its own, if it were uttered with genius—with bovine genius (and in the case of Hemingway that is what has happened). . . ." And DeVoto had declared, "So far none of Ernest Hemingway's characters has had any more consciousness than a jaguar"; they live "on an instinctual level" and their "mindlessness" has come "to dominate his work."[20] Indeed, Hemingway, who once boasted that he had a "'rat-trap memory,'" may have had these very critical gentlemen in mind when he created his bull (who, incidentally, "was not a bully"), for twice in the fable he points out that his hero "never thought at all." But whether or not he recalled these particular barbed reviews, quite clearly critics were on his mind when he was, to use his phrase, "'jamming in the stretch'" to finish his long-awaited novel and when he composed his fable of "The Faithful Bull."[21]

The fable of "The Good Lion" also harkens back, I believe, to criticism from the 1920's and 1930's. The hero of this tale is a good lion who has wings and who refuses to partake of the diet of the other lions—zebras, wildebeestes, antelope, and people, especially the blood and flesh of Hindu traders. The bad lions make fun of the good lion because of his wings and his diet of pasta and scampi. They snarl and roar with laughter. The wickedest of them all is a lioness who calls him a liar and "the son of a griffon" when he tells of his father who "lives in a city where he stands under the clock tower and looks down on a thousand pigeons."[22] This very wicked lioness with the bad breath and the blood-caked whiskers threatens to kill him and eat him "wings and all." But when she springs, "he rose into the air on his wings." "'What savages these lions are,'" he thinks as he looks down at the pride of roaring, growling lions. He circles "higher and higher" and sets his course for Venice. When he arrives, it is evening and the pigeons are going to their nests. He greets his father and then goes to Harry's bar, where he orders a very dry martini with Gordon's gin and—to the surprise of the reader—a Hindù trader sandwich. But after all, as the narrator points out, "Africa had changed him."

Hemingway's good lion rises above the jealousies, anger, and

hatred of the wicked lions. Although they growl, snarl, and laugh at
him, he refuses to conform to their savage ways, takes to his wings,
rises higher and higher, and sets his own course. Again, this may be
seen as a flattering self-portrait of a dedicated writer who faithfully
adheres to his own distinctive style and subject matter, despite
rejection by editors, hostile attacks by reviewers, and laughter and
scorn from former friends.

Hemingway's winged lion calls to mind Pegasus, the fabulous
winged horse which is the symbol of poetic inspiration. And the
wicked lioness's term of contempt—"griffon"—actually serves to
enhance the self-portrait. A griffon (variously spelled griffin,
gryphon) is a species of vulture and a breed of dog, but it is also the
fabulous creature of Greek mythology, part eagle and part lion,
which guards the gold mines and hidden treasures. Griffons were
called by Aeschylus "the hounds of Zeus who never bark." Thus the
good lion may be seen as an inspired writer who refuses to follow the
conventions, faithfully guards his artistic treasures, and remains
silent before his critics.

Since the wickedest character in the fable is a lioness, one suspects
that Hemingway had a particular female critic in mind. The list of
candidates would have to include Martha Gellhorn, his former wife,
whom he would attack without mercy in *Across the River;* and
Diana Trilling, who intemperately attacked him in a November,
1949, *New York Times* book review.[23] But the evidence suggests that
Gertrude Stein is once again his target.

Hemingway never forgave Miss Stein for trying to put him out of
business with her cutting and patronizing remarks in *The
Autobiography of Alice B. Toklas.* Later in *For Whom the Bell
Tolls,* he has Robert Jordan mock her: "'A rose is a rose is an onion.'
'Thy onions are affecting thy brain,' Agustín said. 'Take care.' 'An
onion is an onion is an onion,' Robert Jordan said cheerily and, he
thought, a stone is a stein is a rock is a boulder is a pebble."[24] And at
the end of his career in *A Moveable Feast,* he attacked her viciously.

The case for the Steinian lioness in the fable is rather strong. Miss
Stein had written on June 18, 1946, that, when people asked her
when she was going back to America, she answered: "Not until I am
a lion."[25] She died about a month after writing that message, which
appeared in her *Selected Writings* published in 1946.

The good lion's request for a Hindu trader sandwich on his return
to civilization may be taken as a warning to all lions and lionesses
who try to clip his wings. Although he is a highly civilized and
polite creature, who has a preference for pasta and very dry martinis,
apparently he has acquired, vicariously, at least a little taste for
blood in "'very savage'' Africa and, unlike the hounds of Zeus, will
soon break his silence and reply in kind to his critics. Hemingway's

later devastating portraits of Wyndham Lewis and Gertrude Stein in *A Moveable Feast* lend credence to this interpretation.

Perhaps Hemingway succeeded in exorcising some of his personal and literary anxieties by writing his two Venetian fables. The tale of the faithful bull apparently did not solve, once and for all, his problems of the heart, but it may have helped to prepare him for the critical onslaught that came with the publication of *Across the River*. And by harking back to an earlier time, when he was a young lion and, according to his version, bested his old adversary Gertrude Stein, he may have been better able to cope with his premonitions of failure. Hemingway told Lillian Ross that, when he was writing *Across the River*, he was "'just as proud as a goddam lion,' "[26] but the Venetian tales suggest that, as he awaited the publication of his new novel, he really felt more like "The Lion Grown Old" in La Fontaine's fable:

A lion who had made his world tremble,
Mourning lost youth and succumbing to distress,
Was attacked by those formerly servile,
Who dared to profit by his feebleness.
The horse came up and let him feel the force of a heel;
The wolf tore off some skin, the ox gave a prod with his horn.
The unfortunate lion, languid, depressed, and forlorn,
Was without strength to roar; age had made him a cripple.
Lying mute, without a moan, he could scarcely draw breath.
When he saw even the ass come running to the lair,
He said, "Die, yes, but ah! this is too much to bear.
To suffer blows from you is die a double death."[27]

Kansas State University

---

[1]Carlos Baker, *Ernest Hemingway: A Life Story* (New York: Scribners, 1969), p. 465.
[2]Ernest Hemingway, "Fathers and Sons," in *Winner Take Nothing* (New York: Scribners, 1933), p. 231.
[3]Ernest Hemingway, *Death in the Afternoon* (New York: Scribners, 1932), pp. 120-121.
[4]*Ibid.*, p. 121.
[5]Baker, p. 476.
[6]*Ibid.*
[7]*Ibid.*, pp. 480, 481.
[8]*Ibid.*, p. 653n.
[9]Ernest Hemingway, "The Faithful Bull," *Holiday*, IX (March 1951), 51. No further page references will be cited for this one-page work.
[10]Baker, p. 653n.
[11]Ernest Hemingway, "Second Poem to Mary," "*Atlantic*, CCXVI (August 1965), 97.
[12]Baker, p. 484.

[13]George Plimpton, "The Art of Fiction XXI: Ernest Hemingway," *Paris Review*, V (Spring 1958), 62-63.

"Interviewer: Thornton Wilder speaks of mnemonic devices that get the writer going on his day's work. He says you once told him you sharpened twenty pencils.

"Hemingway: I don't think I ever owned twenty pencils at one time. Wearing down seven No. 2 pencils is a good day's work" (*Ibid.*, 67).

[14]Lillian Ross, "How Do You Like It Now, Gentlemen?" *New Yorker*, XXVI (May 13, 1950), 49.

[15]Ernest Hemingway, *Green Hills of Africa* (New York: Scribners, 1935), p. 26.

[16]Plimpton, 68.

[17]Baker, pp. 474, 475.

[18]Ross, 41.

[19]*Ibid.*, 61.

[20]Aldous Huxley, *Music at Night and Other Essays* (London: Chatto & Windus, 1931), pp. 201, 202; Max Eastman, "Bull in the Afternoon," *New Republic*, LXXV (June 7, 1933), 94; Wyndham Lewis, "The Dumb Ox, A Study of Ernest Hemingway," *Life & Letters*, X (April 1934), 33, 40, 45; Bernard DeVoto, "Tiger. Tiger!" *Saturday Review*, XVI (October 16, 1937), 8.

[21]Baker, pp. 539, 475.

[22]Ernest Hemingway, "The Good Lion," *Holiday*, IX (March 1951), 50. No further page references will be given to this two-page work.

[23]Diana Trilling devoted nearly half of her review of Elio Vittorini's novel *In Sicily* to Hemingway's two-page introduction, sharply criticizing Hemingway's anti-intellectualism. "He makes it an occasion for an attack upon criticism," she wrote. "It is not the first time Mr. Hemingway has voiced his animus against the critical intelligence." She placed him in the "ranks of the irresponsibles" ("The Story of One Man's Odyssey," *New York Times Book Review* [27 November 1949], 37).

Hemingway had provoked the attack by his withering description of Academic America "that periodically attacks all writing like a dust storm." The good writer, he said, brings rain to the dry country "so that it will not be a desert where only such cactus as New York literary reviewers grow dry and sad. . . ." Their only flowering, he wrote, is "a desicated criticism as alive as stuffed birds, and their steady mulch the dehydrated cuds of fellow critics. . . ." The introduction was written at Cortina D'Ampezzo in 1949 (Introduction to Elio Vittorini, *In Sicily*, trans. Wilfrid David [New York: New Directions, 1949]).

Robert O. Stephens (*Hemingway's NonFiction: The Public Voice* [Chapel Hill: Univ. of North Carolina Press, 1968], pp. 127-128) writes that the lioness in the fable is "suspiciously suggestive of Lillian Ross with her reputation for doing the savage *New Yorker* portraits." But she must be ruled out because her profile did not appear in *The New Yorker* until after the composition of the fable. Hemingway read the profile in galley proof two weeks before its appearence in *The New Yorker* on May 13, 1950. The typescript of "The Good Lion" was dated January 17, 1950.

[24]Hemingway, *For Whom the Bell Tolls* (New York: Scribners, 1940), p. 289.

[25]"A Message from Gertrude Stein," in *Selected Writings of Gertrude Stein*, ed. Carl Van Vechten (New York: Random House, 1946), p. vii.

[26]Ross, 46.

[27]*The Fables of La Fontaine*, trans. Marianne Moore (New York: Viking, 1954), p. 69. The original title in French is *"Le lion, terreur des forêts"* (The lion, terror of the forests). It is relevant to note here that Col. Richard Cantwell in *Across the River and into the Trees* is called " 'The lion-hearted' " by Renata (Hemingway, *Across the River and into the Trees* [New York: Scribners, 1950], p. 229).

NOEL FITCH

ERNEST HEMINGWAY—c/o SHAKESPEARE AND COMPANY

During the years Hemingway lived in Paris, his postal address was 12 Rue de l'Odeon—a mailing address he shared with James Joyce, George Antheil, Sherwood Anderson, Robert McAlmon, Stephen Vincent Benet, and scores of other English and American travelers and expatriates. Number 12 was the home of Shakespeare and Company, the American bookshop and lending library of Miss Sylvia Beach, publisher of James Joyce's *Ulysses*. Shakespeare and Company, and La Maison des Amis de Livres the French bookshop of Adrienne Monnier across the street, made this section of old Paris the hub of post-World-War-I literary activity. These two women were "like those bleary persons hanging around Pelleport [boxing] Ring on the lookout for talent," Sylvia Beach declares in her memoirs.[1]

Both Sylvia Beach and Ernest Hemingway[2] have recorded briefly their friendship, which spanned four decades from 1922 to 1961. Although their memoirs cast a warm light on their personal relationship, they faintly illuminate Hemingway scholarship. Hemingway's lending library cards, which are a part of the Sylvia Beach Collection at Princeton University Library, elucidate his development as a reader and author. Only recently published in the *Fitzgerald/Hemingway Annual 1975*[3] and as yet uninterpreted, this list of books reveals a distinct preference for Russian literature, particularly the fiction of Ivan Turgenev, whose works account for a fifth of the books Hemingway borrowed.

On 28 December 1921, the twenty-two year old roving

correspondent for the *Toronto Star* returned to his two-room, cold-water flat to tell his wife Hadley about the "wonderful place" he had found and the lady who had trusted him to borrow books without payment. This was soon after the newly married Hemingways had set sail for Paris, 8 December 1921, with a letter from Sherwood Anderson introducing the Hemingways to Sylvia Beach.[4] Sylvia first saw this introductory letter years later. Trusting instead to his own tactics, Hemingway just walked in one day and borrowed four works: Turgenev's *A Sportsman's Sketches* (2 vols.), D. H. Lawrence's *Sons and Lovers,* Tolstoy's *War and Peace,* and Dostoevsky's *The Gambler and Other Stories.*[5] His choice of books by three Russian authors is consistent with his preference for Russian literature through several decades of borrowing. With only a promise to return with the subscription fee, which he did, Sylvia Beach allowed him to take five volumes instead of the usual two. "We're going to have all the books in the world to read and when we go on trips we can take them,"[6] he told his wife. The financial records of the bookshop show the date of his first subscription to be Wednesday, 28 December 1921.[7] Hemingway could only afford a month's subscription: 12 francs. Shakespeare and Company became that day one of his chief sources of books. He was a heavy reader and took Sylvia's books with him on fishing and skiing trips and visits to Spain and Italy.

For Sylvia Beach, who had opened her lending library and bookshop only two years earlier, Hemingway was not the first nor the last American expatriate who was too poor to buy books in Paris. In his sketches of these days in Paris, published four decades later, he remembers the warmth of the shop on that cold winter day, the photographs of famous writers on the walls, the big stove and the proprietress:

> Sylvia had a lively, sharply sculptured face, brown eyes that were as alive as a small animal's and as gay as a young girl's, and wavy brown hair. . . . She had pretty legs and she was kind, cheerful and interested, and loved to make jokes and gossip. No one that I ever knew was nicer to me.[8]

And Sylvia remembered that he was "exceptionally wise and self-reliant" for his age (twelve years her junior) and that she "felt the warmest friendship for Ernest Hemingway from the day we met."[9] Shy as he was at that first visit to the bookshop, they sat down for a long personal conversation in which he spoke about his childhood and the war, showing her his scarred leg and foot.

In his recollections of the early Paris years Hemingway reserves his greatest praise for Sylvia, in sharp contrast, for example, to his recollections of Ford, Fitzgerald, and Gertrude Stein.[10] Sylvia never received the satiric abuse he aimed at other expatriates. Although she made no claim as his tutor nor was she a fellow writer, in any competitive sense, their friendship did involve matters of trust which could have soured their cordiality. But there is no evidence of any disharmony between them. Their friendship was a genuine one, unstrained through four decades. Hemingway undoubtedly saw in Sylvia the qualities he most admired: personal integrity, a devotion to the arts, and a willingness to work hard.

Although Sylvia demanded quality in the books she put on her shelves, she never offered unsolicited literary advice to her writer friends. She was a close friend of two such unlike people as Gide and Hemingway—respecting the achievements of both. She gave Hemingway advice only on his eating habits (he skipped too many meals). And she gave him sympathy in his quarrels. For example, when he mentioned a desire to patch up his quarrel with Gertrude Stein who had claimed credit for his literary style and his love of bullfighting, Sylvia encouraged his plan, and at his request walked him to her doorstep.

Hemingway came to the bookshop each day to read the latest magazines, get his mail, and meet any newly arrived writers from America. Although he did not borrow books of poetry—with the exception of Yeats's *Early Poems and Stories* and Sandburg's *Selected Poems*—he read the latest poetry in the coterie magazines on the bookshop tables. He helped edit the serious little magazines, such as *transatlantic review* and *This Quarter,* which were distributed at the bookshop. A working (not a loafing) expatriate, he spent his mornings writing in a rented room or in the Closerie des Lilas and reading at Shakespeare and Company. Soon he was calling himself her "best customer," and being invited for dinner with Sylvia and Adrienne—often with a few French writers for company, for Hemingway spoke French quite well by ear.

One Frenchman whom Sylvia introduced Hemingway to was Jean Prévost, assistant editor of Adrienne Monnier's *Le Navire d'argent* and a devoted friend and member of both bookshops who later wrote favorable criticism of Hemingway's works, quickening Hemingway's literary reputation in France. Prévost, in his middle twenties, boxed and prided himself on his hardheadedness, which he proved by banging his head against an iron pipe in the bookshop. Amused and impressed by Prévost's head-banging display, Sylvia organized a boxing match between Prévost and Hemingway which resulted, she claimed, in a broken thumb for Hemingway. This seems to be the only "violent" American-French encounter which she mediated. Otherwise, Hemingway was amicably involved in the French literary activity of the two bookshops. His zest for French literature is also reflected in his borrowing of modern classics by Flaubert, de Maupassant, Stendhal, Balzac, and Zola. His reading of Emil Ludwig's *Genius and Character* and J. G. Huneker's *Egoists,* which treat these authors, reveals his interest in the criticism of French literature.

Of the many French, English and American writers he met through Sylvia, the most significant meeting occurred one day when Hemingway was reading in the library and the Pounds sauntered in. Hemingway claimed he had come to Paris in part to see Pound. Probably the greatest literary influence on the modern writers, Pound was advocating *le mot juste*—which the French writers, particularly Flaubert, practiced—and the imagist principles of directness, precision, and economy.[11] In his fiction, Hemingway presented the sequential action of his characters, directly and simply. To present his world with the terseness of poetry, he avoided unnecessary adjectives and the analysis of emotion.

Hemingway was certainly influenced by Pound's distrust of the adjective and by the writing of Flaubert—whose statue he passed each time he walked from the Closerie de Lilas through the Luxembourg Gardens to the bookshop. Yet the influence of Flaubert's style may be less than readers have assumed. According to bookshop records, Hemingway borrowed only Flaubert's *Sentimental Journey.* His major passion was for the Russians— even for Dostoevsky, who cared little for *le mot juste* yet made his people "come alive" for Hemingway. Pound disappointed Hemingway when he said he did not read Dostoevsky or other "Rooshians." There is no record of Hemingway's borrowing any book by Pound, though he certainly read his poetry.[12]

Among the early influences on Hemingway's style was the painting of Paul Cézanne. The Sylvia Beach Collection records the impact of Cézanne on Hemingway. During September of 1926 he studied a book on the paintings of Paul Cézanne, from whom he learned to arrange his landscapes and evoke a sense of scene. In what is certainly an early version of the second part of "Big Two-Hearted River," published for the first time in 1972, Hemingway expressed a desire to "write about country so it would be there like Cézanne had done it in painting."

> He [Nick] knew just how Cézanne would paint this stretch of river. [Nick,] seeing how Cézanne would do the stretch of river and the swamp, stood up and stepped down into the stream. The water was cold and actual. He waded across the stream, moving in the picture.[13]

Both Hemingway and Cézanne expressed ideas and emotions purely in forms—Hemingway in noun words, Cézanne in colors. The detached, lean, taut style of each avoided the emotional and decorative. They favored painting nature simply, crisply and convincingly, to reveal its basic design and its relation in space. Cézanne focused on the solid presence of the object or sphere. He worked with layers of space on the flat painted surface—as Hemingway worked in words on the flat page—moving these planes of his landscape forward and into the center of vision. Cézanne moved these planes back and forth, dissolving the distance of space, yet creating a canvas with dimension, in which the culminating point of objects is in the foreground—where they begin for the writer of fiction. Tilting up the horizontal plane to bring the object forward, Cézanne gives attention to each plane—as, for example, in his paintings of Monte Sainte Victoire. Similarly, Hemingway brings his landscape up front. When he takes Nick from the railroad tracks through the burned-out field, up to the trees, and into the big Two-Hearted River, he brings each essential element directly to the reader's eye.

Some of his library borrowings reflect his work in progress. For example, when he was finishing his satire of Sherwood Anderson's style, *The Torrents of Spring,* he borrowed on 23 November 1925 Donald Ogden Stewart's *A Parody Outline of History.* When he was writing *A Farewell to Arms* he borrowed several books on war: Darrell Figgis's *Recollections of the Irish War* (borrowed February 1928), Beaverbrook's *Politicians and the War* (borrowed June 1929), and Ludwig Renn's *War* (borrowed September 1929). War, he had told Fitzgerald, is the best subject for fiction because much of life is crowded into wartime experience.[14] And several months after beginning *For Whom the Bell Tolls* in March of 1938, he borrowed *Life and Death of a Spanish Town,* which he never returned. Elliott Paul's *Life and Death of a Spanish Town* tells of the fascist invasion of Santa Eulalia. Paul has a sympathy for the people and a hatred of political oppression. He is concerned for the effects of war on the people and their natural environment. Hemingway had vividly portrayed the destruction of nature by war in his opening lines of *A Farewell to Arms.* In *For Whom the Bell Tolls* he expresses a sympathy for the peasants, which he shared with Paul. Hemingway borrowed a second book that fall which portrayed the Spanish Civil War with human compassion. *Homage to Catalonia* reveals George Orwell's feeling for the land, love of the people and understanding of the political background of the war in which he had fought.

Earlier Hemingway revealed this interest in comparing his own experiences and observations with others' written accounts. On 30 January 1926, while rewriting *The Sun Also Rises* (manuscript mailed to Maxwell Perkins April 24), he briefly borrowed a book on

196 Wed
December 28

Extras		1 20
The Nation		2 25
Extras & Junes		12 85
1 Tauchnitz		4
Dubliners		22 50
Subs Mr Hemingway 1 mo 2 vols		12
" Mrs Peats 3 mos 2 vols Dep 14		30
		84 80

Fri
December 30

Almayer's Folly		6
Jude the Obscure		13 50
A Portrait of the Artist (not paid		22 50
Subs Mr Tipple 2 wks 2 vols Dep 14		8
Dr Jeckyl & Mr Hyde		6
		56 00

Sat
December 31

Subs Capt. Davies ren. 1 mo 2 vols		12
" Mrs Arnold ren. 1 mo 1 vol		8
" Mr Kershaw " 6 mos 1 vol		35
Metaphysical Poets		20
Leaves of Grass		15
Subs Mr Ashworth 1 mo 1 vol Dep 7		8
" Baronne Chaulin ren. 6 mos 2 vols		50
Prologue Chinen		4 50
		152 50
The Tables of the Law		4
		156 50

Page from the 1921 ledger of Shakespeare and Company which records Hemingway's first subscription to the lending library. Sylvia Beach Collection, Princeton University Library.

1927

Norman Douglas (pub. privately)	Birds & Beasts of The Greek Anthology, Norman Douglas Sept 27 2 copies (ordered & paid for) $1-1 1927
Putnam's	Blessing of Pan, Lord Dunsany, 1 c 7/6 Sept 30 $6.00 1927
Putnam	Bismarck, Emil Ludwig, 1 c 12/6 Sept 30 1927
Albert & Chas Boni	Blues, ed. by Handy, ill. by Covarrubias 1 c $3.50 1927 Oct 4
Warne	Kate Greenaway's Book of Games, 1 c 4/- Oct 4
Benn	Blue Murder, Edmund Snell, 1 c 7/6 Oct 5 1927
Scribner's	Blue Voyage, Conrad Aiken, 3 c $2.50 Oct 7 1927
Hutchinson	Black Cap, Cynthia Asquith, (14 authors) 1 c 7/6 Oct 17
Macmillan	Bacon's Essays of Good & Evil, g. t. 1 c 3/6 Oct 18
Fisher Unwin (Benn)	Big Request, Ethel M. Dell, 1 c 7/6 Oct 27 1927
Simpkin Marshall (Routledge)	Book of The Saints, Miniature Reference Library, 1 c 1/- Oct 26
Heinemann	Brook Kerith, George Moore, 3 c 7/6 Nov 3 1927
Boni & Liveright	Boss Tweed, Dennis Tilden Lynch, 1 c #4 Nov 3
Allen & Unwin	Bismarck, Emil Ludwig, 1 c 21/- Nov 10 1927
Faber & Gwyer	Black Book of Edworthstown 1 c 18/- Nov 12 1927
Kegan Paul	Baschets, Shand, Today & Tomorrow Series, 1 c 2/6 Nov 24
A & C Boni	Bridge of San Luis Rey, Thornton Wilder, 3 c $2.50 Nov 28
Cape	Beethoven, a critical Study, J. W. N. Sullivan, 1 c 7/6 Dec 7 1927
Herbert Jenkins	1928 Bindles on The Rocks, Herbert Jenkins, 1 c 2/6 Jan 21 1928
Heinemann	Babyons, Clemence Dane, 1 c 7/6 Jan 26 1928
Boni & Liveright	Blues, W. C. Handy, ill. by Covarrubias, 2 c $3.50 Feb 1 1928
Cape	Best Short Stories of 1927 Am. 2 c 7/6 Feb 11 1928
Cape	Best Short Stories of 1927 Eng. 1928
Routledge	Byrd, Frank Howes, 1 c 7/6 Feb 17 1928
Routledge	Boris Godounov, Alexander Pushkin, 1 c 2/6 Feb 18 1928
Constable	Bliss, Katherine Mansfield, 2 c 5/- Feb 25 1928
Cape	Book of Marriage, Keyserling, 1 c 21/- Feb 25 1928
Longmans, Green & Co	Bridge of San Luis Rey, Thornton Wilder, 1 c 6/- Mar 5
A & C Boni	Bridge of San Luis Rey, " " 2 c $2.50 Mar 7
John Lane Bodley Head	Bloom of Life, Anatole France, 1 c 2/6 March 10 1928
A & C Boni	Bridge of San Luis Rey, Thornton Wilder, 6 c $2.50 March 21
A & C Boni	Blues, Handy, ill. by Covarrubias, 3 c $3.50 March 21
Longmans	Bridge of San Luis Rey, Thornton Wilder, 2 c 6/- March 29 1928

Page from purchase records of Shakespeare and Company. Sylvia Beach Collection, Princeton University Library.

bullfighting (probably T. W. Jones' *Bullfighting*). Of course, Hemingway knew bullfighting first-hand. As he was fond of telling Sylvia Beach in letters and postcards, he saw scores of fights on his vacation trips to Spain. But this interest in bullfighting is technical as well as theoretical; he was interested in the clean, unadorned lines, its clarity of style, the study of a confrontation with death. In the Sylvia Beach Collection are several bullfight scenes on picture postcards Hemingway brought back to the bookshop.

Though Hemingway obviously preferred to read fiction, he borrowed several works of drama. As early as 1927, he had discussed with his editor, Maxwell Perkins, the possibility of writing a play. During February of 1928, Hemingway borrowed O'Casey's *Plough and the Stars* and O'Neill's *Emperor Jones*. These were the only plays he borrowed. In the fall of 1937, ten years after first speaking about becoming a playwright, he wrote his only play, *The Fifth Column.* In March of the following year he purchased three plays: Christopher Isherwood's *Lions and Shadows: An Education in the Twenties,* Charles Bennett's *Blackmail,* and Stephen Spender's *Trial of a Judge.* That same month he left his play with Sylvia Beach, who mailed it to Perkins on the 27th. As is indicated in the records kept by Sylvia Beach, Hemingway read very few plays. With some justification he was uncertain about his success as a playwright, waiting until August to make the decision to include the play with a collection of his short stories.

Hemingway remembers that, in addition to lending him books, Sylvia lent him money "plenty of times." Her bookshop records show a $100 loan on 3 August 1923, probably extended at the Hemingways' return to Toronto for the birth of their baby, nicknamed Bumby. On October 3, a week before the baby was born, the records show the money refunded.[15] In a letter from Toronto Hemingway declares that, had the child been a girl, they would have named her Sylvia. And, he adds, "Being a boy we could not call him Shakespeare."[16] Upon the Hemingways' return to Paris in January of the following year, Sylvia added the occasional care of Bumby to her other assistance in Hemingway's behalf. She put him in contact with the English publisher, Jonathan Cape, and enthusiastically supported all his endeavors. Hemingway in turn taught her the intricacies of boxing and cycling and bullfighting. He and Hadley took Adrienne and Sylvia by Metro to the region of Ménilmontant, where they saw what the women thought was a very bloody boxing match. Reassured by Hemingway, they proceeded to learn the rules of the sport, listening with close attention to his explanation of each move. Soon he became engrossed in the action and forgot all about them. The evening ended in a free-for-all which Sylvia deemed "a real Western."[17]

He not only gave lively cycling and boxing lessons, but also read all of the French publications and had "the true writer's temperament," observed Adrienne Monnier, Hemingway's first French enthusiast. Bryher, English novelist and loyal member of the Company of Shakespeare and Company, recalls Adrienne quietly predicting that "Hemingway will be the best known of you all. He cares for his craft."[18] Adrienne's enthusiasm for his work manifested itself when she published "L'Invincible" ("The Undefeated") in *Le Navire d'argent* (March 1926), his first story translated into French.

This contact with the small French and English presses in Paris was a valuable service which the bookshop provided. Hemingway had his *Three Stories and Ten Poems* published by McAlmon's Contact Publishing Company (address 12 Rue de L'Odeon) in 1923, and *in our time* was published by Willian Bird's Three Mountain Press in 1924. A year after Adrienne and Prévost published "L'Invincible," the *Nouvelle Revue Francaise* published "Cinquante mille dollars" (May 1927), corrected proofs of which are in the Sylvia Beach Collection. The influential literati who were members of the two bookshops continued to publish and translate Hemingway, who was admired by French critics even before he became famous in the United States.

Sylvia admired his "skillful workmanship, his tidiness, his storyteller's gift and sense of the dramatic, his power to create." She also wrote that his titles, an aspect of a book which a librarian and bookseller would notice, are poems in themselves: "His titles have a life of their own, and they have enriched the American vocabulary."[19] Of course, Hemingway took some of his titles from poetry: *The Sun Also Rises* from "Ecclesiastes," *For Whom the Bell Tolls* from John Donne, and *A Farewell to Arms* from George Peele's poem of the same title.

The list of books borrowed by Hemingway from the lending library gives an accurate portrayal of his reading. Because he spent time browsing and reading in the library, we can assume that if he took a book home he intended to read it with greater care. He travelled a great deal and could not have carried much of a library with him. Had he any personal library, he would certainly have had all of Turgenev's titles—especially *A Sportsman's Sketches*, which he borrowed four times in eight years.

Hemingway was a keen student of literature because he considered writing to be a competitive profession. Shakespeare and Company was Hemingway's library at a critical period of his learning. Although the absence of any of his library cards before October of 1925 is an unfortunate loss, one can still assess the impact of his reading from a look at the books he checked out between that date and 1929—with occasional borrowings in the 1930's. There appears a consistency of literary interests, beginning with the first books he claims he borrowed in 1921. His reading, as indicated by his borrowings and by the comments he makes in *Green Hills of Africa* and in occasional interviews, focussed on the great works of realism in continental literature—particularly Russian fiction. He had a keen sense of the literary tradition, of his relationship to those whose pictures surrounded him on the walls of the bookshop.

On several occasions Hemingway listed the books which had given him so much pleasure that he would rather read them again for the first time, he declared, than have a million dollars guaranteed annual income. At times he admitted these books were his literary inheritance. Those titles which occur most frequently on his lists include the major works of Tolstoy, Stendhal, Flaubert, Joyce, Fielding, Dostoevsky, Twain, James, and Turgenev. With the exception of Turgenev works, which account for 13 of the 85 borrowed books (children's titles excluded), only the following titles from these lists appear on his library cards: Mann's *Buddenbrooks*, Flaubert's *Sentimental Education*, Dostoevsky's *The Gambler*, Tolstoy's *War and Peace*, W. H. Hudson's *Far Away and Long Ago*, and Stendhal's *The Charterhouse of Parma*. One can assume that most of the other works he considered excellent he had read before the October 1925 date of the earliest surviving library card.

The author who appears most frequently on the library cards is Turgenev, whose *A Sportsman's Sketches* was the first book Hemingway remembered borrowing. Hemingway admired the realistic portrayal of the peasants and the figure of the observant hunter. He borrowed *A Sportsman's Sketches* four times in eight years, *Torrents of Spring* and *On the Eve* twice, and *Lear of the Steppes, House of Gentle Folk, Fathers and Children, Knock, Knock, Knock,* and *Two Friends* once each. He kept some of these books for months. Excluding the children's books and periodicals, nearly a fifth of the books he borrowed from the bookshop were Turgenev titles, two of which (*Fathers and Children* and *The Torrents of Spring*) Hemingway used for his own titles. Hemingway was concerned primarily with style and the power to create scene. He admired Turgenev's creation of country scenes and his power to confer on the reader a sense of participation: "I knew that I have lived there," he declares in praise of Turgenev in *The Green Hills of Africa*. Although he recast any influence into his own art, Hemingway inherited his classical style of clear, lean prose detail as much from Turgenev as from any other writer.

Hemingway admired Turgenev's precise observation and his effort to call attention not to his language but to his material. Turgenev's economy is evident in his creation of character, in which he bares the psyche of a character through action and landscape—a method Hemingway used markedly well in "Big Two-Hearted River." Here, the personal pain and the process of healing which Nick undergoes are correlatives of the burned-out landscape and the ritual of fishing. This use of economy and understatement Hemingway described as his "iceberg" theory, in which the writer reveals one-eighth of his material, implying the remainder. Turgenev also believed that the writer uses part of reality to suggest the whole: he once asserted that the writer "must know and feel the roots of phenomena, but he must represent only the phenomena themselves—in their blossoming or fading."[20]

In addition to the pursuit of clear prose, Turgenev and Hemingway shared a stoical, perhaps nihilistic, view of life and the inevitability of death. In the final pages of Turgenev's *On the Eve*, death fells the man of action, Insarov, in the midst of life. His stoical pessimism is echoed in Frederic Henry's ruminations about fate and the game of life in the final pages of *A Farewell to Arms:*

> Now Catherine would die. That was what you did. You died. You did not know what it was about. You never had time to learn. They threw you in and told you the rules and the first time they caught you off base they killed you.[21]

Both Turgenev and Hemingway treat the metaphysical tension between the individual and the cosmos. Turgenev, in *Fathers and Children*, dramatizes the tragic collision of Bazarov with history and the immutable force of nature, stressing the frailty of man in the midst of nothingness. Hemingway acknowledges this void also but stresses human dignity and a clean, well-lighted place to repel the darkness. Both writers adopt a strong naturalistic stance by depicting nature as indifferent, almost identifying it with impersonal Fate.

Hemingway's interest in Russian literature extended beyond Turgenev. He borrowed Dostoevsky's *The Gambler* (twice), *The Insulted and Injured*, *The Idiot*, and the autobiography of Dostoevsky's wife. In *A Moveable Feast* he expresses admiration for the power and madness in Dostoevsky's works. He borrowed also Tolstoy's *War and Peace* and a volume on contemporary Russian literature. In German literature he admired Thomas Mann, borrowing *The Magic Mountain* and *Buddenbrooks*.

Although he could not have been more dissimilar from the life and style of James Joyce, Hemingway admired and defended Joyce, whom he called "the greatest writer in the world," and became involved with Shakespeare and Company's launching of *Ulysses*. According to Sylvia Beach, one of Hemingway's services for the bookshop and the American reading public was his part in the importation of *Ulysses* from Canada into the United States. After the United States shipment was confiscated and destroyed at the port of New York, Hemingway, according to Sylvia, supplied the name of a "certain Bernard B." The unpublished letters of this mysterious man to Sylvia are signed "Barnet Braverman" and occasionally appear below the letterhead of the Curtis Company Limited, an advertising service in Windsor, Ontario.[22] He rented an apartment in Windsor, where he received the *Ulysses* shipment, and then each day, according to Sylvia, he carried in his pants one or two copies of the book across on the ferry to Detroit, a ten minutes' ride away. From Detroit they were sent by express to each subscriber. His letters declare that he paid duty on at least forty copies. Fearful that the Canadian customs official would discover the U. S. ban on *Ulysses*, he announced that it was a cheap novel worth no more than fifty cents. He thus avoided a higher payment from the 25% tax. Shakespeare and Company paid all his expenses ($53.34), but he worried about the danger involved and the inconvenience of unwrapping each book at the border and retying the book on the other side. In the account by Sylvia of this voyage of *Ulysses* across the Detroit River she implies that Hemingway handled the intrigue, although there is no reference to Braverman in any Hemingway letter. The correspondence in the Beach Collection indicates that, although Hemingway may have originated the idea and suggested the name of a friend, Sylvia carried on all the details and correspondence. In Braverman's undated first letter he asserts he is pleased to be "putting one over on the Republic and its Methodist smut hounds." When the task was completed, he wrote to ask what Chicagoan referred her to him. The letter itemizing his expenses is dated 3 January 1923. In his last letter, undated, he thanks her for the expense check and adds: "my small performance, dangerous as it was, simply enabled me to be of service to a fellow artist and his daring publisher."

Hemingway also assisted the Shakespeare and Company launching of Joyce's *Ulysses*. He helped collect subscriptions for *Ulysses*, and records show that he bought at least two copies of the book himself. Out of his friendship for Sylvia and his admiration for Joyce, he helped distribute *Ulysses*. Bookshop records also show that in 1926 he signed a protest against the pirating of *Ulysses*— receiving a French Academy membership designation after his name, a mistake which apparently no one protested. Joyce revealed his affection for Hemingway in a remark that Sylvia records:

> I am going to say this whether Hemingway shoots me or not—I have always felt that he was a deeply religious man. Hemingway was a great pal of Joyce's, and Joyce remarked to me one day that he

thought it was a mistake, Hemingway's thinking himself such a tough fellow and McAlmon trying to pass himself off as the sensitive type. It was the other way around, he thought. So Joyce found out, Hemingway.[23]

The friendship which Sylvia and Hemingway shared is briefly documented in their unpublished letters.[24] In postcards from Pamplona and letters from Austria and later from Key West, Hemingway gives her boxing news and tells her of his writing progress. He also asks her for literary news and informs her when he has read all the books she lent him. Each letter includes personal news of his family and reveals his warm regard for her. When he returned to Paris he joined the literary activities of the bookshop: letters of protest, a French edition of Joyce, and Sylvia's Walt Whitman exhibit in April of 1926. On the first day of the exhibit, Hemingway signed the guest book on the third line, along with Joyce, Adrienne, Valéry, Romains, and Eliot.

The chief subject of Hemingway's correspondence, except for occasional news of family and fishing, was his books. For example, he sent her cards, in lieu of signatures, to insert in his books (probably *Men Without Women*), which she was to send out to thirty "influential" people (keeping him out of it). He later wrote, in a letter addressed to "Madame Shakespeare," apologizing for asking her to do this chore. He also occasionally asked that books be sent to others, as in his 18 August 1929 letter where he asks that she send a copy of *Torrents of Spring* to Owen Wister, adding that he will send the money when he can. In the margin of this letter he writes that literature is on the "bum" and they both had better try another line of work. She wrote him about Paris literary news and the sale of his books.[25]

During his frequent visits to Paris during the 1930's, Shakespeare and Company was his address. Although most of the hours at the bookshop were pleasant, two incidents in March of 1934 show his temper or touchiness. The first was a minor incident when Sylvia Beach made the mistake of introducing Katherine Anne Porter and Hemingway to each other as "the two best modern American writers." When Sylvia went to answer a phone call, Hemingway, after a long stare at Miss Porter, walked silently out the door.[26]

The second incident occurred on the 24th of that month when, after reading Wyndham Lewis' criticism of him entitled "The Dumb Ox: A Study of Ernest Hemingway," Hemingway took a swing at a vase of tulips, breaking the vase and ruining thirty-eight books—an incident which culminated years of hostility between Lewis and Hemingway. Hemingway had met him in those early years in Paris, while sparring with Ezra at the Pound studio.

Although Pound admired Lewis, to Hemingway Lewis looked "nasty," with the face of a frog and the "eyes of an unsuccessful rapist."[28] After Lewis' attacks on James Joyce, antagonism grew. Lewis deplored the naturalism of modern literature with its aimless people to whom things happen. Lewis debunked Hemingway's "art of the surface" and his cult of "action" (without will) and accused him of imitating the "Stein-stutter," which he called "dull-witted" and "dreamy." His *Men Without Art* parodied Hemingway's title *Men Without Women*. Hemingway's anger was sudden and intense, but when it subsided he wrote Sylvia a check for 1500 francs to replace the vase and the books.[29] Financial records show that she returned 500 francs.

A high moment for Sylvia, but a miserable one for Hemingway, occurred in the spring of 1937 when Hemingway gave one of his rare public readings on behalf of Friends of Shakespeare and Company, a group organized by André Gide to lend financial support to the bookshop. Hemingway appeared with Stephen Spender—he would not go it alone—in a double reading 12 May. Both men had just returned from the war in Spain. Although previous readings by Prévost, Valéry, Schlumberger, Eliot, Maurois, Gide, and Paulhan were always announced formally by printed invitation, the announcement for the Hemingway-Spender evening was

1937. Invitation to Hemingway/Spender reading. Sylvia Beach Collection, Princeton University Library.

handwritten on small calling cards. The evening must have been arranged in haste or uncertainty. Hemingway had been covering the war in Spain for forty-five days and had returned to Paris only three days prior to this time. And Sylvia certainly knew that he was a reluctant reader. He is quoted as saying that evening that he would never again give a reading—even for Sylvia Beach.

At approximately 9 P.M., more than generously fortified with beer and obviously uncomfortable, Hemingway began to stammer through his comments on the war and writing. By the time that Sylvia brought him more beer and he had begun his reading of "Fathers and Sons" from *Winner Take Nothing,* he was able to put more expression into his speaking voice. Although all reports[30] of the evening stress his discomfort and drinking, Sylvia, who had years before heard him read from *in our time* (his "first bout"), thought the event a "great sensation." Perhaps her positive report was a result simply of Hemingway's presence or the rarity of his public reading.

According to the guest list in the Sylvia Beach Collection, the guests included French men of letters—Romains, Maurois, Paulhan, Prévost, Claudel, Valéry—and Joyce, Eugene Jolas, Janet Flanner, Gisèle Freund, and Martha Gellhorn, whom Hemingway had been with in Spain and was to marry three years later. Joyce, who had been sitting in a corner, slipped out before Stephen Spender began reading six of his unpublished war poems.

As Hemingway continued to publish and receive the highest literary praise, Sylvia collected newspaper clippings of his activities. Although she closed her bookshop at the end of 1941, she remained a family friend—attending Bumby's wedding in Paris in the winter of 1949. In a 29 January 1954 letter, she confesses that she and Adrienne had "wept at" the news of Hemingway's plane crash in Africa. With this letter she sent a few French papers for him to see "what a fuss" the French had made about his crash—they had almost gotten "the Pantheon ready" for him. Paris had not forgotten Hemingway and Hemingway did not forget Paris, his "moveable feast." Her final newsclipping was of his death, just fifteen months before her own.

The bookshop was a major literary stimulus for Hemingway. Shakespeare and Company was his main source of books, his library, post office, and club house. Here he borrowed Turgenev's books, met Pound, made contacts with translators, editors, and the great and soon-to-be great writers. The friendship between Hemingway and Sylvia Beach was based upon a shared love for Paris and literature. Sylvia remained his noncritical and loyal friend, seeing him always as the charming young Hemingway of the 1920's. In her memoirs she casts Hemingway in the role of a hero on several occasions. He played an active role in the major literary events connected with the bookshop: the publishing and smuggling of *Ulysses,* the pirating protest, the Whitman exhibition, and the 1937 reading for the Friends of Shakespeare and Company.

Of all the events involving Hemingway at the bookshop, the most dramatic occurred during the liberation of Paris in 1944. Adrienne and Sylvia had joined a premature victory march down the Boulevard Saint Michel and narrowly escaped death when German soldiers, leaving the Luxembourg Gardens, fired into the crowd. Several days after this incident, Sylvia saw four little cars (she was to remember them as jeeps) parked at her house:

> I heard a deep voice calling: "Sylvia!" And everybody in the street took up the cry of "Sylvia!" "It's Hemingway! It's Hemingway!" cried Adrienne. I flew downstairs; we met with a crash; he picked me up and swung me around and kissed me while people on the street and in the windows cheered.[31]

The husky shirtsleeved Hemingway and his sixteen-man "Hem division" had come to liberate the Rue de l'Odeon. For the neighbors this incident was the most exciting of a number of "Westerns" staged by these Americans who, for so many important years, had enlivened their quiet little street.

---

[1]*Shakespeare and Company* (New York: Harcourt, Brace, 1959), p. 81.

[2]Hemingway's memoirs of the Paris years are entitled *A Moveable Feast* (New York: Scribners, 1963). Both Hemingway and Sylvia Beach feature each other with laudatory recollections.

[3]Richard Layman, "Hemingway's Library Cards at Shakespeare and Company," pp. 191-207. Although valuable for the photographic reproductions of the library cards, Layman's essay contains errors and omissions in his identification of the titles on the cards. A full interpretation of the entries and an identification of the books—checked against the shop records of stock purchases—follows this essay.

[4]This letter is reproduced in *Mercure de France,* CGCXLIX (Août-Septembre 1963), 102. Although Anderson was the only U.S. writer of stature whom Hemingway had met before coming to Paris, Sylvia introduced him to many others, including Ezra Pound, Allen Tate, and Katherine Anne Porter.

[5]*A Moveable Feast,* p. 36. Although Carlos Baker believes the style of these memoirs belongs to the 1950's, this specific remembrance of titles may be based on notes he took in the 1920's and presumedly stored in a trunk in the Ritz Hotel basement. To date no evidence of early notes for *A Moveable Feast* has been found in the trunk material at the John F. Kennedy Library.

[6]*A Moveable Feast,* p. 38.

[7]He renewed his subscription on 27 February 1922 for three months. Thereafter, his subscriptions were by the year. His library cards from 28

December 1921 to 8 October 1925 have been lost.

[8]*A Moveable Feast,* p. 35.

[9]*Shakespeare and Company,* pp. 79, 77.

[10]It was not until March that he began visiting Gertrude Stein. The surviving library cards reveal that he only borrowed her *Composition as Explanation* (November 1926) and *Three Lives* (June 1928). She undoubtedly read portions of her work to him in the early years of their friendship.

[11]These principles were set forth in three rules of imagist poetry: "(1) Direct treatment of the 'thing,' whether subjective or objective; (2) To use absolutely no word which did not contribute to the presentation; (3) As regarding rhythm: to compose in sequence of the musical phrase, not in sequence of a metronome." F. S. Flint, "Imagisme," *Poetry,* I (March 1913), 99.

[12]Hemingway uses the title "The Age Demanded"—a title from Pound's "Hugh Selwyn Mauberley." *Der Querschnitt,* V (February 1925), 111.

[13]"On Writing," *The Nick Adams Stories* (New York: Scribners, 1972), pp. 239-240. In *A Moveable Feast,* Hemingway proclaims that what he learned from Cézanne "made writing simple true sentences far from enough to make the stories have the dimensions that I was trying to put in them" (p. 13).

[14]1 January 1926 letter in the F. Scott Fitzgerald Collection, Princeton University Library. In *A Moveable Feast,* Hemingway expresses his admiration for "the wonderful Waterloo account" in Stendhal's *Charterhouse of Parma,* which he borrowed from the lending library December 1925. Except for Tolstoy's accounts of war, this was the first treatment of war which Hemingway felt was authentic.

[15]The only other loan recorded was $100.00, 17 February 1928. In early drafts of her memoirs she claims Hemingway generously helped in financial crises of young painters and writers.

[16]6 November 1923 letter entitled "Dear Seelviah" published in *Mercure de France,* CCXLIX, 106-7.

[17]Letter from Mrs. Hadley Hemingway Mowrer, June 1969. See also *Shakespeare and Company,* p. 79.

[18]Bryher, *The Heart of Artemis: A Writer's Memoirs* (New York: Harcourt, Brace & World, 1962), p. 213.

[19]*Shakespeare and Company,* pp. 81, 83.

[20]Turgenev letter to Konstantin Nikolaevich Leontiev, 3 October 1860. Edgar H. Lehrman, ed. *Turgenev's Letters: A Selection* (New York: Knopf, 1961), p. 11.

[21]New York: Scribners, 1929, p. 327.

[22]Barnet Braverman's unpublished letters are in the Sylvia Beach Collection, Princeton University Library. In her memoirs, Sylvia refers to him only as "Bernard B."

[23]*Shakespeare and Company,* p. 78.

[24]For copyright reasons, all Hemingway letters which have not previously been published must be paraphrased. The unpublished Hemingway letters to Sylvia Beach are at Princeton University Library. Sylvia Beach's letters to Ernest Hemingway are at the John F. Kennedy Library.

[25]In total sales of American titlés, according to bookshop ledgers, his books ranked second only to those of Eliot (and followed by Whitman, Stein, Poe, Pound and Cummings, and James). Hemingway's four

best-selling titles at the bookshop were *A Farewell to Arms, The Sun Also Rises, In Our Time,* and *Men Without Women.*

[26]Katherine Anne Porter, "Paris: A Little Incident in the Rue de l' Odeon," *Ladies Home Journal,* LXXXI (August 1964), p. 55.

[27]Hemingway read this either in *Life and Letters* (April 1934) or *The American Review* (June 1934). It was reprinted with shortened title as a chapter in *Men Without Art* (London: Cassell, 1934).

[28]*A Moveable Feast,* p. 109. Interestingly, Lewis' occasional remarks to others about Hemingway and his works in his letters of the 1940's are affirmative.

[29]The list is in the Sylvia Beach Collection. The most expensive was Eliot's *Selected Essays* at 56 francs.

[30]Francis Smith, "Hemingway Curses, Kisses, Reads at Sylvia Beach Literary Session," *Paris Herald Tribune,* 14 May 1937. Clipping in Sylvia Beach Collection. Interview with Gisèle Freund, Paris, August 1969. Carlos Baker, *Ernest Hemingway: A Life Story* (New York: Scribners, 1969), p. 312.

[31]*Shakespeare and Company,* pp. 219-220. Sylvia's version embellishes the facts when she asserts his company fired shots from the roof. In a copy of *Winner Take Nothing,* from which he had read "Fathers and Sons" in 1937, he added "Lu et approuve" and signed his name and the date 25 August 1944. Adrienne Monnier remembered the voice as that of Maurice Saillet and the day as "Saturday the 26th, the day of the assassination attempt on General de Gaulle." Her full account of this incident is found in *Les Gazettes d' Adrienne Monnier* (first published in *Fontaine,* 1945), reprinted in *The Very Rich Hours of Adrienne Monnier,* ed. Richard McDougall (New York: Scribners, 1976), pp. 413-417.

Shakespeare and Company's Borrower's
Cards for Ernest Hemingway[1]

Note: Following is an interpretation of all entries on Hemingway's
library cards, including identification of the books. All titles
were checked against shop ledgers of book purchases.

1925

Oct.	8	Upton Sinclair, *Mammonart* (Pasadena: Privately published, 1925)	b.b.[2]
	12	Gustave Flaubert, *Sentimental Education* (London: Nichols, 1898)	Oct. 27
	14	Joshua Slocum, *Sailing Alone Around the World* (New York: Century, 1900; London: Sampson, Low, 1900)	22
	14	Henry Major Tomlinson, *The Sea and the Jungle* (London: Duckworth, 1912; New York: Dutton, 1913)	22

	22	Ivan Turgenev, *A Lear of the Steppes*[3]	27
	22	Ivan Turgenev, *A Sportsman's Sketches,* Vol. 2	Nov. 16
	25	Ivan Turgenev, *The Torrents of Spring*	16
Nov.	9	Marie Adelaide (Belloc) Lowndes, *Bread of Deceit* (London: Hutchinson, 1925)	24
	16	Hermann Alexander, Graf von Keyserling, *The Travel Diary of a Philosopher,* 2 vols. (London: Cape, 1925)	24
	23	Donald Ogden Stewart, *A Parody Outline of History* (New York: Doran, 1921)	Dec. 10
	24	Violet Hunt, *More Tales of the Uneasy* (London: Heinemann, 1925)	1
	28	Edward Phillips Oppenheim, *The Terrible Hobby of Sir Joseph Londe, Bart.* (London: Hodder & Stoughton, 1921)	1
Dec.	1	Marie Henri Beyle (de Stendhal), *The Charterhouse of Parma,* 2 vols. (New York: Boni & Liveright, 1925)	10
	10	Thomas Mann, *Buddenbrooks,* 2 vols. (London: Secker, 1924)	Jan. 19
	10	Knut Hamsun, *Children of the Age* (New York: Knopf, 1924)	Apr. 13
	10	Ivan Turgenev, *A House of Gentlefolk*	Feb. 2
	10	Ivan Turgenev, *Fathers and Children*	Jan. 19

1926

Jan.	28	Joseph Collins, *The Doctor Looks at Literature* (London: Allen & Unwin, 1923)	Feb.	2
Jan.	30	Ernest Hemingway, *In Our Time*/new copy/bought		
	30	*Bullfighting*[4]	Jan.	30
Mar.	29	Edward J. O'Brien (ed.), *The Best Short Stories of 1925* (Boston: Small, Maynard, 1926)	May	10
Apr.	1	Violet Hunt, *The Flurried Years* (London: Hurst & Blackett, 1926)	Apr.	13
	11	Aldous Huxley, *Along the Road* (London: Doran, 1925)		24
	13	André Gide, *Strait Is the Gate* (London: Jarrolds, 1924)		24
	17	Carl Sandburg, *Selected Poems*[5] (London: Cape, 1926)		24
	21	Ralph Hale Mottram, *The Crime at Vanderlynden's* (New York: Dial, 1926; London: Chatto & Windus, 1926)	b.b.	
	26	*Salve* [crossed out] *Vale*[6]	b.b.	
	26	William Butler Yeats, *Early Poems and Stories* (New York, London: Macmillan, 1925)	b.b.	
	29	Joseph Conrad, *An Outcast of the Islands* (London: Appleton, 1896)	b.b.	
May	4	James Gibbons Huneker, *Egoists; a Book of Supermen* (New York: Scribners, 1909; London: Laurie, 1909)	May	10
	4	James Gibbons Huneker, *Steeplejack*, Vol. II (New York: Scribners, 1921)		10
	4	William Henry Hudson, *Far Away and Long Ago* (New York: Dutton, 1918; London: Dent, 1918)	Oct.	1
	5	Friedrich Nietzsche, *Thus Spake Zarathustra* London: Reeves, 1900)	Sep.	13
	10	Ivan Turgenev, *Knock, Knock, Knock and Other Stories*	Nov.	2
	10	Ivan Turgenev, *The Two Friends and Other Stories*	Sep.	10
	10	Ivan Turgenev, *On the Eve*		10
	14	*Problems of Philosophy*[7] (July 3rd forwarded letter and little review to Madrid, Thomas Cook)		13
Aug.	26	Ford Madox Ford, *A Mirror to France* (New York: Boni, 1926; London: Duckworth, 1926)		10
Sep.	10	Ivan Turgenev, *A Sportsman's Sketches*	Oct.	1
	10	Ambroise Vollard, *Paul Cézanne* (Paris, 1914; London: Brentano's, 1924)		1
	25	*New Republic* (Sep. 15)		1
Oct.	1	Giovani Verga, *Mastro-Don Gesualdo*, translated by D.H. Lawrence (London: Cape, 1925) Subscription due since March 23, 1926	11	

11 *Saturday Review* to March 23, 1927 = 150 frs.
11 Robert Sherard, *The Life, Work and Evil Fate of Guy de Maupassant* (New York: Laurie, 1926; London: Brentano's, 1926) — b.b.
11 Alexander McDannald (ed.), *The Americana Annual;* an encyclopedia of current events. 1926 (New York: Americana, 1926) — b.b.
29 Roy Chapman Andrews, *On the Trail of Ancient Man* (New York, London: Putnam, 1926) — Feb. 28

Nov. 4 Gertrude Stein, *Composition as Explanation* (London: Hogarth Press, 1926) — 28
18 David Garnett, *The Sailor's Return* (London: Chatto & Windus, 1925)

Dec. 16 Julius Meier-Graefe, *The Spanish Journey* (London: Cape, 1926) — Mar. 12

1927

brought back Virginia Woolf, *The Common Reader* (London: Hogarth Press, 1925) — Feb. 28
Feb. 17 [indecipherable] paid
Mar. 12 David Garnett, *Go She Must!* (London: Chatto & Windus, 1927) — Mar. 12
Apr. 23 Alan Lawson Maycock, *The Inquisition from its Establishment to the Great Schism* (London: Constable, 1926) — b.b.
May 31 St. John Ervine, *Parnell* (London: Bean, 1925)
Jun. 11 Ring Lardner, *The Story of a Wonder Man* (New York: Scribners, 1927) — Jun. 13
Sun Also Rises 42+4.80 = 46.80 paid [crossed out]
11 *Transition*
ask Hemingway about "Grandmother"
Sep. 20 Glenway Wescott, *The Grandmothers* (New York & London: Harper, 1927) — Oct. 18
20 *Aloysius Horn* [crossed out] [no author] (London: Cape, 1927)
Oct. 18 Wyndham Lewis, *Time and Western Man* (London: Chatto & Windus, 1927) — 19
19 **Lady Cynthia Asquith (ed.), *The Black Cap; new stories of murder and mystery* (London: Hutchinson, 1927)** — 25
25 Phineas Taylor Barnum, *Barnum's Own Story* (New York: Viking, 1927) — Nov. 15
25 Katherine Mayo, *Mother India* (London: Cape, 1927) — 15
Nov. 3 *Sun Also Rises* 42 one [crossed out]
14 *Dial* Nov. — Dec. 7
14 Marie Adelaide (Belloc) Lowndes, *The Story of Ivy* (London: Heinemann, 1927) — Nov. 26
23 Walton Hall Smith, *Shadow River,* (Boston, New

York: Houghton Mifflin, 1927; London: Allen &
Unwin, 1928)   Dec.   7

26   Osbert Sitwell, *Before the Bombardment* (New York:
Doran, 1926; London: Duckworth, 1926)   7

?   **Thornton Wilder, *The Bridge of San Luis Rey* (New**
York: Boni, 1927; London: Longmans, 1927)   7

Dec.   7   Feodor Dostoyevsky, *The Gambler and Other Stories* Feb. 13
(London: Heinemann, 1917)

7   Feodor Dostoyevsky, *The Insulted and Injured*
(London: Macmillan, 1915)   Feb. 13

7   Henry Major Tomlinson, *Gallions Reach* (London:
Heinemann, 1927)   6

1928

Feb.   4   Robert Graves, *Lawrence and the Arabs* (London:
Cape, 1927) Post card, Feb. 21.   Feb. 24

9   Ivan Turgenev, *The Torrents of Spring*   Mar.   3

11   Darrell Figgis, *Recollections of the Irish War* (Garden
City: Doubleday, Doran, 1927; London: Benn,
1927)   3

John Chartres Molony, *The Riddle of the Irish*
(London: Methuen, 1927)   Feb. 13

?   *Dial* Jan. 1928   13

13   Jakob Wassermann, *The World's Illusion*, 2 vols.
(New York: Harcourt, Brace, 1920)   28
(loancd 100 frs. Feb. 17) [crossed out]

24   Eugene O'Neill, *The Emperor Jones* (New York: Mar.   3
Boni & Liveright, 1921)

24   Sean O'Casey, *The Plough and the Stars* (New York
& London: Macmillan, 1926)   3

28   Thomas Mann, *The Magic Mountain*, 2 vols. (New
York & London: Knopf, 1927)   b.b.

Mar.   3   Harry Golding (ed.), *The Wonder Book of the Wild*
(London: Ward, Lock, 1924)   Mar.   8

8   Emil Ludwig, *Genius and Character*, translated by
Kenneth Burke (London: Cape, 1927)   *8

1929

Sylvia Beach received cheque for 350 frs. for E.H.'s
account.

Apr.   23   *Dial* Dec. 1928   *

23   Lord Alfred Bruce Douglas, *The Autobiography of
Lord Alfred Douglas* (London: Secker, 1929)   May 16

26   Matthew Josephson, *Zola and His Time* (New York:
Macaulay, 1928; London: Gollancz, 1929)   14

26   Louis Gosselin (pseud. G. Lenotre), *The Guillotine
and Its Servants* (London: Hutchinson, 1929)   14

26   *Dial* Jan. 1929   *

May 16 George Gordon Coulton (ed.), *Life in the Middle Ages* (Cambridge: Cambridge University Press, 1928-1930) Vol. II: *Chronicles, Science and Art* (1929); vol. III: *Men and Manners* (1929)   b.b.

    21 Anna Dostoevsky, *The Diary of Dostoyevsky's Wife* (London: Gollancz, 1928; New York: Macmillan, 1928)   Jul. 2

Jun. 1 Four parcels/signed sheets/by regular post= 42.80

    3 Burton Rascoe, *A Bookman's Daybook* (New York: Liveright, 1929)   Jun. 5

    5 Gertrude Stein, *Three Lives* (London & New York: Lane, 1920)   *

    21 Dmitrii Svyatopolk-Mirskii, *Contemporary Russian Literature, 1881-1925* (New York: Knopf, 1926)   *

    24 Samuel Beach Chester, *Round the Green Cloth* (London: Paul, 1928)   probably   b.b.

    29 William Aitken Beaverbrook, *Politicians and the War, 1914-1926* (London: Butterworth, 1928)   Jul 2

Aug 22 Sent *Torrents of Spring* see letter[9]
        gave *Sun Also Rises* and *In Our Time* to A. Maurois

Scp. 19 D.H. Lawrence, *Lady Chatterley's Lover* (Florence: Privately published, 1928)   Sep. 27

    19 Ludwig Renn, *War* (New York: Dodd,Mead, 1929; London: Secker, 1929)   27

    19 *This Quarter* No. 5   27

    25 *Adventures of Sir W. Raleigh*[10]   Oct. 19

    27 Ivan Turgenev, *On the Eve*   *

    27 Ivan Turgenev, *A Sportsman's Sketches*   *

    27 Feodor Dostoyevsky, *The Idiot* (London: Heinemann, 1913), brought by a gentleman Jan. 23   *

Oct. 11 Leon Gozlan, *Balzac in Slippers* (New York: McBride, 1929)   Oct. 19

Nov. 7 To his credit   29 frs.
        —regular postage   5.40
                      —————
                      23.60

    20 George Jennison, *Natural History, Animals* (London: Black, 1927) 87.50

    20 Jakob Grimm, *Fairy Tales* (London: Collins, 1929) 35.

    20 Andrew Lang (ed.), *Yellow Fairy Book* (London: Longmans, Green, 1929) 35.

    20 Johann Wyss, *Swiss Family Robinson* (Philadelphia: Winston, 1929) 35.
                  192.50
                   23.60
                  —————
    23 Paid[11]—108.90

1931

Sep.   7   D.H. Lawrence, *The Virgin and the Gipsy* (New
                 York: Knopf, 1930)   Sep. 23
          7   *Pagany*[12]   23

1933

Nov.   10   Margaret Barton and Osbert Sitwell (eds.), *Sober
                 Truth* (London: Duckworth, 1930)   Nov. 21
         10   Osbert Sitwell, *Discussions on Travel, Art and Life*
                 (New York: Doran, 1925; London: Richards,
                 1925)   21
         10   Eric Linklater, *The Men of Ness* (London: Cape,
                 1932)   21
         10   W.H. Auden, *The Orators* (London: Faber & Faber,
                 1932) 33frs. paid Nov 21

1937

May   7   Rudyard Kipling, *Something of Myself* (Garden
                 City: Doubleday, Doran, 1937; London:
                 Macmillan, 1937)
          7   John Lehmann (ed.), *New Writing*, No. 1, Spring,
                 1936 London.
          7   John Lehmann (ed.), *New Writing*, No. 2, autumn,
                 1936 London.

1938

Dec.   Borrowed *New Masses* and other papers returned
March   Sylvia Beach sent off on Queen Mary Hemingway's
                 play to Maxwell E. Perkins, Scribner's, 547 5th
                 Ave., N.Y. 1st class mail letter post, sealed   18.00
Mar.   26   Hemingway gave Adrienne Monnier $50.00
                 changed at 32 francs   1600
                 he bought from Adrienne Monnier   636
                                  BALANCE   964
Mar.   27   Bought at Shakespeare and Company   113
                                                                              851
                 Sylvia Beach refunded   787
                 Credit Ernest Hemingway   64
                 less reviews (forgot to charge?)
Sep.   7   Elliot Paul, *The Life and Death of a Spanish Town*
                 (New York: Random House, 1937; London: Gone
                 Davis, 1937)
          7   Jonathan Latimer, *The Dead Don't Care* (Garden
                 City: Doubleday, Doran, 1938; London: Sep. 10
                 Methuen, 1938)
         10   Sent instead Margaret Halsey, *With Malice Toward
                 Some* (New York: Simon & Schuster, 1938;
                 London: Hamilton, 1938) for library

30 George Orwell, *Homage to Catalonia* (London:
        Secker & Warburg, 1938)

Oct.   26   Nine *Saturday Reviews*

Nov.   Leonard Ross, *The Education of H*Y*M*A*N
        K*A*P*L*A*N (New York: Harcourt, Brace,
        1937; London: Constable, 1937)*

28   Five copies of *The Fifth Column*, arrived from Paris
        branch Brentano's (!?) to replace 5 copies Sylvia
        Beach gave to Ernest Hemingway.

Point Loma College

Footnotes for Borrower's Cards

[1]Although Hemingway recalls in *A Moveable Feast* his first borrowing on December 28, 1921, the cards from that date to 8 October 1925 have been lost. Only titles are recorded on the borrower's cards, with date of borrowing to the left and date of return to the right. Most of the titles and authors can be confirmed by the lists of Sylvia Beach's purchases from publishers and bookstores. Most were English editions, although for some titles it is impossible to determine whether they are New York or London editions. Titles recorded, usually without first articles, are quite reliable.

[2]The abbreviation b.b. could represent 'brought back' or 'bought book.' Sylvia Beach's financial records, which show her daily sales of books, have no evidence that the b.b. titles were purchased. The 30 January 1926 purchase of *In Our Time*, in which she writes "bought" is in the records. Her use of the words "brought back" on 28 February 1927 and "brought by" on 27 September 1929 further indicate that the books in question were returned, not purchased.

[3]The titles by Ivan Turgenev are the 1916 editions published by Heinemann with translations by Constance Garnet, whom Hemingway preferred.

[4]There is no record for the purchase of this book. It is probably a title by Thomas Wallace Jones (Cincinnati, 1904). Jones' book is small and illustrated, which would explain the one-day borrowing time.

[5]Although the card reads "collected," the book (which she purchased from Jonathan Cape) is entitled *Selected Poems*.

[6]These two words are written in different hands. The title or titles are not identifiable. The only book with a similar title purchased by Beach was A. E.'s *Vale and Other Poems*, which was not published until 1931.

[7]This could be one of several books by this title including Gustavus Watts Cunningham's *Problems of Philosophy* (New York: Holt, 1924; London: Harrap, 1925) or Bertrand Russell's *Problems of Philosophy* (London: Williams & Norgate, 1912).

[8]These books are listed on a "Please Return" card, which accompanies a drawing of William Shakespeare pulling out his hair. Except for *The Idiot*, these books were probably not returned.

[9]*Torrents of Spring* sent to Owen Wister (Ernest Hemingway letter to Sylvia Beach, 18 August 1928).

[10]No book with this title has been located. Possibly it is Milton Waldman's *Sir Walter Raleigh* (London: Lane, 1928).

[11]This price, total for the four children's books, is crossed out.

[12]Probably Volume 2 (March 1931).

The Connable residence.

RICHARD WINSLOW

GREG AND HEMMY:
WRITING FOR THE
Toronto Star IN 1920

After Christmas [1919], when I was still writing for the Saturday Evening Post and had twenty dollars left of my salary, I was promised a job at the pump factory by an old friend, John McConnell, and was looking forward to laying off writing for the magazines for a time when I was offered a job or rather a position as companion and good influence to the not too forward in his studies son of rich parents living in Toronto, Canada. I met this boys mother in Petoskey through Dutch Paltrop [Pailthorp] who was at that time reading law in his fathers law office, a warm and pleasant place to which I used. . . . .[1]

In this fragment, Ernest Hemingway recalled his opportunity to live in Toronto. He was then twenty years old. Unable to place his stories, and still very unsettled, Hemingway quickly accepted Ralph Connable's invitation to spend the winter in Canada as a companion for his son.

Ralph, Jr., the son, was a year younger than Ernest and lame since birth; while the rest of the family wintered in Florida, Hemingway could accompany the boy around the city at sports and cultural events. With an estimated population of 560,000 in 1920, Toronto offered Ernest much more to do than remaining all winter in the closed-down summer resort of Petoskey, Michigan. After a brief Christmas visit with his family, he left Chicago by train on 8 January 1920. Ralph Connable furnished the money for his employee's transportation.[2]

A successful fifty-four-year-old businessman, Ralph Connable was a popular figure around town. Originally from Chicago and a summer resident of Petoskey, Connable moved to Toronto in 1912 to head the Canadian division of F. W. Woolworth. Well known for his generous nature and practical jokes, Connable welcomed Hemingway to his comfortable mansion at 153 Lyndhurst Avenue, in the fashionable "Hill" section of the city. Ernest always called him "Uncle Ralph."[3]

For the first few days, Hemingway enjoyed his new home, skated on a makeshift hockey rink, and played billiards in the basement. With young Ralph, Ernest explored the city on the way to Massey Hall and the Mutual Street Arena Gardens for concerts and boxing matches. The boys often stopped by the YMCA, to see Dutch Pailthorp, now working for Connable at his Woolworth store.

Within a week, Hemingway became restless. Before Connable left for Palm Beach, Ernest kept asking about working for the *Toronto Star,* the city's leading newspaper. With his many contacts, Connable was glad to help. One January afternoon he took Hemingway to the Star Building at 18-20 King Street West in downtown Toronto.

After being introduced to a few people, Hemingway was finally directed to the small office of Gregory Clark, the features editor of the *Toronto Star Weekly.* With Clark was the paper's cartoonist, James L. Frise. Clark remembers:

> The door of our dingy little room opened and there stood a dark, tall, gangling boy in short leather coat and carrying a walking stick.
> We stared at the kid in the doorway, for apart from being an incongruous figure in his cap and carrying his walking stick, he was obviously suffering from great stress and strain.[4]

There was no chair for their unexpected visitor. "He needed to sit. He was almost limp with nervousness." Clark invited him to rest on an "old rusty radiator." The boy's heavy boots creaked on the floor. After mentioning his previous work on the *Kansas City Star,* Hemingway began hinting he wanted a job. Believing him to be "an utter fraud," Clark's early impressions

> were of a curiously inarticulate and puzzled youth whom I mistook for the characteristic young hanger-on we had around newspaper offices such as the Weekly.[5]

Greg Clark, as he has always been known, almost seemed destined to become a newspaperman. Born in Toronto in 1892, he joined the *Star* "through the back door" in 1911, as he still insists, because his

father was editor-in-chief. Back from the fighting in France during
World War I, where he had been a major in the infantry, Clark was a
married man with responsibilities at home and on the paper.

"Don't lend him any money, Jimmie," he told Frise after
Hemingway had left. "He'll borrow five bucks off you, and that's
the last you'll ever see of him."[6] Jimmie, however, was the "first to
appreciate the young Yank"; they had common interests and Clark
recalls that Hemingway "hung around Jimmie's and my room
every day."[7] At the end of a week, Clark finally suggested to J.
Herbert Cranston, editor of the *Star Weekly*, that "Hemmy," as they
now called him, be given a job.

These chance occurrences thus determined Hemingway's
association with the paper for the next four years. Once Clark saw
his new friend's obvious sincerity and energy, Greg supplied him
with tips for stories and "wrangled him a small space rate job or
two. . . ."[8] Himself a veteran of the war, Greg sensed this job would
provide a much needed outled for Hemingway.

> How he sweat, it was all over his lips. Hemmy had veal-like eyes,
> the large, dark, rolling eyes of a bull calf, and couldn't pronounce
> certain words. He was nervous. I had been in the war and recognized
> it. I think because of his speech impediment he was trying to
> overcompensate.[9]

Sympathetic to the boy's problems, Clark took into account
Ralph Connable's solemn remark, "What can you do with a guy
like that, a cripple."[10] But along with the job's therapeutic
importance, Clark sensed the making of a newspaperman:

> Now that I have read the family history, etc., the idea grows in my
> mind that the young Hemmy Jimmie and I knew was not so much
> inarticulate and puzzled, as a kid realizing in rising excitement that
> he had a chance to break into newspaper writing in an up and
> coming outfit and not knowing how to go about it. At that stage, Feb.
> 1920, I was the little Lord Fauntleroy of the Weekly, dashing off copy
> in all directions, and Hemmy was watching me as much as anybody
> to learn the trick of pleasing Cranston, who was just having it dawn
> on him that he had a growing publication on his hands, full of
> prospects it had never had prior to 1919. . . .[11]

Writing for Cranston, as Hemingway was well aware, would be
an exciting experience. The *Star's* reputation as the best newspaper
in the country was known throughout Canada and the United
States. Thousands of copies were shipped to Montreal, Windsor,
and to American readers in Detroit, Buffalo, and Chicago. During
January 1920, the *Star Weekly*, the Saturday weekend paper,

enjoyed a circulation of 105,469 copies; the daily *Star* trailed with 93,170. Attracting the best talent with many free-lance contributors, Cranston stressed human-interest features.

At Clark's suggestion, Ernest wrote during February a story about art collecting among Toronto's social set. Cranston paid $5 for it.[12] His writing attracted attention from the start. Hemingway's second article, "Taking a Chance for a Free Shave,"[13] brought him recognition from Cranston and other reporters. Proud of his work, he cut out his story from the page and placed it in his wallet. Eager to impress new acquaintances, Hemingway gladly fished out the clipping to show them.[14]

His next contribution, "Sporting Mayor at Boxing Bouts,"[15] presenting a satirical portrait of Mayor Tommy Church, caught the eye of John Bone, the managing editor. Bone immediately recognized a hot, controversial article. Ernest's humorous sketch of Toronto's political boss would delight the paper's readers.[16]

Hemingway's articles were now bringing a penny a word, a raise from the half cent he was previously earning as a free-lancer. As the story goes, Clark once told him, "You'll never get anywhere with all those damned little short sentences."[17] Greg, however, corrects this legend, saying. "That's not it at all. What I was trying to tell Hemmy was how to write for the *Star*, the way Cranston wanted it."[18]

Ernest, in turn, had some advice for Greg. Always carrying a copy of Sherwood Anderson's *Winesburg, Ohio*, in his pocket, Hemingway urged Greg repeatedly to read it. "I haven't to this day," Greg remarks.[19]

Ernest's kiddish antics around the Star offices were often taxing. "Hemmy was a posturer, the biggest one in the world," Clark remembers. "He was always throwing punches, going through boxing stances. He wasn't any good. Heavy on his feet and a sucker for a short left." The sound of Hemingway's heavy boots striking the floor indicated to others it could be nobody else. "Except for not having a beard, you would call him a hippy today. He was broke and needed the job."[20]

There was no posturing, however, about his wanting to write; the young Yank worked diligently. From February until mid-May, 1920, Hemingway contributed twelve articles to the *Weekly*, and one piece to the daily *Star*. Concentrating on the topics he knew best, he wrote about boxing, fishing, and the veterans. Until the ice melted, he was releasing his pent-up yearnings by writing articles such as "Are You All Set for Trout?" and "Fishing for Trout in a Sporting Way."[21] He often mentioned his high school friend, Jack Pentecost, who appears as Jacques Pentecost, "an old-time north shore fisher," or as Jock. Cranston had no idea who Pentecost was; it amused Ernest to give his buddy different disguises. Soon everyone on the *Star* considered Hemingway an expert on camping and trout fishing.[22]

An extant typescript and an ink manuscript indicate Hemingway's patience for revision and the painstaking accuracy he strived for in his work. On a four-by-six notecard, he typed out a rough draft, "Slacker is a dead word," which he incorporated into a March contribution.[23]

For another piece, eventually titled "Lieutenants' Mustaches the Only Permanent Thing We Got Out of War,"[24] he penned a three-page sketch. Bill and Jack are two "returned boys," Canadian slang for veterans back from France. They watch a building being demolished, brick by brick, on King Street. Everything rankles them, the slow progress of the demolition work, the quality and operation of the streetcars, and women shopping in the department stores. Coming back to observe such incompetence and trifles, Bill and Jack quickly conclude that the war was fought for nothing.[25]

"He was avid to hear me talk of World War I," Clark writes.

> I never had such an audience. His dark eyes would blaze as I took him over the top and through the barrages and out on patrol.[26]

The slang of the discharged Canadian soldier is caught so accurately that Hemingway obviously listened closely to Greg. The pen sketch ends:

> . . . We ain't got nothing out of this war. What are you doing now, Jack?"
> 'Resting up for the next war, Bill!'[27]

However, Hemingway may have felt on second thought that this ending was too cynical, or perhaps the phrase had already become hackneyed. Having revised and expanded his story, he submitted his final version to Cranston before sending it to the composing room. In the final version two vets shout to one another as they stand on the rear platform of a crowded streetcar.

> 'Who was he?' Jack shouted back.
> 'Used to be a batman to the R. T. O. at Boulogne,' grunted Bill, as a milling passenger stepped on his pet corn.[28]

Jack and Bill, barely developed in this vignette, anticipate Hemingway's early fiction with their sharp dialogue and disgruntled attitude. Bill is disgusted at a "batman," an officer's servant, who was going out with his sister. A Railway Transport

Officer, or R. T. O., was considered to be a bombproofer by frontline
troops, especially if he were stationed at the channel port of
Boulogne. There he would be "just as far as he could get from the
firing-line and still be able to boast that he was serving overseas."
His batman, accordingly, "would be even lower in the military
scale, a lackey quite beneath contempt."[29]

By now Hemingway was a familiar figure around the *Star*.
Jimmie Frise took him skiing that first winter. These outings
developed into a life-long hobby. In keeping with his outdoor tastes,
Hemingway usually appeared in the newspaper offices with the
coming of warm weather in

> a vivid vermillion red shirt, a sport shirt, and a black tie. He wore
> sport shirts all the time, which was something different in those days.
> He said he couldn't stand a collar button rubbing his Adam's apple.
> It drove him crazy.[30]

The Connables returned home in the spring. During late April,
Ernest discovered he had a scoop within the household. Chatting
with Uncle Ralph, he learned that Connable had been preparing a
report for Ottawa about co-ordinating all the purchasing
departments of the country. Hemingway wrote an excellent article,
"Buying Commission Would Cut Out Waste." This story appeared
in the *Star* on 26 April. The next day, the *Toronto Globe*, a rival
paper, excerpted a lengthy paragraph from Hemingway's article for
its lead editorial, "A National Purchasing Board." Joseph E.
Atkinson, the *Star's* owner, congratulated Hemingway. Ernest was
greatly pleased. To exert influence on governmental policy was
quite a thrill for a youth, new to the country, who was considering a
factory job a few months before.[31]

With the Connables back and his duties with young Ralph almost
over, Ernest decided to spend still another summer in the Michigan
woods. Shortly before he left, Hemingway yearned to do what he
had been writing about all winter, to go fishing. Greg Clark, an
ardent sportsman, needed no coaxing. One of his favorite places was
the fast-flowing Credit River, fifteen miles west of Toronto.

> I took him fishing on the Credit; it was in early May. We went after
> Nipigon trout. He had a split-bamboo fishing rod his father had
> given him. He knew how to cast, and got two or three eight-to-ten
> pound trout. I never took him bass fishing, never was in a canoe with
> him.[32]

During the second week in May, Hemingway boarded the train for
Windsor and on to Chicago.

The Selby Hotel, home of the Hemingways during August 1923.

The four months Hemingway spent in Toronto in 1920 were critical at this stage of his career. He might have chucked writing, simply relaxing at the Connable home, content to be nothing more than a companion. But Ernest grasped his chance; he would not quit. Working as a professional for the first time in two years, he was competing with the best journalists in Canada.

After a stint as the *Star's* roving foreign correspondent in Europe, Hemingway returned to Toronto during the summer of 1923. Greg welcomed him back to "the land of trouts and deers and spaces." With Hemingway was his pregnant wife, Hadley. Immediately checking into an old hotel, the Selby, in a decaying section of the city at "the end of August," the Hemingways began apartment-hunting. (The Selby is mentioned as "the Shelby," boxer Jack Brennan's hotel in "Fifty Grand.") Soon Clark found them a place at 1599 Bathurst Street, not far from the Connable home.[33]

"We all loved Hadley," Greg says. "She was wonderful, had lovely red hair, and could play the piano beautifully." After Hemingway's son was born in October,

> my wife taught Hadley how to bathe the baby. But by that time, he was more with younger friends on the Star, Mary Lowery Ross, [Morley] Callaghan, and Jimmie Cowan, etc. Though I was only eight years or so older than he, there was an obvious generation gap between him and me.[34]

Perhaps Hemingway could repeat his idyllic times of 1920. At first all seemed well, renewing his friendship with Jimmie Frise, whom Hemingway called "the best fellow I know,"[35] and earning $75 a week "on staff." A dictatorial new boss, however, along with the temporary loss of his byline, and grueling out-of-town assignments soon convinced him that returning was a big mistake. "After Paris, Hemingway thought Toronto was a sad place, a hick town," remembered one reporter. "Naturally, he didn't like the place."[36]

After several unhappy months, Hemingway resigned. To switch to another newspaper and stay on in Toronto was not for him. Secretly moving his belongings out of his Bathurst Street residence, Hemingway broke his lease. David Garfield, who remembered Hemingway as a tenant in his father's apartment building, "wishes the writer never had come near the place." "When he died" Garfield said, "he still owed us three months' rent."[37]

On 12 January 1924, Hemingway was back, four years to the month from his initial happy arrival, at Toronto's Grand Central Station, waiting to catch a train. This time, however, he was unemployed with a wife and baby.

For the rest of his life he savored his pleasant times with the Connables and "the wonderful dry cold of the Toronto winter. . . ."[38] "I never enjoyed myself so much," he once wrote to Cranston, "as working under you and with Greg Clark and Jimmy Frise."[39]

University of Pennsylvania

---

[1]"We never caught them as big after the war . . ." Pencil, p. 4, Manuscript fragment. Item 820, Ernest Hemingway Papers, John F. Kennedy Library, Federal Records Center, Waltham, Massachusetts. The author appreciates the assistance of Jo August, Curator of the Hemingway Papers, in locating valuable sources. For permission to quote directly from the Papers, he thanks Mary Welsh Hemingway.

Hemingway's statement about writing for the *Saturday Evening Post* is somewhat misleading. Although he was at this time trying to place his stories with various magazines, he was not on staff and never sold anything to the *Post*.

[2]Standard published books and articles for Hemingway's life and work in Toronto during 1920 include: Carlos Baker, *Ernest Hemingway: A Life Story* (New York, Scribners, 1969), pp. 66-70, 115-122, 575, 582-583; Charles A. Fenton, *The Apprenticeship of Ernest Hemingway* (New York: Viking, 1954), pp. 74-95, 242-263, 272-274, 286-290; J[ames] H[erbert] Cranston, *Ink on My Fingers* (Toronto: Ryerson Press, 1953), Chapter 27 "His Hero Was a Matador," pp. 107-110; Roy Greenaway, *The News Game* (Toronto, Vancouver: Clarke, Irwin, 1966), pp. 20-21; Ross Harkness, *J. E. Atkinson of the Star* (Toronto: University of Toronto Press, 1963), pp. 163-166; Madelaine Hemingway Miller, *Ernie: Hemingway's Sister "Sunny" Remembers* (New York: Crown, 1975), pp. 95-96; Marcelline Hemingway Sanford, *At the Hemingways: A Family Portrait* (Boston, Toronto: Little, Brown, 1962), pp. 200-201; Donald St. John, "Hemingway and the Girl Who Could Skate," *The Connecticut Review*, II (October 1968), 10-19.

[3]*Buffalo Evening News* (20 April 1939), 24; *Toronto Star* (19 April 1939), 35. Obituaries of Ralph Connable, Sr. *Toronto Star Weekly* (5 July 1924), 17, contains an excellent article by Gregory Clark, stressing Connable's love of practical jokes and kindly nature.

[4]"Hemingway Once Star Cub Reporter: Friends Recall Him," *Toronto Star* (3 July 1961), 1; Gregory Clark, "Work in Toronto Important to Hemingway Career," *Toronto Telegram* (3 July 1961), 23.

[5]*Ibid,*; Gregory Clark, personal interview with the author, Toronto, 4 March 1975, hereafter referred to as Clark interview; Gregory Clark, 4 Nov. 1974 letter, to the author, hereafter referred to as Clark letter; Gregory Clark, 28 May 1965, letter to William McGeary, Gregory Clark Folder, William L. McGeary Collection, *Toronto Star* Library, Toronto, Ontario. This collection consists of nine looseleaf notebooks, McGeary's typescripts of Hemingway's newspaper articles (1920-1924), appearing in the daily *Toronto Star*, and the *Toronto Star Weekly*, a Saturday edition, with excellent annotations. In addition, there are many folders of related newspaper and magazine clippings, Xeroxed pages from published books, and personal correspondence relating to Hemingwayana. As *Star* librarian during Hemingway's second (1923-1924) period in Toronto, McGeary had a "nodding acquaintance" with him. For permission to do extended

research and for every courtesy, the author is grateful to librarians Carol
Lindsay and Donald Swogle. The three above-mentioned sources
constitute much of the material for this essay.

[6]Gregory Clark, *May Your First Love Be Your Last and Other Stories*
(Markham, Ontario: Simon and Schuster of Canada, 1969), p. 12. An
excellent profile of Clark, by Frank Lowe, editor of the *Weekend Magazine*,
appears as an "Introduction," pp. 5-21. For another sketch on Clark, see
"Five Foot Two, Eyes of Blue," *Ink on My Fingers*, pp. 86-91; *The
Canadian Who's Who*, XII (1970-1972) (Toronto: Who's Who in Canadian
Publications, 1972), p. 196.

[7]Clark interview.

[8]*Toronto Telegram*, 3 July 1961, 23.

[9]Clark interview.

[10]*Ibid.*

[11]Gregory Clark, 28 May 1965, letter to McGeary, Gregory Clark Folder,
McGeary Collection.

[12]Ernest Hemingway, *The Wild Years*, ed., Gene Z. Hanrahan (New
York: Dell, 1962), pp. 15-16; Notebook 1, p. 4, McGeary Collection;
William McGeary, Toronto, 17 Dec. 1965, letter to L. H. Brague, New
York, McGeary Collection. McGeary refers to Cranston's office ledger to
establish exact amount of payment. "Circulating Pictures a New High-Art
Idea in Toronto," *Toronto Star Weekly*, 14 Feb. 1920, 7; Audre Hanneman,
Ernest Hemingway: A Comprehensive Bibliography (Princeton:
Princeton University Press, 1969), pp. 130-131, lists all the signed and
unsigned Hemingway articles written during his stay in Toronto in 1920.

Regarding possible "lost" Hemingway contributions, McGeary writes,
"The Cranston tally also includes some stories of which no trace can be
found in the printed pages of the *Star Weekly*. What happened here is
probably that the articles were bought and paid for on acceptance, the
practice at that time. But in the case of the missing MSS, they may have not
fitted into the meagre space jigsaw and, being elbowed aside by higher
priority material, perhaps lost their topicality before they could be used
and thus finally had to be killed unprinted. Or, if the overmatter was
running heavy, the type might have been buried in the composing-room
storage racks until, forgotten, it was covered with dust. Then in some spring
housecleaning flurry, it would get dumped into the hellbox with other
mouldy articles to make way for newer, fresher stories." Notebook 1, p. 4,
McGeary Collection.

[13]*Toronto Star Weekly*, 6 March 1920, 13.

[14]*Toronto Telegram*, 17 June 1967, 64.

[15]*Toronto Star Weekly* 13 March 1920, 10.

[16]Clark interview; *Toronto Telegram* 3 July 1961, 23.

[17]*Ernest Hemingway: A Life Story*, p. 68; John Robert Colombo, ed.,
Colombo's Canadian Quotations (Edmunton: Hurtig, 1974), pp. 113-114;
Clark interview.

[18]Clark interview.

[19]*Ibid.*

[20]*Ibid.*

[21]*Toronto Star Weekly*, 10 April 1920, 11; 24 April 1920, 13.

[22]*Ernie*, p. 96.

[23]"Slacker is a dead word. . ." Item 699, typescript, no corrections, 2
pp., Hemingway Papers; re-titled "How to be Popular in Peace Though a
Slacker in War," *Toronto Star Weekly*, 13 March 1920, 11.

[24]*Toronto Star Weekly*, 10 April 1920, 17.

[25]"Two Returned Men Stood Looking. . ." Item 787, ink manuscript, 3 pp., Hemingway Papers.

[26]*Toronto Telegram*, 3 July 1961, 23.

[27]Item 787, p. 3, Hemingway Papers.

[28]*Toronto Star Weekly*, 10 April 1920, 7.

[29]Notebook 1, p. 52, McGeary Collection.

[30]Clark letter; Roy Greenaway, Toronto, 31 Aug. 1962, letter to McGeary, Roy Greenaway Folder, McGeary Collection.

[31]*Ernie*, p. 96; *Toronto Star*, 26 April 1920, 3, excerpted in the *Toronto Globe*, 27 April 1920, 6.

[32]Clark interview.

[33]Hadley Scott Mowrer, Chocorua, New Hampshire, 23 Nov. 1963, filled out questionnaire and letter to McGeary, Hadley Mowrer Folder, McGeary Collection. For the observation about the "Shelby" Hotel, mentioned in "Fifty Grand," the author is indebted to Dr. Raymond W. Kearney.

[34]Clark interview and letter.

[35]*Ernest Hemingway: A Life Story*, p. 120.

[36]Roy Greenaway, 31 Aug. 1963, letter to McGeary, Greenaway Folder, McGeary Collection.

[37]"Ernest Hemingway Slept Here. . . Or Was It Here?" *Toronto Star* (23 May 1963), 7.

[38]Ernest Hemingway, 17 Feb. 1953, letter to Dorothy Connable, Dorothy Connable Folder, McGeary Collection. The letter is Dorothy Connable's own typescript of Hemingway's original letter.

[39]*Ink on My Fingers*, p. 110, excerpts from a Hemingway letter to Cranston.

DICK PENNER

THE FIRST NICK ADAMS STORY

"Indian Camp" was a first for Hemingway in several respects: it was the first Nick Adams story from the standpoint of Nick's probable age, the first story in Hemingway's first collection of short stories, *In Our Time*, which was also his first important book. "Indian Camp" has also been one of the most controversial stories with regard to critical interpretation. Four questions have been at issue: whether or not the story is a parable of a conflict between Anglo and Indian cultures, and the related question of the paternity of the Indian child; whether or not the story is an expose of Dr. Adams' professional ineptness and personal insensitivity, and the correlative question of the meaning of the experience to Nick. Much of the confusion can be eliminated by a careful reading of the story and of "Three Shots," Hemingway's original, deleted, opening of "Indian Camp."

The action of "Indian Camp" is fairly simple. Two Indians arrive at a camp where Nick, his father, and Uncle George are staying, and they ask Dr. Adams' help in delivering an Indian baby. The Indians row the party across the lake to the Indian village in two boats, Uncle George in the forward boat and Nick and his father in the second boat. Inside the Indian shanty, they find that the pregnant woman has been in labor for two days; the husband, who cut his foot seriously with an ax a few days before, is lying in the upper bunk of the bed in which his wife is to have her baby. Dr. Adams, without the aid of anesthetics or proper operating instruments, delivers the child by Caesarean section with a jack-knife, sewing up the incision with gut fishing leaders. Nick observes the operation and assists his father by holding the bowl into which the afterbirth is placed. Once the baby boy has been successfully delivered and the operation completed, Dr. Adams pulls back the quilt covering the father and finds that the man has slit his throat with a straight razor; the doctor tries but is unable to prevent his son from witnessing the suicide's body. On the way back to the fishing camp, Nick asks his father several questions about suicide and death. Following the discussion, Nick "felt quite sure that he would never die."[1]

The significance of the story has been the subject of some debate. It has been described by G. Thomas Tanselle as "a parable of the gradual supplanting of one culture by another" in which "the central character is actually the Indian father" and Uncle George is "a harbinger of the new order."[2] Kenneth Bernard, expanding on this theory, has asserted that Uncle George is the father of the Indian child inasmuch as he has given cigars to the two Indians who rowed the party across the lake, is bitten by the Indian woman who is giving birth, and disappears following the operation.[3] The George-is-the-father theory is not utterly impossible, but it is well to remember that offering cigars to others is a common courtesy when you are smoking one yourself, particularly if the others have just performed some service such as rowing your party across a lake, that delirious women in childbirth are apt to bite anyone, indiscriminately, and that there is nothing remarkable about a man wandering off by himself after having witnessed a Caesarean birth under primitive conditions topped off with a throat-slitting suicide. (Philip Young has put the whole issue in perspective by acknowledging publicly that *he* is the father of the Indian child.)[4]

Bernard's theory, however, is ultimately cultural rather than paternal in focus, with Dr. Adams as the central villain:

> The baby, a half breed, is thus a mixture of the two cultures. Nick's father is the cold, unfeeling midwife of this birth. Nick is not only recoiling from the crudity of the medical details, or from the life and death situation, but also from the cruelty of the cultural Caesarean, most represented by his father's comments, "But her screams are not important." Those screams are the screams of the death of a civilization, a way of life. Nick's father's stoicism is the indifference of the newer civilization to the death of the older; progress can ignore human values.[5]

To interpret the doctor's comment in this way is to ignore the circumstances of the operation and to misread a typical Hemingway understatement. When Nick asks his father if he can't "give her something to make her stop screaming" the doctor's full reply is: "No. I haven't any anaesthetic . . . . But her screams are not important. I don't hear them because they are not important" (p. 17). What the abbreviated response means, obviously, is that as a surgeon, he must operate under adverse circumstances with a disciplined disregard for the screams (which he is powerless to alleviate), for the crucial task is to save the life of the mother and child, which Dr. Adams does.

The doctor comes in for more adverse criticism from another source. Joseph DeFalco, who has written a book on the hero in Hemingway's short stories, charges that "Certain revelations concerning the doctor's character emerge because of the method of delivery, for he has failed to bring along the proper equipment. The operation must be performed with a jack-knife and without benefit of an anesthetic."[6] He sees the primitive equipment and the doctor's failure to prevent the Indian father's suicide as evidence of the "ineptitude of the father as a man of science and representative of a rational and civilized world in his dealings with dark forces that lie outside his province."[7] DeFalco seems too eager to prove Dr. Adams' "ineptitude." First, no one in the room—Uncle George, the two Indians, the Indian midwife, or Nick—had anticipated that the father would slit his throat beneath the blankets, and it is certainly not a "failure" on the doctor's part that he did not prevent the clandestine suicide while he was engaged in performing a Caesarean delivery on a screaming woman. Second, DeFalco faults the doctor for not bringing along the "proper equipment," but it seems apparent that the doctor and his party are staying at a temporary camp at a remote location and that he had no reason to believe that he should bring along on a sporting outing equipment to perform a Caesarean delivery. The author states that the Indian "shoved off the *camp* boat" (italics mine) to row Uncle George across the lake, and Dr. Adams comments after the operation, "The nurse should be here from St. Ignace by noon and she'll bring everything we need" (p. 19).

Quite simply, the foregoing theories about Uncle George and the supposed clash between Anglo and Indian cultures are both barking up the wrong critical trees. As Philip Young has pointed out, "'Indian Camp' is Nick's story."[8] More specifically, as I intend to demonstrate, the story has two major and interconnected themes: the relation between Nick and his father, and Nick's awareness of death. This has been made clearer as a result of the publication of Hemingway's original opening for the story, entitled "Three Shots" in *The Nick Adams Stories.* Carlos Baker notes that what Hemingway "revealed to no one was that he had cut his story rigorously, omitting an entire preliminary episode covering eight longhand pages. This was the story of Nick Adams, a small boy afraid of the dark, firing off a rifle to bring his father and his uncle back from jacklight fishing in the lake."[9] The fragmentary episode reveals clearly that Nick's fear is of something more profound than the dark:

He was not afraid of anything definite as yet. But he was getting very afraid. Then suddenly he was afraid of dying. Just a few weeks before at home, in church, they had sung a hymn, "Some day the silver cord will break." While they were singing the hymn Nick had realized that some day he must die. It made him feel quite sick. It was the first time he had ever realized that he himself would have to die sometime.

. . . . .

Last night in the tent he had had the same fear. He never had it except at night. It was more a realization than a fear at first. But it was always on the edge of fear and became fear very quickly when it started. [10]

For the first time, a consciousness of his own mortality has come home to Nick. It is this consciousness, even more than sexual maturity, which demarcates a loss of childhood innocence, the voyage out of Edenic security into an adult recognition and, possibly, an acceptance of mortality. In the fragment "Three Shots," Nick recognizes his mortality, but he has not learned to cope with it. He simply escapes his fear by calling back his father with the agreed-upon signal: *"As soon as he began to be really frightened he took the rifle and poked the muzzle out the front of the tent and shot three times. The rifle kicked badly. He heard the shots rip off through the trees. As soon as he had fired the shots it was all right."* [11] It is "all right" because Nick knows his father's presence will enable him to escape the fear of death momentarily. When his father and an irate Uncle George return, Nick does not confront the fear directly, but rather makes up a story about an animal that "sounded like a cross between a fox and a wolf" frightening him. The following morning, Dr. Adams is concerned about his son's fear and tries to probe the source. He finds two basswood trees that might have made a frightening sound by rubbing together in the wind, and the following conversation ensues:

"Do you think that was what it was, Nick?" his father asked.
"Maybe," Nick said. He didn't want to think about it.
"You don't want to ever be frightened in the woods, Nick. There is nothing that can hurt you."
"Not even lightning?" Nick asked.
"No, not even lightning. If there is a thunder storm get out into the open. Or get under a beech tree. They're never struck."
"Never?" Nick asked.
"I never heard of one," said his father.
"Gee, I'm glad to know that about beech trees," Nick said.

The whole conversation is ironically inconsequential. Nick has been unable or unwilling to discuss his real fear—of death—with his father. This is in marked contrast to the conversation that Nick and Dr. Adams have after the suicidal death of the father in "Indian Camp." Following the discussion of lightning and beech trees, there is a quick transition to the following night when Nick is again undressing for bed. He hears his father talking with someone who has pulled up in a boat, and then his father tells him to get dressed. At this point, "Three Shots" ends and "Indian Camp" begins.

The failure of communication continues in "Indian Camp" as Nick asks his father about the purpose of the journey. Instead of stating straightforwardly that he is going to deliver a baby, Dr. Adams replies obliquely, "There is an Indian lady very sick." "Oh," Nick replies (p. 15). This exchange between Nick and his father establishes a pattern of non-communication that is to recur throughout the Nick Adams stories (most notably in "Fathers and Sons," in which Nick remembers the misinformation he has received from his father concerning sex). When they are inside the Indian cabin and the nature of the "sickness" is apparent to Nick, the following dialogue takes place:

> "This lady is going to have a baby, Nick," he said.
> "I know," said Nick.
> "You don't know," said his father. "Listen to me. What she is going through is called being in labor. The baby wants to be born and she wants it to be born. All her muscles are trying to get the baby born. That is what is happening when she screams" (p. 17).

Without being unduly harsh in judging Dr. Adams, it is fair to say that he is a better talker than he is a listener. He disregards his son's acknowledgment that he has some understanding of pregnancy and proceeds to give a simplified, authoritative lecture on the process of birth, breech fetus positioning, Caesarean delivery, and suturing. After completing the operation successfully, he is exhilarated and filled with pride, as is evidenced in his saying, "That's one for the medical journal, George `. . . Doing a Caesarian with a jack-knife and sewing it up with nine-foot, tapered gut leaders" (p. 19). It is only when he throws back the covers to see the "proud father" and discovers that the Indian has slit his throat from ear to ear that Dr. Adams finally attains some humility. He has been the real "proud father," so quick to supply the right answers that his son has been unwilling to speak honestly with him about his fear of death. After his confrontation with the unexpected suicide, Dr. Adams drops his pose of infallibility, saying to his son, "I'm terribly sorry I brought you along, Nickie . . . . It was an awful mess to put you through" (p. 20). This comment opens the way for one of the few real

communications between father and son that occur in any of the
Nick Adams stories.

When he and his father are rowing back across the lake, Nick no
longer hides his feelings concerning death behind fabricated stories
of "a cross between a fox and a wolf" but states them openly:

> "Why did he kill himself, Daddy?"
> "I don't know, Nick. He couldn't stand things, I guess."
> "Do many men kill themselves, Daddy?"
> "Not very many, Nick."
> "Do many women?"
> "Hardly ever."
> "Don't they ever?"
> "Oh, yes. They do sometimes."
> "Daddy?
> "Yes."
> "Where did Uncle George go?"
> "He'll turn up all right."
> "Is dying hard, Daddy?"
> "No, I think it's pretty easy, Nick. It all depends" (p. 21).

The story ends on a remarkably optimistic note:

> The sun was coming up over the hills. A bass jumped, making a
> circle in the water. Nick trailed his hand in the water. It felt warm in
> the sharp chill of the morning.
> In the early morning on the lake sitting in the stern of the boat with
> his father rowing, he felt quite sure that he would never die (p. 21).

For years the ending of the story had seemed to me simply, and
beautifully, appropriate in describing Nick's feelings. Ultimately,
however, the first doubting thoughts began to show their devils'
heads: Why should a young boy who is perhaps no more than eight
or nine years old feel that he "would never die" after having just
witnessed an agonizing, painful birth and a pointless suicide which
the author had described in these terms: "His throat had been cut
from ear to ear. The blood had flowed onto a pool where his body
sagged the bunk. His head rested on his left arm. The open razor lay
edge up in the blankets" (p. 20).

The published interpretations of the story's ending seem less
than satisfactory. Joseph DeFalco connects Nick's reassurance with
Dr. Adams "failure": "When his father fails to sustain the expected
role, Nick reverts to infantile dependence . . . . Nick's denial of
the learning experience begins when he addresses his father as
'Daddy' instead of 'Dad,' as he had at the beginning . . . . Both the
denial of the experience—or admission of his insensitivity to it—
and the attempt to recreate the father as a man into the infantile

father-*imago* likeness are sublimated at this point."[13] DeFalco concludes that the ending of the story is ironic in that Nick's "'feeling' is depicted as illusory and child-like because it is a romantic reaction to the experience he has undergone."[14] The interpretation is plausible, but it disregards the import of the final conversation between Nick and his father, which is the culmination of the father-son relationship that Hemingway has developed throughout the story. Moreover, when Hemingway wishes to be ironic, his tone is not that gentle. One need think only of "Hills Like White Elephants," "God Rest You Merry, Gentlemen," "A Natural History of the Dead," or "The Capital of the World," the last of which deals directly with the type of illusion vs. reality that DeFalco attributes to "Indian Camp." Delmore Schwartz gives essentially the same reading to the story that DeFalco does, but without a psychoanalytical basis. For Schwartz, as well, the concluding sentence "Illustrates the extreme illusion about existence which is native to the Hemingway hero and which makes disillusion, when it occurs, so astonishing and disastrous."[15]

The only reading of the story which comes near to my own was written a quarter of a century ago by Harry Levin, who concludes, "This, for Nick, is an initiation to suffering and death; but with the sunrise, shortly afterward, youth and well-being reassert themselves; and the end of the story reaffirms the generalization that Hazlitt once drew: 'No young man ever thinks he shall die.' It is easy enough for such a young man to stand things, for he is not yet painfully involved in them; he is not a sufferer but a wide-eyed onlooker . . . ."[16]

Levin's interpretation is more appropriate, for it is an expression of understanding rather than of judgment, and Hemingway's first Nick Adams story is, after all, about understanding. Had Levin had access to the original opening to "Indian Camp," he doubtless would have revised the connection which he makes with Hazlitt, for the fragment "Three Shots" makes it clear that it *has* occurred to Nick that he will someday die, that "Some day the silver cord will break." Such a realization comes to one quite suddenly, and the Edenic sense of immortality is gone. One senses, with a sudden, and lonely clarity, that everything dies. Why then, does Hemingway stress Nick's sense of reassurance at the end of "Indian Camp"? I submit that he does so because "Indian Camp" is one of the very few stories in which Hemingway allowed himself to explore the hopeful paradox, "out of ugliness comes beauty," or "out of death, life." Two other stories in which this occurs are "The Light of the World" and "Big Two-Hearted River." His more frequent themes were, of course, out of love comes death, as in *A Farewell to Arms* and "In Another Country"; or, out of love comes pain, as in *The Sun Also*

Rises and "The End of Something"; or, most hopeless of all, out of death comes still more death, "A Natural History of the Dead." But in "Indian Camp," Hemingway suggests the paradox expressed by Wallace Stevens, "Death is the mother of beauty."

The key to reading "Indian Camp" is to recognize the inherent ambiguity of the ending. On a literal, biological level, Nick's assurance that he will "never die" is ironic. He will die. On an experiential level, however, the ending is not ironic. To *sense* death, as Nick does in "Three Shots," in the abstract, as a vague and unknown presence that threatens life, is to know fear. To *experience* death, to meet it head on, as Nick does in "Indian Camp," is to know its reality. In effect, Nick has faced the fact of death and learned that it is, after all, only the Great Death. Moreover, Nick knows from that final conversation that his father loves him, and that love reinforces his sense of being,and of immortality. Thus, the ending of the story is appropriate in a sense that is neither illusory nor ironic: "In the early morning on the lake sitting in the stern of the boat with his father rowing, he felt quite sure that he would never die."

University of Tennessee

[1]Ernest Hemingway, *In Our Time* (New York: Boni & Liveright, 1925), p. 21. Subsequent references are cited in text.

[2]G. Thomas Tanselle, "Hemingway's 'Indian Camp,'" *Explicator*, 20 (1962), Item 53.

[3]Kenneth Bernard, "Hemingway's 'Indian Camp,'" *Studies in Short Fiction*, 2 (Spring, 1965), 291.

[4]Philip Young, Letter to the Editor, *Studies in Short Fiction*, 3 (Fall, 1965), ii-iii.

[5]Bernard, p. 291.

[6]Joseph DeFalco, *The Hero in Hemingway's Short Stories* (Pittsburgh: University of Pittsburgh Press, 1963), p. 28.

[7]*Ibid.*, p. 30.

[8]Philip Young, *Ernest Hemingway, A Reconsideration* (University Park: Pennsylvania State University Press, 1966), p. 32.

[9]Carlos Baker, *Ernest Hemingway, A Life Story* (New York: Scribners, 1963), p. 125.

[10]Ernest Hemingway, *The Nick Adams Stories*, ed. Philip Young (New York: Scribners, 1972), p. 14.

[11]*Ibid.*, p. 14.

[12]*Ibid.*, p. 15.

[15]DeFalco, p. 32.

[14]*Ibid.*

[15]Delmore Schwartz, "The Fiction of Ernest Hemingway," *Perspectives: USA*, No. 13 (1955), 84.

[16]Harry Levin, "Observations on the Style of Ernest Hemingway," *Kenyon Review*, 12 (1951), 606-607.

EUGENE B. CANTELUPE

STATUES AND LOVERS IN
A Farewell to Arms

Much recent criticism has centered on Hemingway's relations
with art and artists: He asserted that Cézanne taught him how to
write landscapes, and his friendships with such painters as Juan
Gris and Henry Strater enriched and deepened his prose. He often
visited galleries and museums in Europe and America,[1] and he filled
his private library in Cuba with books on art and architecture.[2]
These studies, of great value in helping us understand the
circumstances and ambiance of the novelist's phenomenal
development and career, seldom make specific the connections
between the visual and verbal modes that are presented, and they
often miss or ignore the impact of the novelist's artistic interests
upon his writing strategies.

Emily Stipes Watts' excellent, detailed study on this subject
describes how Hemingway "could lead a group through a museum
with running commentary which was both intelligent and
personal. It was the paintings which held his interest; he liked very
little sculpture." The passage adds that perhaps Hemingway voiced
his indifference to sculpture through the hero of *A Farewell To
Arms*. Lieutenant Henry, waiting for Catherine Barkley in a
hallway decorated with classical busts, thinks, "Sculpture has
always seemed a dull business." After four more similar references,
the critic concludes that for Hemingway, sculpture was not as
"dynamic and vibrant" as paintings and therefore not as influential
or formative on his writing.[3]

Yet the "dull business of sculpture"—no matter what the nature
of Hemingway's response to this mode—provided him the most

memorable of images for one of the most famous endings in the
modern American novel: the statue icon in the concluding
paragraph of *A Farewell To Arms*.[4]

Frederic's agonized farewell to Catherine Barkley in a hospital
room in Lausanne—isolated in the Swiss Alps from the chaos of war
raging on the Italian peninsula below[5]—is both prepared for and
anticipated in the first part of the novel when the lovers meet in the
Gorizia hospital that "had been the villa of a very wealthy
German."[6] Two meetings occur in the garden: In the first
encounter, Catherine takes the initiative, talking freely enough to
reveal her near-shattered emotional state resulting from her fiancé's
death in the trenches in France; during the second visit, Frederic,
"seeing it all ahead like the moves in a chess game" (p. 26), attempts
a kiss and receives a stinging slap in the face. But the third meeting
marks a crucial and decisive stage in their relationship, from sexual
pass to committed love. This meeting begins inside the converted
hospital, in the office and adjoining hall, both of which are lined
with marble busts that remind Frederic of "a cemetery." Still
considering the affair with Catherine a diversion better than visiting
the girls in the officers' whorehouse and another game—this time of
bridge, "in which you said things instead of playing cards"—
Frederic leads her through the hall decorated with sculpture and out
into the garden, where she confesses that she loves him in such a way
that he thinks "she was probably a little crazy." Later, in the officers'
barracks, Rinaldi observes that "Baby is puzzled." Thus, Frederic
has started to fall in love with Catherine, the first phase in the
fulfillment of her cryptic remark that they were "going to have a
strange life."[7]

The final episode of their strange life is played in the Swiss
hospital where Catherine hemorrhages to death from childbirth.
This dénouement becomes even more ironically prophetic when
Frederic orders the room cleared, only to discover that "It was like
saying goodbye to a statue." Hemingway does not permit Frederic
to recall his thoughts about statues that evening when the American
officer waited for the English nurse in the hall of the Gorizia
villa-hospital. But these are the thoughts that Hemingway surely
wants the reader to remember:

> I [Frederic] had to wait in the office of the hospital until she came
> down. There were many marble busts on painted wooden pillars
> along the walls of the room they used for an office. The hall too, that
> the office opened on, was lined with them. They had the complete
> marble quality of all looking alike. Sculpture had always seemed a
> dull business—still, bronzes looked like something. But marble busts
> all looked like a cemetery. . . . I tried to make out whether they were

members of the family or what; but they were all uniformly classical. You could not tell anything about them (p. 29).

On her deathbed, Catherine joins the pedestaled sculptures that lined the walls of the office and hall in the Italian hospital. Frederic cannot say goodbye to her because she, like the portrait busts, cannot be identified, one from another. Yet the reader recalls vividly Catherine's physical radiance and abiding passion that converted each improvised bedroom of the lovers into "a home" and a refuge.[8]

Thus the statue image of Catherine in the daringly muted ending of the novel echoes the mortuary sculpture that Hemingway introduces in the beginning, both becoming a part of the iconography of pain, love, death, and violence that supports the symbolic structure of what Carlos Baker calls the novelist's "first study in doom." Indeed, when Frederic walks back to the hotel in the rain, he leaves behind him the stony existential fact of their strange and all-too-briefly-happy life in a world that he is struggling desperately to understand.

Wright State University

[1]Emily Stipes Watts, *Ernest Hemingway and the Arts* (Urbana: University of Illinois Press, 1971), *passim.*

[2]Hans-Joachim Kann, "Ernest Hemingway and the Arts—a Necessary Addendum," *Fitzgerald/Hemingway Annual* (Englewood, Colorado: Microcard Editions Books, 1974), pp. 145-154.

[3]Watts, pp. 21, 121-122, 177, 178-179, 224-225.

[4]Carlos Baker, *The Writer as Artist* (Princeton: Princeton University Press, 1971), p. 97. He comments that the present ending was probably rewritten seventeen times.

[5]*Ibid.*, pp. 94-116. Baker finds in the novel a "central antithesis" that he summarizes in terms of "mountain and plain."

[6]Ernest Hemingway, *A Farewell to Arms* (New York: Scribners, 1929), p. 29. Subsequent page references are noted in the text.

[7]The developmental stages in the love between Catherine and Frederic are convincingly analyzed by Robert O. Stephens, "Hemingway and Stendahl: The Matrix of 'A Farewell to Arms,'" *PMLA*, 88 (1973), 276-279.

[8]Hemingway's use of "home" and "statue" echo both Donne and Shakespeare. In "Songs and Sonnets," Donne often refers to the lovers' bedroom as "an everywhere"; in *Romeo and Juliet* Capulet and Montague vow at the end to cast the unfortunate lovers in statues of gold as "Poor sacrifices of our enmity!" Carlos Baker, p. 98 and fn. 4 refers to Hemingway's calling Catherine and Frederic his Juliet and Romeo.

GEORGE MONTEIRO

DATING THE EVENTS OF
"THE THREE–DAY BLOW"

First I shall take up a statement made by James Barbour and Robert Sattelmeyer regarding my short piece, "Hemingway's Pléiade Ballplayers" (*Fitzgerald/Hemingway Annual 1973*, 299-301),[1] and then I shall consider the notion that the incidents of Hemingway's early story, "The Three-Day Blow," can be dated through its baseball references.

"The pitfalls for literary scholarship seem endless," write Barbour and Sattelmeyer, for having pointed out Roger Asselineau's errors, "George Monteiro . . . is himself in error . . . in consenting to Asselineau's assumption [in *Oeuvres Romanesques: Poèmes de Guerre et D'Après-Guerre*] that the events of 'The Three-Day Blow' transpired in 1916. Nick's reference to Heinie Zimmerman as a 'bonehead' places the story sometime after the 1917 World Series when the third baseman pulled his well-publicized mental error" (p. 286).

First of all, it should be pointed out that there is in Asselineau's work nothing to indicate that he dated the events of "The Three-Day Blow," by assumption or otherwise, as having taken place in 1916 or, for that matter, in any other year. In fact, in suggesting the 1916 date I followed neither Asselineau nor anyone else.

No matter, however; a more interesting question is whether or not the incidents of "The Three-Day Blow" can be legitimately dated through its baseball references. Barbour and Sattelmeyer begin their disagreement with my suggested date—1916—by pointing out that the reference to Heinie Zim [Henry Zimmerman] as "that bonehead" recalls "the final game of the 1917 World Series, when

Zimmerman had a runner trapped between third and home; rather than throw the ball, he held it and chased Eddie Collins of the White Sox across home plate for the run that opened up the game for the American League team" (p. 282). So far so good. Zimmerman, who had been traded from the Chicago Cubs to the New York Giants during the 1916 season, was for several reasons the "goat" of the 1917 World Series between the Giants and the White Sox. Yet, although his own manager, John J. McGraw, exonerated him from blame for the play that gained him undying notoriety (since neither the pitcher nor the first baseman had moved to cover home plate, Zimmerman was justified in asking, "Who the hell was I going to throw the ball to? Klem? [Klem was the umpire]"[2]), it remains true that, no matter what, Heinie Zim would never live down his "boner." But, as even Barber and Sattelmeyer admit, Zim did have a lasting "reputation for making mental errors" (p. 282). In any case, Barber and Sattelmeyer skate on thin ice when, after concluding that the exchange between Nick and Bill—

> "He can hit," Nick offered. . . .
> "He's a sweet fielder, too," Bill said. "But he loses ball games."
> "Maybe that's what McGraw wants him for," Nick suggested.
> "Maybe," Bill agreed—

refers to the possibility that "McGraw, who had a reputation as a gambler, acquired him [Heinie Zim] to lose games," they go on to conclude further that the exchange reflects the "general suspicion about baseball that resulted from the fixed World Series of 1919" (p. 282).

To begin with, it would be anachronistic to see this remark about Heinie Zim's penchant for losing games as related to the fixed World Series of 1919. By the time the White Sox played the Reds in 1919 Zimmerman was already out of major league baseball. His last season as a major league player was 1919, but he did not even complete that season. Trailing the Cincinnati Reds late in the season, the Giants' manager, John McGraw, rid his team of two established players, Hal Chase (who before joining the Giants had already acquired a reputation for gambling and fixing games) and Heinie Zim. As McGraw's biographer puts it,

> The Giants trailed, the mutterings of the players continued. One day Chase failed to appear at the Polo Grounds. "He's sick," McGraw said. "He hasn't been feeling well for a long time. I doubt if he will play again this year."
> A few days later Zimmerman was gone.
> "He's tired," McGraw said. "His eyes have been bothering him. He's been complaining that he can't judge the hops on a ground ball

as it comes down to him. I told him to knock off for the rest of the season."[3]

"Neither Chase nor Zimmerman ever wore a Giant uniform again"; in fact, a year later, "during the investigation following the exposure of the White Sox perfidy in the 1919 World Series," McGraw would insist that "he had dropped the players because they had thrown ball games and [had] attempted to bribe" some others to do the same.[4] Rather than the fixing of the 1919 World Series, which involved neither Zim nor the Giants, Nick and Bill are more likely referring to those rumors concerning the gambling and game-fixing that filled the air in the two years preceding the series fixed by the White Sox.

The salient facts concerning Henry Zimmerman, who had led the National League in hitting in 1912 with a batting average of .372, are that during the 1916 season the Chicago Cubs sold his contract to the New York Giants. He played for the Giants in 1917, a season culminating in their participating in the World Series for the first time since 1913 and the last time until 1921. Before the end of the 1919 season, however, Zim was sent home by the Giants, never again to play in the major leagues. In fact, in 1921, along with several players from the 1919 Chicago White Sox, and players from other teams, including Hal Chase (his Giants teammate), Zimmerman was himself barred from professional baseball.[5]

Consequently, because of the reference to the Giants' winning ways ("'What did the Cards do?' 'Dropped a double-header to the Giants.' 'That ought to cinch it for them' [in 1917]"; they had not done well in 1916 and would not do well in 1918 either), I shall withdraw my original suggestion that the events of "The Three-Day Blow" must refer to 1916. Indeed, because Bill puts his statement in the future tense ("That bonehead will do him a lot of good"), the fact that the Giants did win the National League pennant in 1917, and because Zimmerman was dismissed permanently from the Giants team *before* the end of the 1919 season, one could more readily opt for a date in 1917, late in the season but before the early October opening of the World Series. As such, in the biography of the young Nick Adams, "The Three-Day Blow" should be placed chronologically immediately before the fragment "Crossing the Mississippi," which can be dated, using the same kind of evidence, as taking place during the 1917 World Series between the Giants and the White Sox.

But there is another possibility. In *A Moveable Feast* (1964) Hemingway informs us that "The Three-Day Blow" was written in Paris in the 1920's, a long way from the Upper Peninsula of Michigan.[6] Hemingway was also a long distance in time from the exploits of the New York Giants and the shenanigans of the likes of John McGraw and Heinie Zim: the Zim trade in 1916, the Giants' National League championship in 1917 and their loss to the Chicago White Sox in the World Series (along with Zim's "boner" in the last game), and the news in 1920 that the Chicago White Sox had fixed the 1919 World Series. It is entirely possible that to enhance the "reality" of his story Hemingway decided to conflate into a single conversational exchange those events dispersed over three or four historical years.

Still, its arrangement in *The Nick Adams Stories* notwithstanding (there it is placed *after* the World War I stories), "The Three-Day Blow" does seem to belong with those pre-war stories presenting Nick as a teen-ager. A companion piece to "The End of Something," this story would seem to deal with Nick's late adolescence, a time when the loyalties of male companionship are still powerful enough to rout the conflicting claims of heterosexual love. Having sorted out and dated the baseball references, we can now, perhaps, accept the strong possibility that Hemingway, making "truth" in Paris as he wished to remember the truth, let several details meld into the composite exchange between two boys about·to get knowingly drunk on someone else's whiskey. As an earlier realist, William Dean Howells, put it, in defending his own use of a seeming anachronism, "it is the effect of contemporaneousness that is to be given, and the general truth is sometimes better than the specific fact."[8]

Brown University

---

[1]"Baseball and Baseball Talk in *The Old Man and the Sea*," *Fitzgerald/Hemingway Annual 1975*, (Englewood, Colorado: Microcard Editions Books, 1976), pp. 281-87. Further references to ·this piece will be incorporated into the text by page number.

[2]Frank Graham, *McGraw of the Giants: An Informal Biography* (New York: Putnams, [1944]), p. 107.

[3]Graham, *McGraw*, pp. 128-29.

[4]Graham, *McGraw*, p. 129.

[5]David Quentin Voigt, *American Baseball* (Norman: University of Oklahoma Press, 1970), II, 144.

[6]*A Moveable Feast* (New York: Scribners, 1964), p. 5.

[7]*The Nick Adams Stories* (New York: Scribners, 1972). Arranging the events of Nick's life chronologically, Philip Young reprints as post-war stories in Section 4 ("A Soldier Home") four stories in order: "Big Two-Hearted River," "The End of Something," "The Three-Day Blow," and "Summer People" (pp. 177-228).

[8]" 'Anachronism,' "*Century*, 29 (Jan. 1885), 477.

MARTIN STAPLES SHOCKLEY

UNCLE TYLER HEMINGWAY

Professor Baker tells us that when Ernest Hemingway went to Kansas City in October, 1917, he was met at the station and driven home by his Uncle Tyler, who took him next day to the offices of the *Star* and introduced him to the chief editorial writer, Henry J. Haskell. Ernest lived with Uncle Tyler and Aunt Arabella in their impressive residence on Warwick Boulevard before moving, "after what he regarded as a decent interval," to share with his friend Carl Edgar a small apartment in Agnes Street. Aunt Arabella was the daughter of J. B. White, "who had made a fortune in lumber and was grooming his son-in-law to succeed him in the business. . . . Tyler was nervous in manner and slight of build. He walked quickly and impatiently, snapping out orders. Of all his uncles, Ernest liked Tyler least."[1]

There was enough ground for dislike in generation gap and personality clash. Uncle Tyler, however, had more than wealth to justify arrogance. Professor Baker does not tell us, but Uncle Tyler was an author. *How To Make Good/ Or /Winning Your Largest Success / A Business Man's Talks / On Personal Proficiency / And Commercial Char- / acter Building — The / Only Success Insurance /* by Alfred T. Hemingway, a publication of the Personal Proficiency Bureau, from the press of Franklin Hudson Publishing Company of Kansas City, Missouri, was copyrighted in 1915. My copy is a second edition, also 1915.

Uncle Tyler's success manual is a small volume of some eighty pages, consisting of a Foreword and thirteen "Talks" on such topics as: "Determine to Succeed," "Check Yourself Up," "Apply the Spurs to Yourself," "Thrift and Contentment," "Credits and Confidence." The Foreword begins by telling us that "The game of business, like life itself, is a great game." The "Talks"proceed to develop the proper relationships among the profit motive, the acquisitive society, "True Nobility," and "Success, Influence, Power." Black type emphasizes such admonitions as: "Decision to 'make good' is the all-important thing"; "Reach out early for success!"; "Think success, hope success, believe success." Young men who would succeed are warned to avoid the evils of tobacco and alcohol: "You will have better control and do a higher type of work if you do not smoke at all" and "liquor is the greatest foe of dependability." The successful salesman will "Be persistent," "Be willing to assume responsibility," "Be honest from top to toe," "Be loyal," "Be a good soldier," and "Obey orders." Under "True Nobility" the aspirant of success learns that "Material possessions alone will not take you far toward success . . . Let your business be the subject of a great, glowing enthusiasm." Talk XII asserts that "Every business man . . . is entitled to a net profit of from twelve to fifteen per cent on his investment."

Tone throughout is smug and hortatory; this is the voice of assurance from the very seat of righteousness. That voice was heard and respected more perhaps in 1915 than now. Although this predecessor of *The Power of Positive Thinking* did not achieve the nation-wide acclaim of its successor, two editions in the first year may be taken as indication of some success. We may assume that in the lumberyards of Kansas City Uncle Tyler made himself felt not just as the son-in-law of J. B. White but as a gentleman of wealth and culture in his own right. We may also assume that he did not neglect his duty in passing on his wisdom and his example to his young nephew.

Here in plain print is what Ernest had to repudiate. The extent of his repudiation is well known.

North Texas State University

---

[1]Carlos Baker *Ernest Hemingway A Life Story* (New York: Scribners, 1969, pp. 32-3. A picture of Alfred Tyler Hemingway appears among those following p. 78.

How to Make Good

OR

Winning Your Largest Success

A BUSINESS MAN'S TALKS
ON PERSONAL PROFICIENCY
AND COMMERCIAL CHAR-
ACTER-BUILDING—THE
ONLY SUCCESS INSURANCE

BY

ALFRED T. HEMINGWAY

PERSONAL PROFICIENCY BUREAU
KANSAS CITY, MISSOURI

ROBERT E. JUNGMAN

A NOTE ON THE ENDING
OF The Sun Also Rises

At the conclusion of *The Sun Also Rises*, we find Jake and Brett once more driving off together in a taxi, a scene which recalls the end of Chapter Three and thus brings us full circle to the opening passages of the novel. Jake recalls:

> The driver started up the street. I settled back. Brett moved close to me. We sat close against each other. I put my arm around her and she rested against me comfortably. It was very hot and bright, and the houses looked sharply white. We turned out onto the Gran Via.

"We turned out onto the Gran Via"—a seemingly irrelevant detail. Or is it? "Gran Via" might be translated "big street" or "large path" or possibly even "great way." But however the two words are rendered into English, they seem to recall Matthew 7:13-14:

> 13   Enter ye in at the strait gate: for wide is the gate, and *broad is the way*, that leadeth to destruction, and many there be which go in thereat:
> 14   Because strait is the gate, and *narrow is the way*, which leadeth unto life, and few there be that find it. [my italics]

That Jake and Brett are on the road to Hell ("It was very hot. . . .") seems to be confirmed by Hemingway's comment in a 1926 letter to Fitzgerald that *The Sun Also Rises* is "a hell of a sad story" whose only instruction was "how people go to hell."[1]

Louisiana Tech University

---

[1]Carlos Baker, *Hemingway: The Writer as Artist*, 3rd edition (Princeton: Princeton University Press, 1963), p. 81.

TAYLOR ALDERMAN

FITZGERALD, HEMINGWAY, AND *The Passing of the Great Race*

Given the sustained interest in F. Scott Fitzgerald and Ernest Hemingway both as major novelists and as writers whose careers can profitably be examined together (the *Fitzgerald/Hemingway Annual* being perhaps Exhibit A to support this assertion), it seems inevitable that one day we will have a "definitive"—or at least a volume-length—treatment of the significance of the literary relationship between the two men: who learned, borrowed, or stole what from whom in which works; how third parties may have influenced both of them in different ways; how the shifting literary reputations of each may have influenced the other in subtle ways from the Dingo Bar in 1925 to the completion of *A Moveable Feast*. We *have* had, of course, a number of closely defined essays on the influence of Fitzgerald on Hemingway, and vice versa, and to these I would add one modest suggestion: a query concerning a possible relationship between the two writers on the social and philosophical question of race.

When Hemingway met Fitzgerald, in 1925, the latter had just published *The Great Gatsby*. At Fitzgerald's suggestion, Hemingway read the novel, and expressed his admiration for it in a letter to Maxwell Perkins.[1] A significant if minor aspect of *Gatsby* is the question of race and racism; early in the novel, Tom Buchanan's vast ignorance and general nastiness are revealed as he laments the decline of civilization and the rise of the non-white peoples of the world, citing *The Rise of the Colored Empires* by "Goddard."[2] Following Arthur Mizener's initial suggestion, Lewis A. Turlish has argued that Fitzgerald was thinking of Lathrop Stoddard's *The Rising Tide of Color* (1920), and more recently M. Gidley has suggested that Fitzgerald referred also to Madison Grant's *The Passing of the Great Race* (1916).[3] Gidley argues in detail for Grant as a source for *Gatsby,* pointing to Grant's connections to Stoddard, to the wide reception and several editions of Grant's work, and to certain parallels between ideas found in Fitzgerald's fiction and in Grant's thesis that history was destroying the primacy of Caucasian Europe. Gidley argues—convincingly, it seems to me—for Grant as a source for *Gatsby;* Hemingway's use of Grant later in the same year is easily demonstrated.

The friendship between Fitzgerald and Hemingway developed quickly, and they spent a good deal of time together during the summer and fall of 1925. Some six months after meeting Fitzgerald and reading *Gatsby,* Hemingway sat down to write his parody of Sherwood Anderson, a short novel about the Indians of Michigan. Hemingway used epigraphs from Henry Fielding, and as Carlos Baker and others have noted, borrowed his title, *The Torrents of Spring,* from Turgenev.[4] But Hemingway's sub-title, *A Romantic Novel in Honor of the Passing of a Great Race,* is taken directly from Madison Grant. The only modification of Grant's title is in the article, which is changed from the definite to the indefinite. The relationship of the title to Hemingway's work is clear. Grant seriously, solemnly, even piously, mourns the endangered white man, presenting his case in a pedantic and quasi-scientific fashion. With his portrayal of the American Indian in a fictional parody, Hemingway satirizes Anderson's sentimental excesses. The ironic use of Grant's title is simply one of many examples of Hemingway's topical and heavy-handed humor in *Torrents.*

Is there a Fitzgerald-Hemingway connection in Madison Grant? Possibly. I have mentioned above the chronology of events from the meeting of the two writers (and Hemingway's reading of *Gatsby*) to the completion of *Torrents,* late in 1925. During this period the two men discussed literature on numerous occasions, including the well-known trip from Paris to Lyon to pick up the Fitzgerald automobile.[5] Grant and his theories could well have been a topic of conversation. Furthermore, Fitzgerald himself appears briefly in *Torrents.* In one of the author's interjections, he mentions Fitzgerald having dropped by the apartment to roast himself and his overcoat before the fire.[6] Finally, Hemingway presented to the Fitzgeralds a typescript of the novel, inscribing it "To Scott and Zelda with love from Ernest."[7] The title page, of course, includes the sub-title derived from Madison Grant. What this sequence of events indicates is simply that Hemingway knew Fitzgerald and *Gatsby* during the six months prior to writing *Torrents,* that his conversations with Fitzgerald may have touched on the question of race and the work of Madison Grant, and that Hemingway thought of Fitzgerald during his work on the novel and at the completion of it.

There is apparently no evidence to justify an assertion that a causal relationship exists between Fitzgerald and Hemingway in this matter, but the person who undertakes an exhaustive study of the relationship between the two writers—or of the difficult issue of racism in the 1920's—would do well to address this possibility.

Youngstown State University

---

[1]Carlos Baker, *Ernest Hemingway: A Life Story* (New York: Scribners, 1969), pp. 145-146.

[2]*The Great Gatsby* (New York: Scribners, 1925), p. 16.

[3]Mizener, *The Far Side of Paradise* (Boston: Houghton Mifflin, 1951), p. 336, n21; Turlish, "The Rising Tide of Color: *A Note on the Historicism of* The Great Gatsby," *American Literature* 43 (November 1971), 442-444; Gidley, "Notes on F. Scott Fitzgerald and the Passing of the Great Race," *Journal of American Studies*, 7 (1973), 171-181.

Apparently unrelated to this aspect of *Gatsby* is a list of names Fitzgerald jotted down some years later, names involving Fitzgerald's use of New York and Long Island: "Goddards Dwanns Swopes." See Matthew J. Bruccoli, ed. *F. Scott Fitzgerald: The Great Gatsby: A Facsimile of the Manuscript* (Washington: Microcard Editions Books, 1973), pp. xvi, xvii.

[4]Baker, p. 159.

[5]Baker, p. 146; cf. *A Moveable Feast* (New York: Scribners, 1964), pp. 154-176.

[6]*The Torrents of Spring*, (New York: Scribners, 1926), p. 119.

[7]Reproduced in *The Romantic Egoists*, ed. Scottie Fitzgerald Smith, Joan P. Kerr, and Matthew J. Bruccoli (New York: Scribners, 1974), p. 129. This TS is presumably a carbon copy; Philip Young and Charles W. Mann list the original among the manuscripts in the Hemingway estate, in *The Hemingway Manuscripts: An Inventory* (University Park and London: Pennsylvania State University Press, 1969), p. 31.

HEMINGWAY FILMOGRAPHY

Fifteen screen adaptions of Ernest Hemingway's works were made during 1932-1977, and he wrote the commentary for a sixteenth film, *The Spanish Earth*. Many of the adaptations are rather loose ones, especially the 1964 version of *The Killers* which makes use only of the title of its source. This list may soon be incomplete since, several additional projects involving Hemingway's life and fiction are being planned.[1]

A Farewell to Arms

Paramount; 1932
Director: Frank Borzage
Screenwriters: Benjamin Glazer and Oliver H. P. Garrett
Cast:

Frederic Henry	Gary Cooper
Catherine Barkley	Helen Hayes
Rinaldi	Adolphe Menjou
Helen Ferguson	Mary Philips
Priest	Jack La Rue
Head nurse	Blanche Frederici
Bonello	Henry Armetta
Piani	George Humbert
Manera	Fred Malatesta
Miss Van Campen	Mary Forbes
Count Greffi	Tom Ricketts
Gordoni	Robert Cauterio
British major	Gilbert Emery

The Spanish Earth

Contemporary Historians; 1937
Director and producer: Joris Ivens
Story by Archibald MacLeish and Lillian Hellman
Commentary written and spoken by Ernest Hemingway

For Whom the Bell Tolls

Paramount; 1943
Director and procucer: Sam Wood
Screenwriter: Dudley Nichols
Cast:

Robert Jordan	Gary Cooper
Maria	Ingrid Bergman
Pilar	Katina Paxinou
Pablo	Akim Tamiroff
Agustin	Arturo de Cordova
Anselmo	Valdimir Sokoloff
Rafael	Mikhail Rasumny
Fernando	Fortunio Bonanova
Andres	Eric Feldary
Primitivo	Victor Varconi
El Sordo	Joseph Calleia
Joaquin	Lilo Yarson
Paco	Alexander Granach
Gustavo	Adia Kuznetzoff
Ignacio	Leonid Snegoff
Andre Massart	George Coulouris
General Golz	Leo Bulgakov
Lieutenant Berrendo	Duncan Renaldo
Captain Gomez	Frank Puglia
Colonel Miranda	Pedro de Cordoba
Staff Officer	Michael Visaroff
Karkov	Konstantin Shayne
Captain Mora	Martin Garralaga
Colonel Duval	Jack Mylong
Sniper	Jean Del Val
Kashkin	Feodor Chaliapin
Don Guillermo	Antonio Vidal
Don Guillermo's wife	Soledad Jiminez
Don Ricardo	Mayo Newhall
Don Benito Garcia	Michael Dalmatoff
Don Faustino Rivero	Robert Tafur
Julian	Armand Roland
Drunk	Luis Rojas

Singer	Trini Varela
Sergeant	Dick Botiller
Cavalry man	Yakima Canutt
First sentry	Tito Renaldo
Girl in cafe	Yvonne de Carlo

To Have and Have Not

Warner Brothers; 1944
Director and producer: Howard Hawks
Screenwriters: Jules Furthman and William Faulkner
Cast:

Harry Morgan	Humphrey Bogart
Eddie	Walter Brennan
Marie Browning	Lauren Bacall
Cricket	Hoagy Carmichael
Hellene de Bursac	Dolores Moran
Paul de Bursac	Walter Molnar
Lieutenant Coyo	Sheldon Leonard
Gerard	Marcel Dalio
Johnson	Walter Sande
Captain Renard	Dan Seymour
Beauclerc	Paul Marion
Mrs. Beauclerc	Patricia Shay
Rosalie	Janette Grae
Horatio	Sir Lancelot
Emil	Emmett Smith
Bodyguard	Aldo Nadi
Bartender	Pat West
Quartermaster	Eugene Borden
Civilian	Pedro Regas
Headwaiter	Major Fred Farrell
Cashiers	Adrienne d'Ambricourt
	Marguerita Sylva
Chef	Joseph Milani
Detective	Hal Kelly
Dancer	Audrey Armstrong
Naval ensign	Ron Randell
Gaullists	Fred Dosch
	Maurice Marsao
	Louis Mercier
	George Suzanne
	Crane Whitley
Urchins	Elzie Emanuel
	Harold Garrison

The Killers

Universal; 1946
Director: Robert Siodmak
Screenwriter: Anthony Veiller
Producer: Mark Hellinger

Cast:

Swede	Burt Lancaster
Kitty Collins	Ava Gardner
Jim Reardon	Edmond O'Brien
Big Jim Colfax	Albert Dekker
Sam Lubinsky	Sam Levene
Al	Charles McGraw
Max	William Conrad
Nick Adams	Phil Brown
Mrs. Hirsch	Vera Lewis
George	Harry Hayden
Queenie	Queenie Smith
Joe	Garry Owen
Kenyon	Donald MacBride
Jake	John Miljan
Lilly	Virginia Christine
Charleston	Vince Barnett
Packy Robinson	Charles D. Brown
Sam	Bill Walker
Dum Dum	Jack Lambert
Blinky	Jeff Corey
Charlie	Wally Scott
Ginny	Gabrielle Windsor
Plunther	John Berkes
Farmer Brown	Charles Middleton
Lou Tingle	Noel Cravat
Stella	Ann Staunton
Gimp	Ernie Adams
Pete	Michael Hale
Paymaster	Harry Brown
Assistant paymaster	Audley Anderson
Timekeeper	Mike Donovan
Customer	Al Hill
Bartender	Wally Rose
Minister	Rev. Neal Dodd
Motorman	William Ruhl
Conductor	Ethan Laidlaw
Housekeeper	Therese Lyon
Nurse	Beatrice Roberts

Doctors	John Sheehan
	George Anderson
Police Chief	Howard Freeman
Police driver	Jack Cheatham
Policemen	Howard Negley
	Perc Launders
	Geoffrey Ingham
Waiters	Milton Wallace
	Nolan Leary
	John Trebach
Man	Rex Dale

The Macomber Affair

Based on "The Short Happy Life of Francis Macomber"
United Artists; 1947
Director: Zoltan Korda
Screenwriters: Casey Robinson and Seymour Bennett
Producers: Benedict Bogeaus and Casey Robinson
Cast:

Francis Macomber	Robert Preston
Margaret Macomber	Joan Bennett
Robert Wilson	Gregory Peck
Police inspector	Reginald Denny
Kongoni	Earl Smith
Aimee	Jean Gillie
Coroner	Carl Harbord

Under My Skin

Based on "My Old Man"
20th Century-Fox; 1950
Director: Jean Negulesco
Screenwriter and producer: Casey Robinson
Cast:

Dan Butler	John Garfield
Joe	Orley Lindgren
Paule Manet	Micheline Prelle
Louis Bork	Luther Adler
George Gardner	Noel Drayton
Maurice	A. A. Merola
Rico	Ott George
Max	Paul Bryar
Henriette	Ann Codee
Bartender	Steve Geray

Published in 1933. Bruccoli Collection.

Katina Paxinou, Mikhail Rasumny, Gary Cooper, and Vladimir Sokoloff in *For Whom the Bell Tolls* (1943).

Joan Bennett and Gregory Peck in *The Macomber Affair* (1947).

The Breaking Point

Based on *To Have and Have Not*
Warner Brothers; 1950
Director: Michael Curtiz
Screenwriter: Ranald MacDougall
Producer: Jerry Wald
Cast:

Harry Morgan	John Garfield
Leona Charles	Patricia Neal
Lucy Morgan	Phyllis Thaxter
Wesley Park	Juano Hernandez
Duncan	Wallace Ford
Rogers	Edmon Ryan
Hannagan	Ralph Dumke
Danny	Guy Thomajan
Concho	William Campbell
Amelia	Sherry Jackson
Connie	Donna Jo Boyce
Mr. Sing	Victor Sen Yung
Macho	Peter Brocco
Gotch	John Doucette
Charlie	James Griffith

The Snows of Kilimanjaro

20th Century-Fox; 1952
Director: Henry King
Screenwriter: Casey Robinson
Producer: Darryl F. Zanuck
Cast:

Harry	Gregory Peck
Helen	Susan Hayward
Cynthia	Ava Gardner
Countess Liz	Hildegarde Neff
Uncle Bill	Leo G. Carroll
Johnson	Torin Thatcher
Beatrice	Ava Norring
Connie	Helen Stanley
Emile	Marcel Dalio
Guitarist	Vincent Gomez
Spanish dancer	Richard Allan
Dr. Simmons	Leonard Carey
Witch doctor	Paul Thompson
Molo	Emmett Smith
Charles	Victor Wood

American soldier	Bert Freed
Margot	Agnes Laury
Georgette	Monique Chantel
Annette	Janine Grandel
Compton	John Dodsworth
Young Harry	Charles Bates
Venduse	Lisa Ferraday
Princess	Maya Van Horn
Marquis	Ivan Lebedeff
Spanish officer	Martin Garralaga
Servant	George Davis
Old waiter	Julian Rivero
Clerk	Edward Colmans
Accordian players	Ernest Brunner
	Arthur Brunner

The Sun Also Rises

20th Century-Fox; 1957
Director: Henry King
Screenwriter: Peter Viertel
Producer: Darryl F. Zanuck

Cast:

Jake Barnes	Tyrone Power
Brett Ashley	Ava Gardner
Robert Cohn	Mel Ferrer
Mike Campbell	Errol Flynn
Bill Gorton	Eddie Albert
Pedro Romero	Robert Evans
Count Mippipopolous	Gregory Ratoff
Harris	Bob Cunningham
Frances Cohn	Rebecca Iturbi
Braddock	Eduardo Noreiga
Mrs. Braddock	Jacqueline Evans
Montoya	Carlos Muzquiz
Georgette	Juliette Greco
Zizi	Marcel Dalio
Doctor	Henry Daniell
Girl	Danik Patisson
English girl	Lilia Guizar
Romero's manager	Carlos David Ortigos
American at bullfight	Lee Morgan

A Farewell To Arms

20th Century-Fox; 1957
Director: Charles Vidor
Screenwriter: Ben Hecht
Producer: David O. Selznick
Cast:

Frederic Henry	Rock Hudson
Catherine Barkley	Jennifer Jones
Rinaldi	Vittorio de Sica
Helen Ferguson	Elaine Stritch
Father Galli	Alberto Sordi
Miss Van Campen	Mercedes McCambridge
Dr. Emerich	Oscar Homolka
Bonello	Kurt Kaszner
Passini	Leopoldo Trieste
Aymo	Franco Interlenghi
Major Stampi	Jose Nieto
Captain Bassi	Georges Brehat
Colonel Valentini	Victor Francen
Nino	Memmo Carotenuto
Nurse	Joan Shawlee

The Gun Runners

Based on "One Trip Across"
United Artists; 1958
Director: Don Siegel
Screenwriters: Daniel Mainwaring and Paul Monash
Producer: Clarence Greene
Cast:

Sam Martin	Audie Murphy
Hanagan	Eddie Albert
Lucy Martin	Patricia Owens
Harvey	Everett Sloane
Eva	Gita Hall
Buzurski	Richard Jaeckel
Arnold	Jack Elam
Sy Phillips	Paul Birch
Peterson	John Harding
Pop	John Qualen
Blonde	Peggy Maley
Carlos	Carlos Romero
Juan	Edward Colmans
Pepita	Lita Leon
Pepito	Steven Peck

Commander Walsh   Ted Jacques
Berenguer   Freddie Roberto

The Old Man and the Sea

Warner Brothers; 1958
Director: John Sturges
Screenwriter: Peter Viertel
Producer: Leland Heyward
Cast:

Old man	Spencer Tracy
Boy	Felipe Pazos
Martin	Harry Bellaver
Cafe proprietor	Don Diamond
Hand wrestler	Don Blackman
Professional gambler	Joey Ray
Other gamblers	Richard Alameda
	Robert Alderette
	Mauritz Hugo
	Carlos Rivera
	Tony Rosa
Tourist	Mary Hemingway

Hemingway's Adventures of a Young Man

Based on the Nick Adams stories and A Farewell to Arms
20th Century-Fox; 1962
Director: Martin Ritt
Screenwriter: A. E. Hotchner
Producer: Jerry Wald
Cast:

Nick Adams	Richard Beymer
Dr. Adams	Arthur Kennedy
Mrs. Adams	Jessica Tandy
George	Michael J. Pollard
Joe Bolton	Simon Oakland
Eddy Bolton	Marc Cavell
Billy Tabeshaw	Pat Hogan
The Battler	Paul Newman
Bugs	Juano Hernandez
Brakeman	Edward Binns
Carolyn	Diane Baker
Contessa	Corinne Calvet
Rosanna	Susan Strasberg
Major Padula	Ricardo Montalban
Turner	Fred Clark

Billy Campbell	Dan Dailey
Telegrapher	James Dunn
John	Eli Wallach
Ludstrom	Whit Bissell
Mayor	Charles Fredericks
Montecito	Philip Bourneuf
Greffi	Tullio Carminati

The Killers

Universal International; 1964
Director and producer: Don Siegel
Screenwriter: Gene L. Coon
Cast:

Charlie	Lee Marvin
Sheila Farr	Angie Dickinson
Johnny North	John Cassavetes
Browning	Ronald Reagan
Lee	Clu Gulager
Earl Sylvester	Claude Akins
Mickey	Norman Fell
Miss Watson	Virginia Christine
George	Robert Phillips
Desk clerk	Seymour Cassel
Receptionist	Kathleen O'Malley
Salesman	Jimmy Joyce
Gym assistant	Ted Jacques
Mail truck driver	Don Haggerty
Mail truck guard	Irvin Mosley

Islands in the Stream

Paramount; 1977
Director: Franklin J. Schaffner
Screenwriter: Denne Bart Petitclerc
Producers: Peter Bart and Max Palevsky
Cast:

Thomas Hudson	George C. Scott
Audrey	Claire Bloom
Eddy	David Hemmings
Captain Ralph	Gilbert Roland
Lil	Susan Tyrrell
Joseph	Julius Harris
Willy	Richard Evans

Tommy	Hart Bochner
David	Michael Wixted
Andrew	Brad Savage

University of South Carolina

¹The sources for these film credits are *The New YorkTimes Film reviews, 1913-1968* (New York: New York Times & Arno Press, 1970); *The American Movies Reference Book: The Sound Era*, ed. Paul Michael (Englewood Cliffs, N. J.: Prentice-Hall, 1969); *Filmfacts.*

REVIEWS

HEMINGWAY'S FIRST WAR: THE MAKING OF A FAREWELL TO ARMS

Michael S. Reynolds

Princeton: Princeton University Press, 1976 $13.50

Through a scrupulous and inventive use of materials which have hitherto failed to be prime sources for Hemingway scholarship, Michael S. Reynolds has placed the making of *A Farewell to Arms* in a new and enriched perspective. Essentially his study aims at accomplishing three goals. Relying on a careful examination of the manuscript, typescript, and galleys of *A Farewell to Arms,* Reynolds attempts to retrace the compositional process of the novel as Hemingway's original conception changed, and revisions in direction and emphasis became necessary. (Reynolds has included generous samples of discarded material as well as several examples of the 35 variant endings which Hemingway worked and reworked.) Secondly, he is concerned to check the historical and geographical accuracy of Frederic Henry's reminiscent account of the Italian campaign which went from the summer of 1915 to the spring of 1918 (Hemingway himself did not arrive in Italy until June, 1918). And, finally, he sets himself the task of describing and assessing the technical, structural, and thematic dimensions of the novel.

Reynold's examination is probing, responsible, and especially successful, I think, in its pursuit of the first two goals. Most particularly, his close study of the military campaign as it historically developed and his comparison of the reality with Frederic Henry's almost-casual observations persuade me that

Hemingway must have composed his love/war story with materials very like the documents (military histories and analyses, memoirs, and government reports) that Reynolds himself has brought to light. In other words, the unfolding progress of Frederic Henry's war is narrated in a manner far too knowledgeable for even the most able and sensitive participant in those events; only a careful historian, privy to a multiplicity of documentary materials, and working well after the events have transpired, could have composed the whole picture which Lt. Henry presents in deceptively casual passing remarks. Further, Reynolds demonstrates that the famous symbolic rain in *A Farewell to Arms* falls as much in accord with actual meteorological reality as it does with aesthetic necessity; and the brief, barely-noticed description of towns and landscapes which pervade the novel tend to be less the impressionistic remembrances of a keen-sighted tourist that the deftly cannibalized extracts from Baedekers and other travel books.

I find these things marvelously curious. *A Farewell to Arms* was Hemingway's first major success, and for thousands of readers, Lt. Henry's poignant tale was authentic testimony of Hemingway's realistic ability to record his own war (and love) experience directly into fiction. Later, of course, critics have come to question Hemingway's reliance on reality; they have tended to focus on the ways and whys he projected his subjective experience (dreams, dreads, fantasies) so vividly and with such a sense of authentic immediacy as to become The Romantic par excellence masked as realistic reporter. Now Reynolds reveals a glimpse of the diligent and laborious study with which Hemingway prepared himself in order to make his fiction take place in a setting that would be as firmly grounded in verisimilitude as possible— to invent, as it were, genuinely real gardens in which to set his imaginary toads.

Reynolds' description and analyses of the shifting directions in the drafting of the novel are fascinating but, I believe, inconclusive. A writer's revisions, his cancellations, the fits and starts of his rejected first and second thoughts, etc. can be useful as reflections of his concrete struggle with form, style, and substance; they can cast light on his methods and strategies of work; and they can record his manifest intentions while he is intimately engaged in attempting to shape his work. I am hesitant, however, to know how heavily to weight such data in assessing a finished work—especially a novel whose first draft was completed in less than five months. The aesthetic intentions of *A Farewell to Arms* must ultimately emerge from the novel itself—from the final published version—and although I welcome the evidence that even Hemingway had to blot a line or two, I resist the intrusion of the writer's wastebasket on the formal autonomy of the published book.

And it is perhaps for this reason that I am less convinced by Reynolds' final chapters in which he moves from scholarly documentation to critical evaluation. Structurally he views the novel as a study in the progressive isolation of Frederic Henry— from country, family, military unit, church, friends, and finally Catherine. This seems to me a somewhat unalarming mouse to emerge from such an ambitious, inventive, and conscientious study of the sources and compositional processes of the novel. I suspect that Reynolds may simply know too many irrelevant and distracting things about the making of *A Farewell to Arms* to be able to read it on its own terms. He has mastered the history of the successive battles of the Isonzo, delineated the topography of northern Italy and Switzerland, and hunted down the possible real-life models for Hemingway's fictional characters. To whatever extent this is possible, he has saturated himself with the discoverable internal and external materials of Hemingway's workroom in the summer of 1928. And although I acquiesce to the justice of Reynolds' attempt to redress the balance between solid scholarship and impressionistic criticism in Hemingway studies, I cannot help feeling that the bent of mind which is intent on discovering *how* art is made must concomitantly underestimate the power of art-materials to take up an undirected life of their own. Reynolds has patiently and intelligently collected many of the bits and pieces within which Hemingway performed the making of *A Farewell to Arms;* not unexpectedly, the novel easily eludes the logic of its assemblage.

The City College of New York

WILLIAM WHITE

HOW IT WAS
Mary Welsh Hemingway
New York: Alfred A. Knopf, 1976 $12.50

With a title of her autobiography that has a Hemingway ring to it, the fourth and last wife of one of the greatest American prose writers of this century tells of their fifteen married years, what came before and what came afterwards. That the long 537-page book takes 93 pages before we even get to the novelist himself shows us that Mary Welsh rightly considered her own career of some importance—thus, this is *her* story as well as *their* story.

Widely reviewed and with decidedly mixed reactions, *How It Was* is a significant contribution to our knowledge and understanding of Hemingway for one indisputable reason: no one knew him as Mary knew him. His brother, two of his sisters, his first wife Hadley, one of his sons, and numerous friends and acquaintances have all told their tales. Now it's his widow's turn, and those who are interested will listen. It's not always a pretty story; yet it is candid and authentic, it is packed to the brim with information (sometimes more than we wanted), and it is as honest as a wife could make a portrait so often bizarre and outrageous.

In addition to her diaries, this major contribution to the Hemingway story is based on unpublished Hemingway letters, from which Mrs. Hemingway has wisely decided to quote despite Hemingway's restriction against publication of this material. For all this new first-hand material and for what seems to be Mary's total recall, we are all grateful to her. However, one must ask just what *How It Was* contributes to our full-length view of Ernest Hemingway beyond what is already known.

I think it is necessary in the first part of the book for the author to show us what kind of a person she was, who her parents were, how she grew up in Minnesota. More important is the account of her years as a reporter in Chicago and London, Mary's story of phoning Lord Beaverbrook from Paris to ask him for a job on the *Daily Express*, her account of his later trying in New York to talk her into going down the Nile with him, and her recollections of reading to him on his yacht all make fine reading. Once we realize how well her own newspaper career was going we can, it seems to me, understand what meeting Hemingway in London meant to her—she was having lunch with Irwin Shaw when he came up and said, "Introduce me to your friend, Shaw." Two brief meetings later, although they were both married, Hemingway proposed to her: "I don't know you, Mary. But I want to marry you."

To suddenly have such a thing happen must have been overwhelming. And that was only the beginning; if Mary didn't realize then what being married to the Myth, the Legend, the Big Man of American Letters was going to be like—what she would be giving up of her life and of her career—she would know full well shortly after that in Paris, where they had their first fight. That was when Marlene Dietrich came to his defense: "He loves you, as you know . . . You must know he is a worthy man. He is good. He is responsible . . . He's a fascinating man. You could have a good life, better than being a reporter." That was only the beginning, because following their marriage in Cuba in 1946, such scenes would be repeated many times, differing only in detail.

Mary approached her coming life with Hemingway with the same spirit of determination that she showed in her writing career: despite everything she had learned about him from personal experience or from hearsay, once she had made up her mind that "this was it," there was to be no turning back. No matter what he did—and he began being dreadful even before they were married, when he called her a "goddamn, smirking, useless female war correspondent"—she apparently decided to put up with the worst for the sake of the best. It is easy to go through *How It Was* and pick out the worst side of Hemingway: his calling Mary a "camp-follower," a "scavenger," a "slut," his smashing her typewriter to the floor in one of his bitter moods, his throwing a glass of wine in her face before friends at a party, and his slapping her in the face, the first time anyone had done this to her since she was a child. Once, in the bad year (for Hemingway) of 1950, after he had kept Mary and a friend waiting at lunch for more than an hour, Hemingway turned up drunk, with a Havana whore in tow. Mary's response was a letter to him on his misbehavior, his inflated ego, and much else that was wrong resulting in her decision to leave. Hemingway's response was

to quote a Shakespeare sonnet and plead, "Stick with me, kitten. I
hope you will decide to stick with me." She did. Then, a few months
later, just after the typewriter and the wine throwing scene, which
was connected with the Adriana Ivancich "affair," Mary told her
husband, "No matter what you say or do—short of killing me,
which would be messy—I'm going to stay here and run your house
and your Finca until the day you come here, sober, in the morning,
and tell me truthfully and straight that you want me to leave." He
never asked her to leave.

Apart from the obvious charm of the man, which many who knew
him have remarked on, there must have been something to make
Mary put up with Hemingway. She typed his manuscripts,
answered his letters, ran the charming Finca Vigia, and brought
some order to his chaotic life; she learned to fish with him on the
Pilar, to hunt with him on African safaris, to feast and drink with
him all over the world, and to listen to his stories, his repeated jokes,
his thin philosophizing. But she saw an element of greatness in him
that somehow made it all worthwhile.

By the time the Ernest-Mary relationship began, when he was
forty-four and she was thirty-six, he had reached his peak: *The Sun
Also Rises, A Farewell to Arms,* and most of those wonderful short
stories had long ago been written, published, criticized, and he was
on the all-time All-American fiction writers team. What was left in
his career was pretty much journalism and uneven novels such as
Across the River and Into the Trees (which Mary knew was awful
before others did) *The Old Man and the Sea,* the unfinished *Islands
in the Stream,* and a piece of nostalgia called *A Moveable Feast,*
begun years earlier and seen through the press by Mary after
Hemingway's death. Clearly, the once great master lost his touch at
wordsmanship and, worse, he knew it. No wonder he was often at
his most impossible neurotic self and finally was driven to suicide.

What Mary Welsh Hemingway adds to all that has been told
before, notably in Carlos Baker's *Ernest Hemingway: A Life Story,*
is the myriad of facts and figures from her years with the restless
novelist. She was with him on those two near-disastrous plane
flights in Africa, she was first to learn from him that he had won
"the Swedish thing," the Nobel Prize, and she was the first to hear a
couple of drawers banging shut and rush downstairs to find "a
crumpled heap of bathrobe and blood, the shotgun lying in the
disintegrated flesh."

Mary's prose has a tendency to be, perhaps, too objective, as if she
were still a staffer on *Time* magazine; the number and names of cats
and how many bags the Hemingways took to Venice or to Kenya
seem to occupy more space in the book than more significant
matters: Mary's opinions of Sinclair Lewis and her asides with

Bernard Berenson slow up the Ernest Hemingway story. But one must not begrudge Miss Mary her innings: she's earned them.

It is difficult to understand the miles-apart reviewer's opinions of *How It Was:* Jane Schermerhorn in *The Detroit News* said, "If you have time for only one book this fall, that book should be *How It Was,* by Mary Hemingway. One might expect Carlos Baker's four pages of praise in the *Saturday Review* ("speedily paced and well written, her narritive hums along like a well-tuned engine"). But why the vehemence of Jean Stafford in *Esquire* and Sheldon Frank in *The National Observer?* Ms. Stafford went to some lengths describing the book: "immodest and cliche-ridden," "makes me want to chew tobacco," "the finished product is lousy," "silly," and "almost exclusively awful"; while Mr. Frank said it is "the most stupefying book I have ever read . . . deeply boring, dreadfully written, scarcely coherent, smug, fatuous, complacent, mildly racist, inept, and extremely stupid." One wonders if these two detractors are talking about the same book I read. We must be looking for different things from a different perspective.

As the editor of *By-Line: Ernest Hemingway,* three other Hemingway titles and numerous reviews and articles, I do not pretend to be an unbiased observer. But to anyone seriously concerned with Hemingway the man and author, Mary Welsh Hemingway's *How It Was* is a major work.

Oakland University

WILLIAM WHITE

PAPA:
A PERSONAL MEMOIR

Gregory H. Hemingway, M.D.
With a Preface by Norman Mailer

Boston: Houghton Mifflin Company, 1976. $7.95

The youngest of Ernest Hemingway's three sons, Dr. Gregory Hemingway, now a practicing physician in New York City, had an impossible task: to write a fair and objective book about his father. It was all the more difficult because the father was a legend, a great writer known to have been a bully, a bore, and a braggart. Being the son of a famous man is just damned bad luck, as *Papa: A Personal Memoir* clearly shows.

Although this short work, which can be read at one sitting and must be read by anyone seriously interested in Hemingway, is not the hatchet job it had been rumored to be, the author of *A Farewell to Arms* is absolutely nobody's favorite father. Dr. Hemingway is sensitive, intelligent, articulate, and most of all, he *is* Hemingway's son and tells what he has to tell from a son's perspective. This, no matter what other values it has, makes the book important.

This 119-page book tells of Gig's relationship with Hemingway at Key West, on the island of Bimini, at the Finca Vigia, on submarine patrol in the Gulf of Mexico, among other places, until the novelist killed himself in Ketchum, Idaho. With all his faults, Ernest Hemingway loved his son. He taught him to fish and shoot, and once saved the boy's life from sharks. But before Dr. Hemingway wrote this touching, and often painful memoir, it was well known from countless other books and articles that his father was far from a perfect man-about-the-house. Dr. Hemingway loved both of his parents—his feeling of distress at seeing them destroying each other certainly comes through—but what a difference there is in reading the son's account as compared with what all the other biographers have said about Hemingway's life. As Whitman said, "I am the man, I suffer'd, I was there."

There is little here about Hemingway's novels and short stories, nor is there meant to be, though you can see how Hemingway developed certain sections of *Islands in the Stream* from real events in which Gig took an active part. In addition to a view of the boy's father and mother, we also get very brief close-ups of Martha Gellhorn (Mrs. Ernest Hemingway No. 3), Mary Welsh (No. 4, and what a crazy story Gig tells about the night he spent in her bed), Gary Cooper, Ingrid Bergman, Adriana Ivancich, and various other walk-on characters in the melodrama of Ernest Hemingway.

If there is little new in the general outline here, there are many, many little details that make, for the Hemingway enthusiast and specialist both, fascinating reading—about a personality whom, it almost seems, we can never have too much. The term "love-hate relationship" has been kicked around a great deal, but in Dr. Gregory Hemingway's unassuming and honest memorial to his father it applies in the fullest sense. As Norman Mailer says in the 2½-page preface, "If it is a portrait written in love, it is with all the sweets and sours of love. . . . For once, you can read a book about Hemingway and not have to decide whether you like him or not. He is there. By God, he exists."

He is there. Not completely realized perhaps, not on a wide screen, but surely from a vantage point that is worth the seeing and the telling. *Papa: A Personal Memoir,* in which "papa" is spelled throughout with a small "p," makes a distinct contribution to Hemingway-iana.

Oakland University

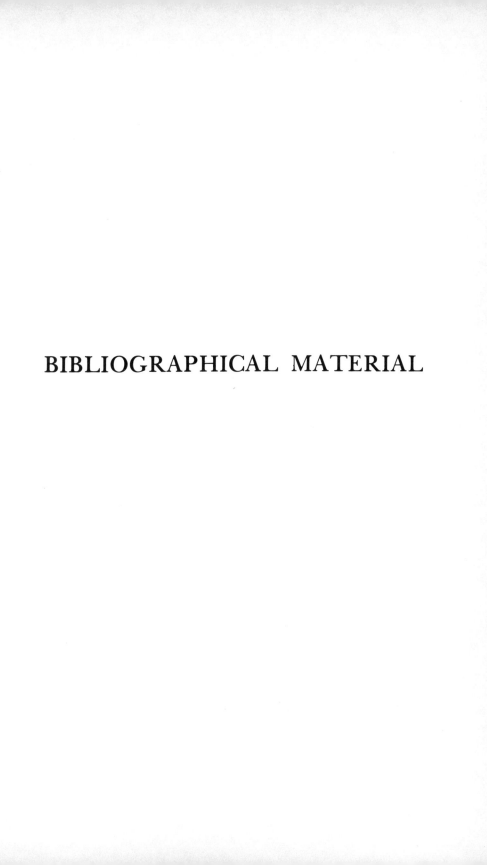

BIBLIOGRAPHICAL MATERIAL

BRUCCOLI ADDENDA

The following items were either omitted from Matthew J. Bruccoli's *F. Scott Fitzgerald: A Descriptive Bibliography* (Pittsburgh: University of Pittsburgh Press, 1972) or appeared after the bibliography was published.

M.J.B.

SECTION A

A9.2 *Tales of the Jazz Age* (London: Collins, [1923]) noted in Times Book Club binding. Wm. Pieper Catalogue #29 [1975].

A10 *The Vegetable*, ed. Charles Scribner, III. New York: Scribners, 1976. Includes unpublished scenes and Fitzgerald's corrections. Published simultaneously in cloth and paper (SL 644).

A11 *The Great Gatsby*. Bath: Lythway Press, [1975]. Large print edition.

Carter, Stella S. *The Art of Book Reading*. New York: Scribners, 1952, pp. 272-274. Passage from *GG* rendered for speed reading.

A18 *The Last Tycoon*. New York: Bantam, [1976]. # 10419-5 Includes movie stills.

A19 *The Crack Up*. [New York]: New Directions, [1975?]. On copyright page: 'ELEVENTH PRINTING'. "Pasting it Together" and "Handle with Care" now have correct titles.

The Basil and Josephine Stories, ed. Jackson R. Bryer & John Kuehl. [New York: Scribners, 1976]. SL 661. New York: Popular Library, [1976]. # 445-08506-175.

Bits of Paradise, ed. Scottie Fitzgerald Smith & Matthew J. Bruccoli. [Harmondsworth]: Penguin, [1976]. # 0 14 00.4071 4. 21 stories.

SECTION AA

The Diamond as Big as the Ritz and other stories, simplified and abridged by Roland John. [London]: Longman, [1974]. Longman Structural Readers: Fiction Stage 5. "The Diamond as Big as the Ritz," "The Long Way Out," "Bernice Bobs her Hair," "The Baby Party," "The Sensible Thing," "The Lees of Happiness," "Gretchen's Forty Winks."

SECTION B

Graham, Sheilah. *The Real F. Scott Fitzgerald.* [New York]: Warner, [1976]. #89-225.
London: Allen, 1976.

SECTION C

C126 Portions of Fitzgerald's review of Thomas Boyd's *Through the Wheat* printed on dust jackets for Boyd's *Shadow of the Long Knives* (New York: Scribners, 1928) and *Mad Anthony Wayne* (New York & London: Scribners, 1929).

C137 Also located as "What Kind of Husbands Do the Rich 'Jimmies' To-day Make?" *Toronto Star Weekly* (29 March 1924).

SECTION D

Sale Number 3842 . . . February 25, 1976 . . . Sotheby Parke Bernet . . . New York . . . # 63: *TITN*, inscribed: "Dear Curtis you've been so appreciative of my books in the past that I thought this might amuse you. Scott Fitzgerald."

SECTION E

E15 "What a Flapper Novelist Thinks of His Wife" also located in *St. Paul Pioneer Press* (30 September 1923), magazine section, 2.

SECTION F

Letter to Don [Swann]. Facsimile. *Architectural Digest,* 33 (July/August 1976), 113.

Rota, Anthony. "F. Scott Fitzgerald Appraises his Library," *Pages 1* (Detroit: Gale, 1976), pp. 82-89. Includes facsimile of Fitzgerald's appraisal; also inscriptions to Fitzgerald.

SECTION H

Keepsake for *Ring Lardner: A Descriptive Bibliography* (Pittsburgh: University of Pittsburgh Press, 1976) by Matthew J. Bruccoli & Richard Layman. [Columbia, S.C.: Privately printed, 1976]. 300 copies. Facsimiles menu on which Fitzgerald made notes on possible titles and selections for Lardner's *How to Write Short Stories.*

APPENDIX 1

The Pat Hobby Stories, ed. T. Koyama & K. Hosokoshi. [Tokyo]: Sansyusya, [1975?]. "Pat Hobby's Christmas Wish," "A Man in the Way," "Pat Hobby and Orson Welles," "The Homes of the Stars," "Pat Hobby's College Days."

The Lost Generation F. S. Fitzgerald E. Hemingway W. Faulkner, ed. H. Okamoto, M. Ochi & T. Niwa. [Tokyo]: Bunri, [1975?]. "Babylon Revisited."

TRANSLATION

Lembi di Paradiso, trans. V. Mantovani & B. Oddera. [Verona]: Mondadori, [1975]. *Bits of Paradise.*

MARGARET M. DUGGAN
<hr>

FITZGERALD
CHECKLIST

Anon. " 'The Roaring Twenties,' " *Building the Future from Our Past A Report on the Saint Paul Historic Hill District Planning Program.* St. Paul: Old Town Restorations, 1975. Brief mention of the Fitzgeralds, with illustration, pp. 60-61.

Boardman, Kathryn. "Designated National Landmark F. Scott Fitzgerald House Cited," *St. Paul Dispatch* (16 February 1972), iv-43. 599 Summit Avenue address.

Bronson, Dan E. *Vision and Revision: A Genetic Study of F. Scott Fitzgerald's Short Fiction with Some Excursions into His Novels.* Doctoral Dissertation, Princeton, 1972.

Bruccoli, Matthew J. "A Great Neck Friendship," *The New York Times* (7 November 1976), 3, 16. On FSF and Ring Lardner.

Bryer, Jackson R. "10. Fitzgerald and Hemingway," *American Literary Scholarship An Annual/1974,* ed. James Woodress. Durham: Duke University Press, 1976, pp. 139-164. Survey of recent criticism.

Dardis, Tom. *Some Time In the Sun.* New York: Scribners, 1976. Study includes chapter on Fitzgerald's Hollywood years (pp. 16-77).

Fenton, Frank. "The Time and the Place," *Vanity Fair*, 45 (September 1935), 35. Includes parody of FSF's description of women.

Fitzgerald, F. Scott. "Bernice Bobs Her Hair," *The Saturday Evening Post*, 248 (July/August 1976), 56-57, 92-100. Special *Post* 1728-1976 Issue.

———. "Foreword," *Colonial and Historic Homes of Maryland*, etchings by Don Swann; text by Don Swann, Jr. Baltimore & London: John Hopkins University Press, 1975, p. ix.

———. "The Intimate Strangers," *McCall's*, 103 (April 1976), 235-240. 100th Anniversary Issue.

———. "A Patriotic Short," *Subject and Structure An Anthology for Writers*, fifth edition, ed. John M. Wasson. Boston: Little, Brown, 1975, pp. 128-131.

Foster, Richard. "Time's Exile: Dick Diver and the Heroic Idea," *Mosaic*, 8 (Spring 1975), 89-108.

Francis, John. "F. Scott Fitzgerald's Women: The Real Romantics," *American Literature*, ed. Lewis Leary and John Auchard. New York: St. Martin's, 1976, pp. 157-173. Sample research paper.

Goodman, Joan. "Undercover Classics," *Club*, 1 (December-January 1975-76), 83. Includes pornographic parody of *Gatsby*.

Graham, Sheilah. "The Most Interesting Men I've Ever Known," *Family Weekly* (7 March 1976), 4-5. FSF makes list, again.

———. "Fitzgerald's Plan for Completing 'Tycoon,'" *The New York Times* (14 November 1976), II-1, II-15.

Hampton, Riley V.   "Owl Eyes in *The Great Gatsby*," *American Literature*, 48 (May 1976), 229.

Hart, Stan. "The Great Gasbag," *Mad Magazine*, 172 (January 1975), 4-10. Cartoon parody of movie.

Highet, Gilbert. *Talents & Geniuses*. New York: Meridian, 1959. Includes three references to FSF.

Korenman, Joan S. " 'Only Her Hairdresser . . .' : Another Look at Daisy Buchanan," *American Literature*, 46 (January 1975), 574-578.

LaHurd, Ryan. " 'Absolution': *Gatsby's* Forgotten Front Door," *College Literature*, 3 (Spring 1976), 113-123.

Lindley, Tom. "Henderson, Ky., Woman F. Scott Fitzgerald's Nurse," *The Evansville* [Indiana] *Courier and Press* (13 June 1976), 2B. Interview with Theodora Gager.

Martin, Marjory. "Fitzgerald's Image of Women: Anima Projections in *Tender Is the Night*," *English Studies Collections*, No. 6 (September, 1976), 1-17.

Marx, Samuel. "The Last Writes of the 'Eminent Authors,' " *Los Angeles Times* (13 June 1976), 3, 12. Recalls FSF, Wodehouse, and Faulkner in Hollywood.

Mason, Franklin. "Scott," *Decade of Short Stories*, 10 (Fourth Quarter, 1950), 12-15. Recounts his meeting with FSF in Baltimore following the publication of *Tender*.

Mayer, Stanley Dehler. " 'A Fine and (Too) Private Place'," *The Pittsburgh Press-Family Magazine* (20 June 1976), 3, 11. Describes a search for FSF's gravesite.

Mencken, H. L. "Newspapers, Women, and Beer," *Harper's*, 253 (September 1976), 41-48. This selection of Mencken correspondence includes his 3 April 1920 letter to FSF.

Miller, Linda Patterson. " 'As a Friend You Have Never Failed Me': The Fitzgerald-Murphy Correspondence," *Journal of Modern Literature*, 5 (September 1976), 357-382.

Mitgang, Herbert. "In search of The Great Gatsby / Retracing Fitzgerald's Footsteps," *The New York Times - Long Island Weekly* (22 February 1976), Section 11 - 1, 11-17.

Moses, Edwin. "F. Scott Fitzgerald and the Quest to the Ice Palace," *CEA Critic*, 36 (January 1974), 11-14.

O'Conor, Bijou. "Bijou O'Conor Remembers F. Scott Fitzgerald," London: Audio Arts, 1975. Cassette recording includes O'Conor's account of her "affair" with FSF.

Pignata, Piero. *Francis Scott Fitzgerald*. Torino: Borla, 1967.

Rees, John. "Fitzgerald's Pat Hobby Stories," *Colorado Quarterly*, 23 (Spring 1975), 553-562.

Romine, Dannye. "Figments of F. S. Fitzgerald: 'Please, Just Call me Scott'," *Charlotte* [N. C.] *Observer* (30 May 1976). Imaginary interview with FSF at Oak Hall, Tryon.

Santa Eulalia, Mary G. "Scott Fitzgerald va a ser enterrado en un cementerio católico," *Informaeiones* (6 November 1975), 6 - XI - 75. On Fitzgeralds' reburial.

Seay, James. "The Wicked Witch of North Carolina," *Esquire*, 86 (October 1976), 116-117, 161-165. Account of his attempt to contact Fitzgerald's spirit through medium Joann Denton during a seance in Fitzgerald's Grove Park Inn room, Asheville.

Thurber, James. "Three Out of All Those Thousands!," *New York Herald Tribune - Weekly Book Review* (25 September 1949), Section 7. Thurber selects *Gatsby* as one of the "three memorable books of the past 25 years."

Whitley, John S. *F. Scott Fitzgerald: The Great Gatsby*. London: Edward Arnold, 1976.

Whitman, William. "They Write Books/The Gin and Jazz Age," *Boston Globe* (13 April 1929), 14. Sketch of FSF's life and career.

Woodward, Jeffrey Harris. *F. Scott Fitzgerald The Artist as Public Figure 1920-1940*. Doctoral Dissertation, University of Pennsylvania, 1972.

Wycherly, H. Alan. "The Fitzgerald Fad," *CEA Critic*, 36 (January 1974), 29-30.

Articles on Movie Version of The Last Tycoon:
"Dialogue on Film/Elia Kazan," *American Film*, I (March 1976), 33-48; "Newsmakers," *Newsweek* (5 January 1976), 42; Hollis Alpert, "Fitzgerald, Hollywood, and *The Last Tycoon*," *American Film*, I (March 1976), 8-14; Stephen Farber, "Film/Hollywood Takes On 'The Last Tycoon'," *The New York Times* (21 March 1976), D15; David Lewin, "I Predict she'll be the Find of '76 (The Surprise Choice for The Last Tycoon)," *London Daily Mail* (30 May 1976), 20; Bob Thomas, " 'Tycoon' by Spiegel,

Naturally," *The Bergen* [N. J.] *Record* (12 January 1976); Alden
Whitman, "Elia Kazan: 'The Movie We Made Is Realistic Holly-
wood,'" *The New York Times* (14 November 1976), II-1, II-15;
Karin Winner, "Secrets of a 'Last Tycoon'," *Women's Wear
Daily* (28-30 January 1976), 9.

Articles on TV Special "F. Scott Fitzgerald in Hollywood":
"F. Scott Fitzgerald in Hollywood," *Media & Methods,* 12 (Febru-
ary 1976), 12-13; "People," *Time* (9 February 1976), 49; "Tele-
vision," *Playboy* (May 1976), 30; Kay Gardella, "Television/
Miller, Like Fitzgerald, finds Success an Enemy," *New York
Sunday Times* (16 May 1976), 1; Aaron Latham, "What Would F.
Scott Think of 'Fitzgerald in Hollywood'?" *The New York Times*
(16 May 1976), D29; Howard Rosenberg, "Scott Fitzgerald in
Hollywood" *The Louisville Times* (15 May 1976), 1-2; Wilfrid
Sheed, "Letter/But Scott and Zelda Were Wordy," *The New York
Times* (30 May 1976), D19 [Reply to Latham's unfavorable
review].

University of South Carolina

HEMINGWAY CHECKLIST

Adair, William. *"A Farewell to Arms:* A Dream Book," *Journal of Narrative Technique,* 5 (January 1975), 40-56.

Anon. "Hemingway Author Wins Libel Suit vs. Doubleday," *Publishers Weekly,* 10 May 1976, 25.

———. "Hemingway Books Clean?" *New York Sunday News,* 16 May 1976, 106. High school library in N. C. to judge the propriety of three Hemingway novels.

———. "Hemingway Libel Suit, A Footnote," *The New York Times,* 30 April 1976, C18.

———. "Preliminary Production Information—'Islands in the Stream'," Paramount (1 October 1975), Xerox, 24 pp.

———. Review of Gregory H. Hemingway, M.D., *Papa: A Personal Memoir, Time* 108 (26 July 1976), 81.

Arnold, Lloyd. *High on the Wild with Hemingway.* Boise, Idaho: R. O. Beatty, 1975? A new limited edition of 1000 copies.

Baker, Carlos. "Mary Hemingway's Years with Ernest," *Saturday Review,* 4 (2 October 1976), 24-28. Review of Mary Welsh Hemingway, *How It Was.*

———. "The Son Also," *Saturday Review,* 4 (2 October 1976), 28. Review of Gregory H. Hemingway, M.D., *Papa: A Personal Memoir.*

_____. Review of Madelaine Hemingway Miller, *Ernie: Hemingway's Sister "Sunny" Remembers*, *Fitzgerald/Hemingway Annual 1975*, pp. 331-332.

Barber, Red. "Ernest Hemingway and the Tough Dodger," *The New York Times*, 14 September 1976, Section 5, 2.

Barbour, James F. "'The Light of the World': The Real Ketchel and the Real Light," *Studies in Short Fiction*, 13 (Winter 1976), 17-23.

_____. and Robert Sattelmeyer. "Baseball and Baseball Talk in *The Old Man and the Sea*," *Fitzgerald/Hemingway Annual 1975*, pp. 281-287.

Beck, Warren. "The Shorter Happy Life of Mrs. Macomber—1955, 1975," *Modern Fiction Studies*, 21 (Autumn 1975), 363-385.

_____. See Mark Spilka, below.

Bennert, Annette. "Survival Through Irony: Hemingway's 'A Clean, Well-Lighted Place,'" *Studies in Short Fiction*, 11 (Spring 1974) 181-187.

Bennett, Warren. "The New Text of 'A Clean, Well-Lighted Place,'" *Literary Half-Yearly*, 14, 1 (1973), 115-125.

Bertrand de Muñoz, Maryse. "Un paralelismo estructural: *Los de abajo* de Mariano Azuela y *For Whom the Bell Tolls* de Ernest Hemingway," *La Torre*, 73-74 (1971), 237-246.

Bolling, Douglass. "Toward *Islands in the Stream*," *South Dakota Review*, 12 (Spring 1974), 5-13.

Bourjaily, Vance. "The Trials and Satisfactions of Being Mrs. Hemingway," *The New York Times Book Review*, 26 September 1976, pp. 3, 18, 20, 22. Review of Mary Welsh Hemingway, *How It Was*.

Braun, Richard E. "Echoes from the Sea: A Hemingway Rubric," *Fitzgerald/Hemingway Annual 1974*, pp. 201-205.

Broer, Lawrence. "The Iceberg in 'A Clean, Well-Lighted Place,'" *Lost Generation Journal*, 2 (Spring-Summer 1976), 14-15, 21.

Bruccoli, Matthew J. "Stan Ketchel and Steve Ketchel: A Further Note on 'The Light of the World,'" *Fitzgerald/Hemingway Annual 1975*, pp. 325-326.

Butcher, Fanny. "Man's Emotions Throb in Novel by Hemingway," *Chicago Tribune*, 21 October 1940. Review of *FWTBT*.

Butler, Arthur T. "Armageddon in Perspective: A Study of the Responses of Six Writers to the First World War," *Dissertation Abstracts International*, 35 (1974), 1649A.

Clark, C. E. Frazer, Jr. "American Red Cross Reports on the Wounding of Lieutenant Ernest M. Hemingway—1918," *Fitzgerald/Hemingway Annual 1974*, pp. 131-136.

Collins, Nancy. "Gregory Hemingway: The Son Also Rises," *Women's Wear Daily*, 23-30 January 1976, 16. Interview.

Cook, Wanda. "Key West Cats Are Papa's Fla. Legacy," *New York Sunday News*, 18 January 1976.

Cousins, Norman. "The Hemingway Letters," *Saturday Review*, 4 (2 October 1976), 4-6.

Currie, William J. "Hemingway's Images of Alienation," *English Literature and Language* (Tokyo), 10 (1973), 183-199.

Daiker, Donald A. "The Pied Piper in *The Sun Also Rises*," *Fitzgerald/Hemingway Annual 1975*, pp. 235-237.

Donaldson, Scott. *By Force of Will: The Life and Art of Ernest Hemingway*. New York: Viking, 1976.

Doody, Terrence. "Hemingway's Style and Jake's Narration," *Journal of Narrative Technique*, 4 (September 1974), 212-225.

Duggan, Margaret M. "Hemingway Checklist," *Fitzgerald/Hemingway Annual 1974*, pp. 323-329.

Elia, Richard. "Three Symbols in Hemingway's 'The Snows of Kilimanjaro'," *Review des Langues Vivantes*, 41 (May-June 1975), 282-285.

Falbo, Ernest S. "Carlo Linati: Hemingway's First Italian Critic and Translator," *Fitzgerald/Hemingway Annual 1975*, pp. 293-306.

Frank, Sheldon. "Life With Papa: Making the Life Less Than the Myth," *The National Observer*, 9 October 1976, 25. Review of Mary Welsh Hemingway, *How It Was*.

Gardella, Kay. "Four Stages in Hemingway's Life," *New York Sunday News*, 2 May 1976, TV section, 1. Review of "The Hemingway Play."

Gellhorn, Martha. "The Indomitable Losers: Spain Revisited," *New York*, 9 (2 February 1976), 42-47.

Goodman, M. "At Sea with Hemingway," *Motor Boating and Sailing*, 137 (June 1976), 43, 115-116, 118.

Gordon, Gerald T. "Survival in *The Sun Also Rises*," *Lost Generation Journal*, 2 (Spring-Summer 1976), 10-11, 17.

Grimes, Carroll. "Hemingway's 'Defense of Dirty Words': A Reconsideration," *Fitzgerald/Hemingway Annual 1975*, pp. 217-227.

Grimes, Larry. "Night Terror and Morning Calm: A Reading of Hemingway's 'Indian Camp' as Sequel to 'Three Shots,'" *Studies in Short Fiction*, 12 (Fall 1975), 413-415.

Gullason, Thomas A. Review of Alice Hunt Sokoloff, *Hadley: The First Mrs. Hemingway*, *Studies in Short Fiction*, 13 (Winter 1976), 100-101.

Hagopian, John V. "Hemingway: Ultimate Exile," *Mosaic*, 8 (Spring 1975), 77-87.

Hand, Judson. "The Gentle Side of Papa, the Many Sides of Rocky," *New York Sunday News*, 6 June 1976, Leisure Section, 17. Review of Gregory H. Hemingway, M.D., *Papa: A Personal Memoir*.

_____. "King Kong's Story, Hemingway Version," *New York Sunday News*, 11 July 1976, Leisure Section, 16. Review of *The Girl in the Hairy Paw* which includes Hemingway parody.

Hemingway, Ernest. "The Tradesman's Return" (Chapters 6-8 *To Have & Have Not*) [London] *Evening Standard, 16 April 1936*, 26, 27.

_____. *House of Books* . . . [1976]. No. 209: *A Farewell to Arms* inscribed, "To Mrs. Guffey with very best wishes."

_____. "Lagniappe" [Letter to James Aswell, 21 October 1929]. *Louisiana Studies*, 12 (Fall 1973), 532.

_____. "On the Blue Water": Excerpts from *By-Line: Ernest Hemingway, Motor Boating and Sailing*, 137 (June 1976), 44-45.

Hemingway, Gregory H., M.D. *Papa: A Personal Memoir*. With a Preface by Norman Mailer. Boston: Houghton Mifflin Company, 1976.

Hemingway, Mary Welsh. *How It Was*. New York: Alfred A. Knopf, 1976.

"Hemingway Sports Special," *Lost Generation Journal*, 3 (Spring-Summer 1975). Issue includes: David Sanders, "Piggott Pandemonium," 2-6; Robert W. Lewis, "Hemingway Ludens," 7-8, 30; Michael Helfand, "A Champ Can't Retire Like Anyone Else," 9-10, 35; Lawrence Broer, "Soldier's Home," 11, 32; Gregory Sojka, "A Portrait of Hemingway as Angler-Artist," 12-13; Philip Bordinat, "Anatomy of Fear in Tolstoy and Hemingway," 14-17; Joseph DeFalco, "Hemingway, Sport, and the Larger Metaphor," 18-20; Christian Messenger, "Hemingway and the School Athletic Hero," 21-23.

Herndon, Jerry A. "No 'Maggie's Drawers' for Margot Macomber," *Fitzgerald / Hemingway Annual 1975*, pp. 289-291.

Holder, Robert Conner, Jr. "The Tip of the Iceberg: The Naturalistic Pattern in the Fiction of Ernest Hemingway," *Dissertation Abstracts International*, 36 (February 1976), 5298A.

Hurley, C. Harold. "Attribution of the Waiter's Second Speech in Hemingway's 'A Clean, Well-Lighted Place,'" *Studies in Short Fiction*, 13 (Winter 1976), 81-85.

Inglis, David L. "Morley Callaghan and the Hemingway Boxing Legend," *Notes on Contemporary Literature*, 4, 4 (1974), 4-7.

Jurado, Maria Rosario. "*The Old Man and the Sea* o la evolución del fatalismo en Hemingway," *Filologia Moderna* (Madrid), 50-51, (1974), 439-459.

Kallapur, S. T. "Ernest Hemingway's Conception of Love and Womanhood," *Banasthali Patrika* 19 (1972), 37-47.

Kann, Hans-Joachim. "Ernest Hemingway and the Arts—A Necessary Addendum," *Fitzgerald / Hemingway Annual 1974*, pp. 145-154.

_____. "Ernest Hemingway and German Culture," *Neusprachliche Mitteilungen*, 28, H.1 (1975), 16-20.

_____. "Review of Carlos Baker," *Die Geschichte Eines Abenteuerlichen Lebens*, tr. Christian Herberg, *Die Neueren Sprachen*, 11 (1972), 674-5.

_____. Reviews of Carlos Baker, *Ernest Hemingway: A Life Story*; Bakker, *Ernest Hemingway: The Artist as Man of Action*; Emily Stipes Watts, *Ernest Hemingway and the Arts*, *Kritikon Litterarum*, 1 (.1972), 240-5.

_____. Reviews of Wayne E. Kvan, *Hemingway in Germany*; Robert Brainard Pearsall, *The Life and Writings of Ernest Hemingway*; Christopher Rudson Longyear, *Linguistically Determined Categories of Meaning: A Comparative Analysis of Meaning in "The Snows of Kilimanjaro,"* *Anglia*, 92 H.¾ (1974), 519-22.

Kesey, Ken. "Hemingway," *The Last Supplement to the Whole Earth Catalog* (March 1971), 69.

Kington, M. "Exclusive—Four Unpublished Early Masterpieces," *Critic*, 34 (Fall 1975), 54-57.

Kobler, J. F. "The Short Happy Illusion of Francis Macomber," *Quartet*, 6 (Winter-Spring 1974), 62-67.

_____. "Hemingway's Four Dramatic Short Stories," *Fitzgerald Hemingway Annual 1975*, pp. 247-257.

Koontz, Leah Rice. "My Favorite Subject Is Hadley," *Connecticut Review*, 8 (October 1974), 36-41.

Kvan, Wayne. "Hemingway's 'Banal Story,'" *Fitzgerald/Hemingway Annual 1974*, pp. 181-191.

Lacasse, Roger. *Hemingway et Malraux: Destins de l'homme*. Paris: Nizet, 1974.

Lajoie, Ronald and Sally Lentz. "Is Jake Barnes Waiting?" *Fitzgerald/Hemingway Annual 1975*, pp. 229-233.

Landis, Arthur. "La Bella Chica Will Rise Again," *The* [Bergen County, N.J.] *Record*, 16 December 1975. Describes meeting with Hemingway in Madrid during Spanish Civil War.

Laurence, Frank M. "5000 Grand: The Plagiarism Suit Against Hemingway," *Fitzgerald/Hemingway Annual 1974*, pp. 193-199.

Layman, Richard. "Hemingway's Library Cards at Shakespeare and Company." *Fitzgerald/Hemingway Annual 1975*, pp. 191-206.

Lehmann-Haupt, Christopher. "The Old Man and His Son," *The New York Times* (16 June 1976), 43m. Review of Gregory H. Hemingway, M.D., *Papa: A Personal Memoir*.

Lichtenstein, Grace. "A Doctor-Author in Hemingway Country," *The New York Times*, 27 July 1976, M27. On Gregory Hemingway.

Lingeman, Richard R. "Publishing: Mary Recalls Papa," *The New York Times*, 27 August 1976, C16.

Lubasch, Arnold H. "Hotchner's $125,000 Libel Award Upheld," *The New York Times*, 3 August 1976, 20C.

Macdonald, Scott. "Hemingway's 'The Snows of Kilimanjaro': Three Critical Problems," *Studies in Short Fiction*, 11 (Winter 1974), 67-74.

Macnaughton, W. R. "Maisie's Grace Under Pressure: Some Thoughts on James and Hemingway," *Modern Fiction Studies*, 22 (Summer 1976), 153-164.

Maddocks, Melvin. "Mary's Museship," *Time*, 108 (18 October 1976), 104, 106. Review of Mary Welsh Hemingway, *How It Was*.

Mansell, Darrell. "When Did Ernest Hemingway Write *The Old Man and the Sea?*" *Fitzgerald/Hemingway Annual 1975*, pp. 311-324.

McClellan, David. "Is Custer a Model for the Fascist Captain in *For Whom the Bell Tolls?*" *Fitzgerald/Hemingway Annual 1974*, pp. 239-241.

Monat, Olympio. "A arte de contar de Hemingway: O narrador, a acao e a consciencia," *O Estado de Sao Paulo, Supplemento Literario*, 4 August 1974, 1.

Monteiro, George. "Hemingway, O. Henry, and the Surprise Ending," *Prairie Schooner*, 47 (1973), 296-302.

———. "The Reds, the White Sox, and *The Old Man and the Sea*," *Notes on Contemporary Literature*, 4 (May 1974), 7-9.

———. "Hemingway on Dialogue in 'A Clean, Well-Lighted Place,'" *Fitzgerald/Hemingway Annual 1974*, p. 243.

———. "Santiago, DiMaggio, and Hemingway: The Ageing Professionals of *The Old Man and the Sea*," *Fitzgerald/Hemingway Annual 1975*, pp. 273-280.

———. Review of Audre Hanneman, *Supplement to Ernest Hemingway: A Comprehensive Bibliography, Papers of the Bibliographical Society of America*, 70 (July-September 1976), 432-433.

Murray, Donald M. "*The Day of the Locust* and *The Sun Also Rises:* Congruence and Caricature," *Fitzgerald/Hemingway Annual 1975*, pp. 239-245.

Nagarajian, M. S. "The Structure of 'The Killers,'" *Literary Half-Yearly*, 15,1 (1974), 114-119.

Nolan, William F. "The Man Behind the Masks: Hemingway as a Fictional Character," *Fitzgerald/Hemingway Annual 1974*, pp. 207-213.

North, Sterling. "Hemingway, Heinz Pol, Connery, Halper!," [21 October 1940]. Unlocated review of *For Whom the Bell Tolls*.

Oldsey, Bernard. "Of Hemingway's *Arms* and the Man," *College Literature*, 1 (Fall 1974), 174-189.

Opre, Tom. "Brookies Still Abound in Hemingway's 'Big Two-Hearted River'—aka the Fox," *The Detroit Free Press*, 23 May 1976, 8-E.

Peper, Jurgen. "Ernest Hemingway: *A Farewell to Arms*," Edgar Lohner, ed. *Der amerikanische Roman im 19. und 20. Jahrhundert*. Berlin: Erich Schmidt, 1974, pp. 275-296.

Prescott, Herman. "A Hemingway Collection: A Moveable Beast," *Lost Generation Journal*, 3 (Spring-Summer 1975), 35. Review of *The Enduring Hemingway*.

———. "Hemingway vs Faulkner; An Intriguing Feud," *Lost Generation Journal*, 3 (Fall 1975), 18-19.

Price, Reynolds. "A Son's Soliloquy—Regret, Love, Thanks," *The New York Times Book Review*, 30 May 1976, 1-2. Review of Gregory H. Hemingway, M.D., *Papa: A Personal Memoir*.

Pritchett, V. S. "The Hemingway," *The New Yorker*, 52 (1 November 1976), 161-164. Review of Mary Welsh Hemingway, *How It Was*.

Prizel, Yuri. "The Critics and *The Old Man and the Sea*," *Research Studies* (Washington State University), 41 (1973), 208-216.

Putney, Michael. "Key West: Papa Still Reigns," *The National Observer*, 23 August 1975, 20.

Redington, Joan Wheeler. "Before the Corrida," *Fitzgerald/Hemingway Annual 1975*, pp. 309-310.

Reuter, Madalynne, "Doubleday Loses Motion to Overturn Hotchner Award," *Publishers Weekly*, 16 August 1976, 58-59.

Reynolds, Michael S. *Hemingway's First War: The Making of A Farewell to Arms*. Princeton: Princeton University Press, 1976.

Rodgers, Bernard F., Jr. *"The Nick Adams Stories:* Fiction or Fact," *Fitzgerald/Hemingway Annual 1974*, pp. 155-162.

Rosen, Kenneth. "Ten Eulogies: Hemingway's Spanish Deaths," *Bulletin of the New York Public Library*, 77 (1974), 276-277.

Ruhm, Herbert. "Hemingway in Schruns," *Commonweal*, 99 (28 December 1973), 344-345.

Russell, Peter. "Hemingway in Italy," *World Review*, 7 (September 1949), 65-67.

Sarason, Bertram D. "Krebs in Kodiak," *Fitzgerald/Hemingway Annual 1975*, pp. 209-215.

Schermerhorn, Jane. "Hemingway Seen as a Real Papa," *The Detroit News*, 9 May 1976. Review of Gregory H. Hemingway, M.D., *Papa: A Personal Memoir*.

_____. "Mary's Memories Make Pulsing Prose," *The Detroit News*, 12 September 1976, H-2. Review of Mary Welsh Hemingway, *How It Was*.

Schonhorn, Manual. *"The Sun Also Rises:* I, The Jacob Allusion; II, Parody as Meaning," *Ball State University Forum,* 16 (Spring 1975), 49-55.

Shaw, Patric W. "How Earnest Is the Image: Hemingway's Little Animals," *CEA Critic,* 37 (March 1975), 5-8.

Skipp, Francis E. "Metempsychosis in the Stream, or What Happens in 'Bimini'?" *Fitzgerald/Hemingway Annual 1974,* pp. 137-143.

Smith, Cecil. "Hem, Wemedge, Ernest and Papa," *The Los Angeles Times,* 11 March 1976. Review of Frederick Hunter, *The Hemingway Play,* Hollywood Television Theater.

Somer, Paul P., Jr. "Sherwood Anderson Introduces His Friend Ernest Hemingway," *Lost Generation Journal,* 3 (Fall 1975), 24-26.

————. "Anderson's Twisted Apples and Hemingway's Crips," *Midamerica: The Yearbook of the Society for the Study of Midwestern Literature,* 1974, pp. 82-97.

Spilka, Mark. "Warren Beck Revisited," *Modern Fiction Studies,* 22 (Summer 1976), 245-255; Warren Beck, "Mr. Spilka's Problems," *ibid.,* 256-269.

Stafford, Jean. "Mrs. Hemingway Remembers," *Esquire,* 86 (October 1976), 28, 30. Review of Mary Welsh Hemingway, *How It Was.*

Tanner, Stephen L. "Hemingway: The Function of Nostalgia," *Fitzgerald/Hemingway Annual 1974,* pp. 163-174.

Telesin, Julius. "For Whom the Scissors Cut; How to Improve Hemingway (Moscow Style)," *Encounter,* 46 (June 1976), 81-86. On emended Russian edition of *For Whom the Bell Tolls.*

Tyler, Anne. "Gregory Hemingway Remembers Papa," *The National Observer,* 5 June 1976, 21. Review of Gregory H. Hemingway, M.D., *Papa: A Personal Memoir.*

Unrue, John. "The Valley of Baca and *A Farewell to Arms,*" *Fitzgerald/Hemingway Annual 1974,* pp. 229-234.

Vanderwerken, David L. "One More River to Cross: The Bridge Motif in *The Sun Also Rises*," *CEA Critic*, 37 (January 1975), 21-22.

Van Gelder, Lawrence. "When the Sun Also Rose," *Pages 1* (Detroit: Gale Research, 1976).

Wagner, Linda Welshimer. *Hemingway and Faulkner: Inventors / Masters*. Metuchen, N.J.: The Scarecrow Press, 1975.

_____. "A Note on Hemingway as Poet," *Midamerica: The Yearbook of the Society for the Study of Midwestern Literature*, 1974, pp. 58-63.

_____. "Juxtaposition in Hemingway's *In Our Time*," *Studies in Short Fiction*, 12 (Summer 1975), 243-252.

Watson, James Gray. " 'A Sound Basis of Union': Structural and Thematic Balance in 'The Short Happy Life of Francis Macomber,' " *Fitzgerald / Hemingway Annual 1974*, pp. 215-228.

Wells, David J. "Hemingway in French," *Fitzgerald / Hemingway Annual 1974*, pp. 235-238.

White, William. Review of Matthew J. Bruccoli and C. E. Frazer Clark, Jr. *Hemingway at Auction 1930-1973*. *Fitzgerald / Hemingway Annual 1974*, pp. 265-267.

_____. "Hemingway Checklist," *Fitzgerald / Hemingway Annual 1975*, pp. 351-368.

_____. "Son's Book Gives Rare View of Hemingway," *The Oakland Press* (Pontiac, Mich.), 7 August 1976. D-10. Review of Gregory H. Hemingway, M.D., *Papa: A Personal Memoir*.

Winn, Harlan Harbour, III. "Short Story Cycles of Hemingway, Steinbeck, Faulkner, and O'Connor," *Dissertation Abstracts International*, 36 (January 1976), 4500A.

Winslow, Richard. " 'A Good Country': Hemingway at the L Bar T Ranch, Wyoming," *Fitzgerald / Hemingway Annual 1975*, pp. 259-272.

Wolff, Geoffrey. *Black Sun: The Brief Transit and Violent Eclipse of Harry Crosby*. New York: Random House, 1976.

Wycherly, H. Alan. Review of Linda Welshimer Wagner, ed. *Ernest Hemingway: Five Decades of Criticism, American Notes & Queries,* 14 (January 1976), 78-80.

Wyrick, Jean. "Fantasy as Symbol: Another Look at Hemingway's Catherine," *Massachusetts Studies in English,* 4,2 (1973), 42-47.

Yannella, Philip R. "Notes on the Manuscript, Date, and Sources of Hemingway's 'Banal Story,' " *Fitzgerald/Hemingway Annual 1974,* pp. 175-179.

Young, Philip. "Hemingway's Manuscripts: The Vault Reconsidered," *Studies in American Fiction,* 2 (Spring 1974), 3-11.

Zayas-Bazán, Eduardo. "Hemingway: His Cuban Friends Remember," *Fitzgerald/Hemingway Annual 1975,* pp. 153-190.

Oakland University

GENERAL
CHECKLIST

Baker, Russell. "The Golden Apple," *The New York Times Magazine* (14 March 1976), 7. Imaginary memoir of New York during 20's with mention of FSF and EH.

Corley, Edwin. *Shadows.* New York: Stein & Day, 1975. Novel with Hollywood setting that includes Fitzgerald as a character.

Friedrich, Otto. *Going Crazy: An Inquiry into Madness in Our Time.* New York: Simon & Schuster, 1976. Includes material about FSF and EH.

Gill, Brendan. "Profiles The Dark Advantage," *The New Yorker,* 51 (15 September 1975), 42-92. On Fitzgerald, Philip Barry, and O'Hara.

Grey, M. Cameron. "Miss Toklas Alone," *Virginia Quarterly Review,* 52 (Autumn 1976), 687-696. Includes mention of FSF and EH.

Hamilton, Ruth. "The Crazily Charmed Life of Donald Ogden Stewart," *The New Haven Register* (21 December 1975), 1D, 4D. Interview includes mention of FSF and EH.

Jaediker, Kermit. "Death of a Gambler The 'Hit' Heard Round the World," *New York Sunday Times* (28 September 1975), 30-31. Article on Arnold Rothstein mentions FSF's use of him in *Gatsby.*

Kazin, Alfred. " 'The Giant Killer': Drink & the American Writer," *Commentary*, 61 (March 1976), 44-50. Discussion of FSF and some mention of EH.

Leary, Lewis and John Auchard, *American Literature A Study and Research Guide*. New York: St. Martin's, 1976. Chapter on FSF, pp. 95-97; chapter on EH, pp. 104-106.

McMillan, Dougald. *Transition The History of a Literary Era 1927-1938*. New York: George Braziller, 1976.

Moser, Barry, illustrator. *Twelve American Writers*. Easthampton, Mass.: Pennyroyal, 1974. Book of 12 engraved portraits with quotations from each author on writing inclucing FSF and EH; signed and numbered edition of 50 copies, $250.00.

Sanford, John. *A More Goodly Country A Personal History of America*. New York: Horizon Press, 1975. Includes fictional sketches of FSF (pp. 272-3) and EH (pp. 200-1).

Shirer, William L. *20th Century Journey [1904-1930]*. New York: Simon & Schuster, 1976. Memoir with mention of FSF and EH.

Wolff, Geoffrey. *Black Sun The Brief Transit and Violent Eclipse of Harry Crosby*. New York: Random House, 1976.

University of South Carolina